MW01291298

COUNTY
1950s

M B Spears

Memory Is My Name

Irish and Southern Art LLC
holds all copyrights to

COUNTY
1950s

Second in the series
Memory Is My Name.

COUNTY follows
MINERAL SPRINGS ROAD 1940s.

For permission to reproduce
any part of
COUNTY 1950s or
MINERAL SPRINGS ROAD 1940s
contact
IRISH AND SOUTHERN ART LLC
through the author
at
Spearsmb@bellsouth.net

All rights reserved.

Thanks to the DARLINGTON (SC) HISTORICAL COMMISSION for permission to investigate and photograph holdings in its files, and for willing and timely assistance, especially from Kay Williamson and Doris Gandy.
The creekside painting on the back cover is from an original watercolour by Martyn Bell of Ireland.
Photography, including the cover, is by M B Spears.

Darlington Edition. December 2013.

COUNTY
1950s

is dedicated to

ST JOHN'S HIGH SCHOOL

-- abandoned but not forgotten --

and all its people through the years,

especially
THE *GOOD* TEACHERS
and
THE *WHOLE* CLASS OF 1957
-- good or not.

**A toast to ourselves and those like us:
the few.**

Memory Is My Name

CHAPTERS

INTRODUCTION
(A View from Farther Away)

My name is not important, nor (in this instance) is my identity. Think of me as simply the writer of this Introduction, which will not be listed on the book's Contents page nor appear in the author's copies of County. Its purpose is to prepare you for the reading experience ahead.

I am not the author and narrator of County. That you not confuse me with her is crucial. I am unlike her in age, experience, habits, social standing, education, accomplishments, taste. We have little in common. I do share with her a respect for those who read often and with energy. Although I myself am convinced that most persons today are teetering along on prejudice and misinformation, I realize that you as a reader may well be one who sees into and beyond the present moment. You have my respect on that basis. Hence this Introduction.

The author of County is 17 in 1957. Note that I use the present tense verb *is*. County is 1957 *now*. The author's world is that world, not the world you and I live in today. She cannot know what has not yet happened. For instance, she knows television in its early years only. "Entertainment" is not thought of as a necessity; her generation, like all generations before it, self-entertains. Church and religious faith play major roles in social and thinking life. Her tastes, values, and beliefs are not unusual for the 1950's – not at all. Her vantage point, however, is uncommon: she and her parents moved to town from farm life but find themselves involved in pivotal events.

Allow me to caution you: Do not underestimate her. Her principal once called her "one of the smartest girls who ever went through St John's High School." Males and females were expected to have separate strengths.

Having praised her mind, I must warn you that her writing style is quirky and inconsistent, even for 17. Her grammar is acceptable but local. She often (annoyingly to me) actually writes *'em* for *them* and continually employs *use to, probly,* and *s'pose* because she intends to "sound the way we talk." (By we, she refers to young people of her part of the Carolinas' coastal plain, which they themselves call the Pee Dee.) Yet she is a devotee of words and a friend of dictionaries and many other books. County's variety in content can be off-putting or engaging, depending on your taste. Descriptions of a midcentury Southern town follow the installing of a superspeedway. Songs are replicated without the use of the expected musical notation. Railroad trains and a legendary hurricane are presented in emotional rhythms.

7

COUNTY

Simplicity vies with complexity, and tantalizing facts hide amidst what appears to me to be deliberate ambiguity.

Most important for readers to remember is that the gaps between her world and ours are many – even for those of us who have experienced both.

She has no personal experience of fast food, violence, nor boredom. To her, China is a far region of underfed children for whom she must "clean her plate" and never waste food. *Obesity, tsumani, mass media, Ayatollah, IED, kalishnikov, couch potato, community organizer*, and *pepperoni pizza* are not heard, and there is not yet a vast industry to manufacture *celebrities*. The term *fan* is so new that most still know its origin: *fanatic*. In Junior High she belonged to a Fan Club for the writer P G Wodehouse. It is doubtful Mr Wodehouse knew of that group.

She is familiar with guitars, dancing beside the ocean to portable radios, *kamikaze*, bomb shelters, tree houses, B-25s, Coventry, John 3:16, and her Uncle Ellison's Packard. To her, *process* is a noun, not a verb, and the concepts imbedded in "media coverage of a mass murder of strangers at a Burger King" would be too foreign to (so to speak) process.

Growing up during World War II and the 1950s, she is often *politically incorrect*, another unheard term, as Russian Communist leaders had not yet invented it as a tool of mass control. She seldom means to hurt anyone's feelings and will usually be unaware when she does. She is busy trying out life, a pursuit we now term "finding oneself." Just as her generation grew up during the violence of war and loves peace, she grew up without "stuff" and therefore views most "stuff" as unnecessary.

A final caution: Those without knowledge of history swallow many lies. As a veteran of both her world and ours, I am familiar with the current view that the only relevance lies in buying the life sold by anointed marketers. Many of us and virtually all our children have bitten the proffered Apple and are in danger of choking on the pieces. Any honest depiction of youthful life in the 1950s will therefore unsettle -- even frighten -- closed minds. I ask all readers to refrain from judging the past as technologically deprived, unenlightened, and irrelevant to today's entertainment-drenched scene. Deprivation is often subjective. A far better approach is to see any past era as a different culture with its own values – possibly superior values.

Take sex. Although County is most assuredly not about sex, no book by a teenager could totally omit either the topic or its attendant activities. Today, however, the mere word "fornication" is seen as shocking, and media have so savaged "love" as to make it an almost unrecognizable concept. Love had a far better chance to survive when acquaintances took time to find each other's heart (a word now frequently reduced to a cartoon shape) before attempting to "make love." Making love is clearly an impossible feat and should be seen as a nonsense phrase. Although love is not a topic taken up in my academic articles, from personal experience I am confident in saying that two persons *find* love after (or while) each of them finds the individual self. Initiallly, love is found, not manufactured.

I have mentioned sex (and love and heart) as a last warning before your plunge into the complex past.

Note: <u>County</u> mentions tangentially the ruthless and still unsolved Darlington County killing carried out in the dark of April 1952. Because our 17-year-old narrator could neither deal with it nor forget it, that crime could neither be a central part of this book nor completely omitted. Few of those whose lives were savaged by the killing have forgotten. Neither, I predict, will she.

At present, without consciously trying and perhaps with no clear idea of what she means to do with it, the narrator is accumulating material for THE LEAVING ROAD.

But then life is unpredictable, as are we all.

A.

COUNTY

The First Chapter

A View from 17

I hardly ever know what to say when I meet somebody new, specially somebody important. One of the first things I do after we get introduced is forget the person's name. I'll call you Reader, if that's okay, and I'd like it if you'd call me Memory.

My address is 120 Warley Street, Darlington, South Carolina, I go to St John's High School, and I'll graduate next month.

Up 'til I was 10, my world was a 3-mile community of farms. It was all the world I needed. I was hungry to learn but not to leave. Then Cap sold the farm we called the Sand Hill -- sold it to a road-construction company. Daddy says with so much owing on the place, Cap's lucky a company was willing to pay good money for it. Cap didn't feel lucky. Neither did I. Cap's last farm was my *place*.

Okay, right, I was just in 5th grade when we left, so I'd already got to live the best part of farm life -- the growing up part. I didn't have hard chores and only had to work in the fields sometimes, like if I wanted money for something, so I was free to roam the woods with our dogs or pester Major and the other grownups or be near wild animals or play cowpersons (cowpersons are Wild West girls who aren't sissies) with Eltas Jean or spend time in my mind in places in books.

I wanted to live on the farm forever, where every season was its own self, where I had all the freedom I could use, and where I'd been all my remembering life.

From Mineral Springs to the Court House Square is barely 4 miles. A countryman'll walk it, finish up his town business, maybe take a short rest in the livery stable or a hardware store and head home again, ready to sit a short spell on the porch after a good dipperful of cold water from the well bucket. Not a far piece for country legs, even without the luck of a lift.

11

COUNTY

But moving away from the honest, wide outdoors, into a house between other pavement-facing houses where air-conditioning units poke out of bedroom windows and new television sets blot out birdsong and peeper-frogs up among the leaves ... that's a different distance.   Different and not easy on the mind.

Farm people start out with an independence that town people don't just naturally have, maybe because we grow up roaming woods and lanes and looking at what's really there, not just *put* there by some*body*.

Mansion or tenant house or shack, growing up country makes you kind of a maverick. Maybe it's all that extra space to think in.   Look at Thomas Jefferson; if anybody thought for himself in the 1700s, it was Jefferson.   Look at the famous Dizzy Dean. Him, a follower? I'd say *not*. Growing up in the country's a blessing. Whether you grow up there rich or grow up there poor, growing up country's got to be best. I don't think many of us ever get over it.

I hope not anyhow.

But farm communities are changing.   Since the War, farmers, want to or not, can wind up selling out if the farm money coming in turns out not to be anywhere near equal to the town money being offered for the land.   Then people start moving in who don't know a plow from a mule's rear. Or maybe they don't even *move* in; they stay in town and pay to get their farming done by people they wouldn't hardly recognize if they passed 'em on the sidewalk. Landowners like that are just landowners, not farmers, is what I think. They're just saying they're farmers to fool the Government.

Now that his last farm's gone, Cap's moved out onto some of his sister Aunt Betty's land their mother accumulated after their father died. Just squattin', you could say. But every so often in a country store there'll be a man who'll remember, and say it too, that Mr Spears "use to be one of the biggest farmers in Darlington County."   Use to be.

And everybody there'll look at Cap and think whatever they're thinking, and they'll go back to talking crops and weather.

Sometimes Daddy takes me out to Mineral Springs Road so I can clear Toby's grave – pull weeds when the weather gets

12

hot and again after the wildflowers shed their summer blooms. Virginia Creeper tries to cover it in October, about the time snakes get sluggish and we can get out there okay I'm not allergic to creeper, and it's really kind of beautiful -- those long-fingered leaves that look like hands and climb like hands onto every kind of thing. When the spidery leaves get tinged with red, it's even kind of a decoration, but I pull it off. Don't and it'd cover the grave completely.

Major, he's still out around there someplace trying to make a living without neglecting his hunting too much. We'll run up on each other now and again. (Lord, have mercy on him please.)

Moaning's not what this book's about. Moaning helps only so long, and then you deal with what you've got. Moaning on is as silly as crying over spilt milk. Just call in the cat.

Still, I can't pretend nothing's changed.

Our mint-green house Daddy worked to make nice for me and Mother -- it sat out on the road where the company wanted its construction office, so after they got moved in all the way, they pushed it down. They pushed down the other tenant house across the big field and even the main house, Cap's house we use to live in. Soon enough the wide red barn, pack house, smoke house, the "store" and the old tobacco barn we never used anyhow -- all that'll be gone and the pecan meadow plowed over. Nothing much'll be left there that was ours, only some pecan grove and the woods.

The Sand Hill (Cap's name for the farm) took up both sides of the big bend on Mineral Springs Road. The main part is still *farmed*, but it's *not a farm*. Nobody *lives* there. On the other side, big track machines sit and wait behind the company office where our mint-green house use to be.

You can't get in; they put up a tall fence.

So we left the ice-cold swimming hole and the pine woods and the streaks of red clay and white sand and the neighbors and openness. Ann Cat was the only living thing we took to Warley Street. Not a single dog, even, nor Nanny's kids JudynTrudy nor our Jersey cow that gave the best milk I bet I'll ever taste.

I never wanted to be a townie. Doubt I'll ever be one, really. My eyes are country eyes. Country eyes just naturally see more

13

COUNTY

because that's what they *do*: they watch.   On farms you can watch how God's working things out around you.

Emily Dickinson was a poet who lived way up North, 100 years ago when everything was sort of country, even people's yards.   Nobody much knew she was a poet or anything else until she was dead. She wrote over 1000 poems, and one was about being nobody, which was how I felt when we first moved into town – like I was nobody. They've got that very poem engraved on a wall at Brookgreen Gardens, which is right near the Myrtle Beach Air Base.

In the country you're somebody; everybody is. You *know* each other.   Towns've got enough people already and don't need any more, is what I think.

Since we moved to town, some of my common sense has up and left me. My diaries from years ago, the ones I used to write the first book, make more sense than the ones today. A few of my teachers think I'm smart, but they could be wrong.

Other people -- they're who I'm about all of a sudden; not as much about me any more.   I can jump from happy to miserable back to happy in a day, depending on who came by or phoned or didn't or just popped into mind. Wishy washy, is what.

Worse, I pick up other people's moods.   Like gloom; I can*not* stay happy around gloom.   Whoever's moaning on, I have to either leave or start moaning too, and next thing is, I'll start trying to solve their problem and they'll get mad because what they really wanted wasn't a solution at all; they wanted a pity party. Pity parties are another thing I'm no good at.

Stuff like that didn't happen on the farm.

Worst of all, I keep deciding I'm in love, but always at the wrong time with the *wrong boys*. Thank goodness it never lasts long.   Besides, it's more fun to go out with a group than with one boy.   Not many boys are all that interesting to be alone with.   (No offense if you're a boy.   You're a reader, which means you have an interesting mind.)

You needn't tell anybody this -- and if you do I won't admit I said it -- but *I don't know what love is*, the kind you fall into. In spite of all the songs about it.

My diaries are full of lines from songs -- whole song lyrics -- lists of titles -- even pieces of songs I could swear I never heard

14

but had to've because there's the evidence, in my own squinched up handwriting trying to fit on tee-niny 5-year-diary pages. I cover a 5-year diary in a year.

You'd think I thought those songs're about me. They're not. Not a chance. No song writer knows *me*. Sometimes I write my own poetry and lyrics for made-up songs, but I throw them away. Silly stuff.

There's no way I could've put together <u>Mineral Springs Road</u> without my diaries from when I first learned to read and write. They were fresh and ... young. Kid stuff, but hey -- being 9's not a bad thing. Better, I sometimes think, than 17. Clearer. I keep all my diaries, but the only person who knows what you really meant then or what you mean now is you yourself.

Sometimes not even you.

So anyhow, Dickinson was a townie with an outdoor mind. She hardly ever left home once she got out of college, but mostly hid out at home, in the yard, admiring hummingbirds and even snakes in a way but she didn't want to pick one up. She thought of trains as like huge mythological horses. She was a watcher. I think she *preferred* being nobody. Maybe I should've got use to it and learned to like it the way she did. Maybe I'd end up famous the way she did, and can go back and buy part of the Sand Hill, live in the country again and not fool with anybody. Only she didn't end up rich, and not famous either 'til too late; she was dead.

Anyhow, famous for what? I'm not even all that good at piano, which is my major talent other than writing. It's not enough to have a good touch; you have to sit there and practice, practice, practice piano, and I don't do it. Converse College wrote and offered me a music scholarship, but I can't take it because they want me to major in piano. I don't know what I'll major in, but it won't be anything I have to sit and practice hours every day. Writing's what I love, but Uncle Bob says you can't make a living writing without working for people who don't know much about it. He loves books and poetry, but what he does for a living is broker hogs and cattle.

You don't have to tell me there's too many buts in that paragraph; no offense but I know it just as well as you do.

COUNTY

That's just the kind of paragraph I end up with when I start talking about the future.

Dickinson was an odd bird at school like me and knew it, but she hung on to who she was. I'm still me I'm pretty sure, but my story and my head shifted when we moved to town. Had to. Out in the country, cross my heart and hope to die if I even knew what *ruthless* was.

But I oughtn't to be bringing that up.

In general, Darlington County's not ruthless -- not the people who live here. But the system -- the best you can say for the system is it's misguided. Now that I'm 17 I see that. The town's misguided too, because Darlington's the county seat.

There's a lot to explain about this town, but one big thing that happened has to wait because it messed with us so bad. The more I thought about it and tried to make it part of this book, the more it tried to take over – it and what-all circled around it. It wore me down and I had to leave it out, because it's too big for us to handle, us at St John's. It's not what we're about.

Just what it is we *are* about, I've been thinking on a lot. I'm not so sure I even know what it is *I'm* about.

Anyhow, County's about us -- my classmates, my parents and me, our kin and our neighbors and others born in and around Darlington that've lived here all along or who came in from the country and turned things inside out, and about St John's on into this very month of April '57.

I've tried to put in chapters that slow things down enough to keep you in the picture, but County kind of crowds in on itself. Things spring out on top of you. Before that starts happening, let's talk about something you and I might have in common: listening to the radio.

I found out in my first book that it purely wears me out to number chapters, specially if I shift some around. I'll just give each one a name.

RADIO

Sometimes I stay home listening to the radio programs I was use to on Mineral Springs Road.   For that little time, it's like being back in the country.

When we first left the farm, I had no plans but to be sad. Radio programs cheered me up, specially when Daddy listened with me.   Other than baseball games, his and my favorite together was Our Miss Brooks. She had a crush, you know, on Mr Boynton the biology teacher, who was so shy she was always getting turned down without Mr Boynton realizing she was even flirting.   Daddy'd get to chuckling and then his shoulders'd be twitching and next thing he'd be laughing out loud. Everybody laughs along with Daddy, even if they weren't happy to begin with. It's catching.

Our Miss Brooks was probly what made me realize teachers are ... you know, *persons*. The lady that plays Miss Brooks is hilarious, even just the way she says words, stopping just long enough for you to get it and then using that drawl of hers to make it even funnier.   Eve something. Arden? After Our Miss Brooks went to tv, I didn't like it as much as when I could get away with picturing her school to be like St John's. Miss Brooks was still perfect, but Mr Boynton looked all wrong. Radio was perfect for that show. Radio lets you *imagine*.

Some people say there won't be any use for radio much longer, now that television's on all day instead of just afternoons and evenings. They're crazy, is what.

Television didn't bring us the world; radio did. Plus, radio lets you be yourself, the way you naturally are; it won't try to change you into something different.

Radio won't make you sit in one place and quit moving around; you can hear it and still do your work or dance or stand on your head if that's your pleasure. We sometimes gather around and look at the radio set during a special broadcast, but it's our choice; we don't *have* to. Television though, it wants to

17

change the way we spend our lives. Television sets *make* you sit and stare, sometimes for hours, like that's normal for a healthy human. Shoot, if I did that every day, I'd be fat as a pig and wouldn't be able to walk even from here to the Public Square, barely 3 miles.

Mother says I'm taking television too seriously. She thinks I'm peculiar anyhow, and maybe this is another way I'm being peculiar, thinking television's about to change the world for the worse by making English-speaking nations fat-bottomed and froze-jointed and having to go to gyms to work out.

With just one tv per household, maybe tv won't be that bad. That way at least, the family won't forget it's a family. They'll be together laughing at I Love Lucy or gaping at a circus act or Senyor Whatshisname the ventriloquist on the Ed Sullivan Show, something they can talk about together, like you discuss your different takes on the sermon over dinner after church. It might not be anything worth discussing, whatever's on tv, but being in the same room, they'll pay some attention to each other. Just so they don't get a tv set for another room.

Around here there's only one channel that comes in with no snow – the Florence one -- but that could change. Sometimes we look at WIS in Columbia to get the news outside the Pee Dee, when the snow's not too bad. Another Florence station's coming, but that's nothing to the radio.

Radios get lots of stations and come in all sizes now, as big as tvs. Our console is a Crosley from Lane's Furniture. "Consoles" have a phonograph *consolidated* in that plays 78s and 33s, plus you can get a middle piece that lets you play 45s too. The woodwork on ours is beautiful. They must've cut the matching doors just at the start of a tree branch. It moved to my bedroom when the tv came. If the phonograph breaks down, we'll take it out and use the space as a cabinet. Radios never quit.

If I come up with some money, I buy a record album. Daddy bought us a set of 33 rpms at Mr Gandy's livestock market. They're all Big Band -- Russell's and C'n Mary's kind of music. Big Bands belong mostly to big cities, but here in the South we've got little bands popping up everywhere. With us it's not trombones and trumpets in hotels; it's guitars in what Mother calls juke joints. Not that we don't get Big Bands ever;

18

COUNTY

Les Brown and his Band of Renown came and played at the Florence Shrine Club last month.

Some people think it was television that made our kind of music famous, but they're wrong. It was radio, and then records -- not 33s and 78s, but 45s. Any single you really like, you can find it as a 45, to listen to until you know it by heart or 'til you don't ever want to hear it again.

Portables go with us to the beach and or anywhere we're roasting hotdogs or marshmallows, and to peanut boilings and parties at cabins, like Dr Mac's at Black Creek.

A lot of cars come with radios now. Our mint-green '53 Ford has one, and Daddy put one in the gray '48 Mercury we had before.

Strings -- guitars, banjos -- that kind of music is the South's music. It's getting to be the whole nation's music since Ed Sullivan noticed Elvis and put him on tv.

Some say our '50s music caused what they call a *generation gap.* I don't know what that is, personally. I know we don't have any such thing here. We're family people. There's all ages in a family.

What I like most on the radio is music and ballgames (don't make me choose which), then comedies, and then Whispering Streets. I like The Inner Sanctum okay too; it lets you use your imagination maybe even a little too much, some dark nights. Besides, I'm not sure it'd be so good 'cept for starting out with the squeaking door. Whispering Streets calls on your imagination and your detective skills both.

Whispering Streets is based on a brilliant idea: in every episode, a minor character that was barely there last week turns out to be the next main character. Trick is to spot next week's main character, and tune in to see if you're right. I love the challenge.

Maybe I should write a series of chapter-long stories on the Whispering Streets plan once I get through writing this book and maybe an Orangeburg County one. But then it'll be time for a book about all of us leaving home, so maybe after that. I've got maybe too many plans, considering how busy I might be if I get to work a job every summer besides going on to school and whatever else comes after graduation.

19

COUNTY

The Blondie and Dagwood radio show didn't last even til the end of the year we moved. I never really missed it. The only really funny thing I remember about it was Mrs Bufforpington, the lady who claimed her husband invented the chicken. (Probly townies don't even know a Buff Orpington *is* a chicken.) Blondie and Dagwood are better in the funny papers, where they're all more interesting looking. The Bumsteads are *meant* to be cartoons. Look at Dagwood's *hair.* And his one huge button.

Fibber Magee and Molly are on, right on. They've still got their hall closet that the stuff it's stuffed with falls on Fibber almost every week. One week a burglar opened it and got buried under the pile, which was maybe the only time I really thought that closet gag was funny. People must like it, though.

Amos 'n' Andy run the Fresh Air Taxi business, but Amos does most of the work. The Kingfish is the leader of their lodge, "The Mystic Knights of the Sea."

Good grief! The light dawns:

You're liable not to believe what I'm fixing to say, but it's true: 'til I wrote that last sentence, I didn't realize Kingfish is his *title,* not his name. All these years and I'm just now figuring out something so obvious. Can't believe I've been so *thick.*

I don't hear Amos 'n' Andy now that I'm a Senior and busy, but Mother says the show's not on any more anyhow. We all really liked it.

When you hear "When Irish Eyes Are Smiling," you know it's time for Duffy's Tavern. Then a phone rings and Archie answers in his Yankee accent:

"Duffy's Tavern, where de elite meet t' eat. Ahchie d'Manageh speakin', Duffy ain't hyeah."

(*very* short pause)

"Oh, h'lo, Duffy."

I ask you, is that not a brilliant start for a comedy? Like the elite would be caught dead meeting to eat at a tavern or any place else run by somebody that talks like Archie. Not that I know any elites myself.

Wait a minute -- I do know some snobs, but they're not particly elite. Just snobs is all. And probly they don't eat anyhow; they dine.

COUNTY

When somebody comes into the tavern, Archie hangs up the phone. 'Til then, Archie's answering Duffy's questions about what's been going on at the tavern. You don't hear the questions.

It'd be good if some time we could hear what Duffy sounds like. He's got to be Irish, right? Even though Duffy's not an Irish name; it's Scottish, like Cap's ancestors the MacDuffies, Cap's christened middle name.

Daddy says you'd think the radio Duffy'd have an Irish Mick's brogue, to go with the theme music "Irish Eyes." Daddy knew some Irish Micks in the Navy. I'd like to hear one talk. There's something wrong with them being called "micks" too; nobody Irish is named Mick. Scots are the ones whose last names start with Mc; Irish names start mainly with O, like O'Sullivan, O'Brian, O'Neill. In the US they generally drop the O and maybe lose the spelling, but they're still Irish.

Over here we think the Scots and the Irish are all mixed in together, but Daddy says it's hard to find any 2 bunches of people who're actually *less* mixed in together. (He went almost all over the world in the Navy; he saw a lot.) The Irish people still in Ireland are all the time feuding, and even in America the Irish won't let it go. The deadliest feud in US history was probly the Hatfields versus the McCoys. McCoy is an Irish name (an exception to the rule of O) and Hatfield sounds English (not Scottish), but the Irish don't like the English any better than they like the Scots. Wouldn't you think they'd get tired and just call it all off?

Archie, he's not either one, I guess; just a reglar New Yorker -- or to write it the way he says it, he's a Noo Yawuhkuh.

Duffy never comes in.

I kept hoping one day he would.

21

WARLEY STREET

Warley Street is on the edge, the last full-length street before town falls down the hill to Black Creek. At its far end, Warley backs on wildness. That's where we built our house.

After the Dovesville Baptists built their new brick church building, Daddy bought their wooden one and built our house out of it. That church didn't belong in Darlington any more than I thought I did. Still, here we both are, country come to town. I'm not letting go of my plan to be country right on.

For a year or so after we moved, we'd drive back out Mineral Springs Road to the Stokeses and get good Jersey milk from our cow we left with them. Now, though, we drink store milk and eat oleo-margarine, which is make-believe butter.

Oleo-margarine was invented during WWII. Town people couldn't get butter -- it was rationed -- so they used oleo.

Daddy says oleo's bad for our insides.

Mother says, "Oh George you just don't trust the government."

I probly don't either. Mama Minnie in Rowesville says Reconstruction, another federal program, was bad enough, and now we've got oleomargarine.

Oleo use to start off lard-white. I'd mash the plastic package to spread the little orange dot until what was in the package was all streaked with yellow, and you were s'posed to keep mashing until you could fool yourself into thinking what was in the bag looked like butter. Then you squeezed some out onto a plate and spread it on bread or cooked with it. Most ladies still cook with lard, specially for biscuits, or with Crisco. Crisco's real popular in the grocery ads in the News & Press.

Lard is pig fat --everybody knows what *it* is. Oleo is an evil of government and of town life. I miss butter.

I had plenty other reasons than oleo not to want to move to town, like having to quit driving because of being 10. In town you're not s'posed to drive a car without a driver's license, and you can't even try for it 'til you're 14.

The minute I turned 14, I took the test and got mine; we all did. The only part anybody said was hard is parallel parking, because who ever does it? All the parking I do in Darlington is head-in.

People who took it before I was old enough (I'm the youngest in my grade now) said, "Whatever you do, don't hit the orange cones even if you end up perpendicular. And take the test in your own car or no telling what kind of car you'll get. You don't stand a chance in some car you've never seen before."

When Southern Bell changed its trucks, Daddy bought one of the old ones. It's army-green like they all are, with lift-up doors on both sides, so Daddy can stand on the ground and open the cabinets and not have to rummage all through the car trunk for tools. Plus while he's working, Mother can use the car. That's why she could take me over to Florence for my test and Daddy wouldn't have to lose time from working.

Turned out they both took me. Daddy said he couldn't let us go alone.

I didn't do bad. The driving part was easy, 'cept for being nervous the whole time because the parallel parking was coming last. I got the car parked and it looked okay, even though the officer said I could've got closer to the curb.

What I missed was on the written test. I didn't really study the Driver's Handbook because nobody said it mattered really and besides I couldn't believe I'd have to know all that. Like how far you've got to stay behind a car in moving traffic: a car-length for every 10 mph you're moving. If you're doing 40, you're s'pose to be 4 car-lengths behind?!? I don't think many drivers know much that's in that handbook.

Anyhow I passed and got my license without having to come back and be tested again. You'd be surprised how many people I know who had to go back the 2nd and even a 3rd time. I wonder do they ever get tired of fooling with some people and say so.

Daddy had me a key made to the car and gave me a FORD key ring for it, the front-door key, and my beautiful license like a military dog tag, engraved with my name, address, and license number.

COUNTY

Actually licenses might not be really engraved. Probly the letters and numbers are pressed in with a machine. Heck, you know what they look like, but this one's *mine*.

Not that I get to use our car alone much, even now, but I *have* had to drive myself home from a date before. Boys don't always know when they've had enough beer at a party. Me, I get a headache right off the bat, plus I can't see how anybody gets to like the taste. Give me sweet tea any *time*.

While Daddy and some men were building our new house next door to where we were renting from Mary (Mrs James) MacInnis, I picked up some of the nails they dropped and dragged some cut treated boards out planning to try to put up a tree house where I could go and be alone. (Our lot's deep, down to the creek.) Daddy figured out what I was up to and built it, only he put it in our big tree farther back; he said nails might kill the smaller one.

So I have a tree house. It's not much like a house -- mostly a floor with 3 walls under a roof-- but for a while it was my frequent place. From there I can look into the tree branches behind us, or down toward the creek where things are always moving around. When there's enough wind, the heavy vines sway over the water. Wisteria, they are. Some are bigger then Daddy's arms.

Once after a hard rain I saw a huge vine fall. It roiled the water and gradually sank out of sight.

Up 'til then, I'd been thinking I'd try swinging across like Tarzan.

I changed my mind.

Daddy likes being in town, as far as his work. He's closer to more of his customers.

We've got our own telephone now; seems like everybody in town has one, and it's not even a party line. We have to have it for Daddy's work. I never talked on telephones when I was growing up; now I do. People call, whether you want 'em to or not.

When we first got here, our number was 373. Then it got to be 373-J. Now Southern Bell's changed it to 1071, and they're about to add a J to *it*. I could understand changing the number

24

if we'd moved, but we've lived right here at the cemetery ever Daddy got the house built.

I wish they had just let us keep 373.

Daddy says Mother's the best secretary in the world; that he gets compliments all the time, about how nice it is to talk with Mrs Spears when they phone him to come. Which is natural, of course: she was brought up in Orangeburg County by Mama and Papa, and knows how to act. She tries to teach me manners too, but finds it discouraging.

Soon as we got to town and Daddy got the truck, Mother started me in to joining things. The Memorial Center (it's a Victorian house on Pearl Street with a huge front porch and big rooms) has activities for children and young people, and judging by what she knew to do in Lamar growing up, she figured that was where I should go. After an older boy in a convertible started hanging around and asking if he could drive me home (and she met him), she decided maybe things are different now and that I should mostly hang around with people I already know at church and through the family.

One activity at the Memorial Center turned out really nice: Mrs Belissary's Brownie Troop. She started it herself – the 1st Brownies in town. We didn't get to go camping in the wilderness, but I enjoyed the meetings. Mrs Belissary did her best to teach us to be good Scouts.

She and Mr Matthew bought acreage and built a brick house on Mineral Springs Road soon after we moved to town. I think they even have horses – horses and room to ride -- my idea of a dream place for a family. I miss the Sand Hill a lot.

Mrs Belissary is a kind lady with fair complexion and shiny black hair. Mr Matthew is handsome and dignified, like Greek Gods in paintings only with clothes on. American clothes.

Daddy and Waldo Davis came up with a plan: they were going to cook their own chitlins. The Chitlin Club is still going, but it meets only every so often when the weather's cold and right, and Daddy *does* like chitlins.

Out of the extra bricks Daddy and Waldo put up an outdoor fireplace at the backyard line between us and the Davises. Waldo and Wilhelmina are who moved into the rental house next door when we moved out. He's a plumber and Daddy's an

25

electrical repairman, a perfect fit. Neither one's a brick mason, but they both grew up on farms so they know how to build anything they need.

So here they go all excited with the new fireplace, cleaning and boiling and doing everything right to serve up chitlins just for us (only I don't eat 'em), and here comes Mother out saying we're liable to be asked to leave the neighborhood.

"We're not out in the sticks now, George. Those chitterlings are too fragrant to cook in town."

Chitterlings. Who says chitterlings; nobody but townies. It's *chitlins*.

Mrs Davis shows up right behind her, asking what in the world they think they're doing stinking up the place so bad she couldn't hardly breathe and her sinuses fixin' to give her a headache to beat the band.

Daddy and Mr Davis kept on and ate their chitlins that night. Mother ate some too; she hates the smell of the cooking but she likes chitlins.

That turned out to be the last hoorah for the home-cooked chitlin plan. Now Daddy uses the fireplace for hamburgers or ribs and sometimes weenies. Mother burns trash in it.

Still, if you have to live in town, here's as close to the country as Darlington gets. Our woods slope down to a real creek, deeper than the on-again, off-again stream in the woods behind the Sand Hill. There's turtles here just like there only bigger, and snakes might come crawling up like in the country, only these don't stay. (No point in it. No barns here, and precious few rats. We've always got a cat on the job.)

I heard a commotion in the back yard during May of '51, soon after we moved into the house Daddy built out of lumber from the old Baptist church in Dovesville. I looked out the bathroom window and saw Mother flailing away with a hoe at something on the ground. It would move and she'd flail some more. Pretty soon it quit moving.

It was a snake, a big one that'd made the mistake of crawling up from the creek. She wouldn't've bothered it, I don't think, if it hadn't messed with her cat Parthenia. Parthy use to be my cat but they all love Mother best of all, no contest.

COUNTY

Whenever a cat takes up at our house, I get to name it, but then Mother feeds it table scraps so it doesn't have to eat normal stuff like mice and roaches from the garage.

I named Parthenia for the mother in Miss Edna Ferber's book <u>Showboat</u>. (We all saw that picture show or read the book.) Parthenia arrived at our house expecting, so a mama name was natural. She's had the kitten since -- an *only* kitten, believe it or not. We kept waiting, there on the back porch, but she just got up and started washing her one baby, and that was that. Then we had her fixed. Later on she wandered off someplace, but at least she's quit being a streetwalker.

I named the kitten Magnolia because it was deep black like Kathryn Grayson's hair. (She played Magnolia.) Then the kitten grew and grew and turned out to be a boy. I changed ~~her~~ his name to Noir, which is French for black. He grew up huge; 22 pounds of muscle, no fat; most prodigious cat anybody around here's ever seen.

There're dogs in the neighborhood, but they don't bother Noir. Daddy says a German Shepherd was sniffing around until Noir roused up from his nap on the front porch and slashed its nose. We don't see the German Shepherd here any more. The dachshund that use to come for scraps won't come here now, and the Galen Elliotts' cocker crosses over to the other side and heads home if he sees Noir.

Everybody calls him Blackie, though. Daddy says I can't expect "us old people" to take to speaking French. Silly talk; Daddy's not old a bit. His hair's thinning but what's there's still wavy and blond and he's very handsome.

If you pass by from Cashua going to the cemetery, you'll see our house on your left. It's small, tight and bright: white with an ink-blue roof and a 2/3 front porch we can sit on, and a garage out back. 'Course we don't put the car in it; it's actually Daddy's shop, and was built to be. He can work on small jobs here, and keep parts, tools and his big ledger with the bills and receipts. He took an old oak sewing machine apart and uses the drawers as files for screws and brads and so on.

I jumped off the roof of the garage under an umbrella as soon as it got built, but Mother says that's dumb; I'm not s'posed to want to do stuff like that. I admit landing on the ground wasn't that much fun, but there's not as much to do in

27

town as on a farm, and you start to experiment. I was hoping the wind would catch up underneath the umbrella and it would feel like flying, but it didn't. I don't know what I weighed then -- not much -- but the umbrella wasn't up to even that.

Mr Davis is a devout fisherman and loves our catalpa tree. We know when the worms hatch out because first thing one morning we'll see Mr Davis in our back yard picking 'em off the tree fast as he can, before birds find out. Mr Davis says fish go crazy over catalpa worms fresh off our tree.

Warley's got no sidewalks, and neither do any of the other streets that cross Cashua. There's not really room, and grass grows to the asphalt almost. That's good; easy to walk along.

Warley Street's natural, 'cept for being paved and too many houses. You can hear the lady over on Spain Street (a block away, running with Warley) calling her son.

"Robert Lee? Robert Lee! You come hyenh 'is *minute*. You don' come right 'is minute, I'm go *tan yo hide*, Robert Lee. You don' bleeve me, you try me. See 'f I don't."

I'm not making fun of her; that's how she *talks*.

Other times, "Boy, you deef in one eah and cain' heah out d' other? I ain' aksin you again. You doe come hyenh right now, you in a worl' a trouble."

And you might see a low dark streak go by. It's not a plane and it's not Superman, it's just Robert Lee, fastest boy on the planet, streaking home.

Sometimes I'd get to feeling right sorry for Robert Lee, hardly ever getting to finish up with whatever he was out there doing. Even yet, I'd say he's not over 12. Loves his mama to death, though.

If a house caught fire, houses on both sides would get singed or worse. When the back of our mint-green house caught fire from lightning that summer afternoon in the country, last thing we had to worry 'bout was somebody else's house. Another time, Eltas Jean and I caught grass on fire fooling around with firecrackers, and we got it stomped out in plenty of time for it not to reach the storage house. Scary though.

The thing that makes Warley Street better than most paved streets is this:

We live one house from the graveyard.

GRAVEYARDS and CREEKS

Time we moved to town, I staked out Grove Hill to be the scene of my meditative moments. I planned to go there a lot and just be miserable. Graveyards are good for that.

Grove Hill came in handy that first year.

Grove Hill's a *big* cemetery. The entrance gate is where Warley ends at the wild end of Broad. The original Cheraw & Darlington track passes through there, north to south. It was mainly a farm-to-market track a hundred years back just before the War Between the States, and for mixed trains. Some years there were passenger trains. Passenger trains don't come here any more.

Walking east on West Broad, you'll pass whole blocks of tall wooden Victorian houses, all well kept up. West Broad was once where everybody wanted to live. Even now some of the town's most interesting people live there, like Miss Emmie Kirven, who got a law degree just to use for her own business investments. And when Russell's Uncle G W Mims moved back rich from New Orleans, he and Mildred (she's half French and half Spanish) and C'n George lived in a Victorian on Broad while they built in G W's old hometown and Daddy's. Their house (the only house I know with an open garden in the middle) got to be the center for a while of where everybody else wanted to build in Lamar.

East Broad – our half of Broad – was *never* the place everybody wanted to live. There were open lots, but nobody but us was building here. Maybe we're the only ones who like cemeteries.

Come all the way east on Broad or all the way south on Warley either one, and you're at the cemetery gate.

Dr H D Fraser was the Darlington County Health officer in 1885. He counted more than 1,500 burial grounds around Darlington -- the town itself, not the county, which was bigger before Florence County formed in 1888. His report shows how big a problem that was, because nobody yet was building secure tombs for reglar people:

> Wells are used exclusively for drinking purposes, the water unquestionably contaminated from surface filtrations, and we believe the greatest source of danger to be from the number of burial grounds within the incorporate limits. ....
> At times odors emanating from these grounds are considerably annoying, especially during damp nights in Summer. The Board of Health have been energetic in trying to have these nuisances abolished and in their stead established cemeteries without the town limits. By a unanimous vote at a mass meeting, the citizens have decided to sustain the recommendation of the Board of Health.

It must've been a chore, getting a new town in shape for healthy living. I use to think towns wouldn't have an odor problem unless they had a paper mill like Georgetown's, but what did I know.

Even after the "mass meeting," Dr Fraser said the town council was slow to establish cemeteries "without the town limits." When they did act, Grove Hill must have been one they established. It and this end of Warley are almost out of town, hanging out here on the edge.

I don't know what Dr Fraser did to solve the "considerably annoying" odors, but Grove Hill smells perfectly fine now, summers and all year long. Anyhow, wouldn't you think back then they'd've known about lime? Any farmer could've told 'em. Nobody uses a concrete vault and casket to bury a mule, no matter how good a friend of yours the mule might've been.

Grove Hill looks flat when you come into it or see it from Warley Street, but walk around among the graves till you come to the tall trees, and you'll see: Behind and below the trees are our same creek and swampy land. It's what the poet Wordsworth would recognize right away to be a *romantic* place, inspiring imagination and emotion and a lot of butterflies -- small yellows and pale tiny blues and showy Monarchs.

All the tombstones here are gray, which is exactly right -- the color of sadness but not of dark despair. Some are marble and started out white, but nature grays them and brings the cemetery into harmony again.

Some of the stones are downright beautiful. The one I visit most often, even without planning to end up there, is the tall marble lady weeping for C'n Mamie Agness that I never knew. The weeping statue could stand for Mamie herself. She died before I was born. Could be the statue was actually cast in her likeness.

C'n Mamie had lots of babies -- I think 9 all together. The last-born was christened Rosa. She lived to grow up, and so did 3 boys. Behind Mamie Agness's grave are the 5 dead babies, side by side, each with its own tiny marker. A few days after Rosa was born, Mamie Agness passed away. I hope she could somehow know before she died that this last and only living girl would not be laid in still another tiny grave.

C'n Monroe's monument is beside the weeping lady and in front of their babies. There's lots of empty space in front within the coping. C'n Mamie's 2 living sons and the daughter are all in Texas now. I wonder will any of them come back here to be buried. And who'll be buried in the rest of the plot if they don't? Nobody at all?

I'm glad Dr Fraser (who was Mother's mother's cousin from the low country, it turns out) and the rest worked to make Darlington healthful and built such a beautiful graveyard. Butterflies love it there, and it's been good for me. The creek behind our house on Warley flows down below the graves, at the back of the property where nothing will ever be built. Down there, it's wild and natural. Just sit on the downslope and listen.

Cemeteries aren't where you go to be happy, but they're some of my favorite places to think -- Grove Hill, and the Florence cemetery that was moved by the Charleston railroad after the War, and the cemetery at Rowesville in Orangeburg County where Barbara Frederick Funchess and James Edward Boone are buried. Some burials were in secret places, off in the woods where Union troops wouldn't find them and maybe desecrate the graves. Usually there'd be no markers at those private burial places, to keep them from being found. Later on, during so-called "Reconstruction" when nothing got reconstructed (like the Federals' new names for every county; *that* didn't stick for sure), there was no money for markers

COUNTY
except wooden ones. Wooden markers decay. Some fell and
were never replaced because no-one still alive knew they were
there.

In a war fought among houses and gardens and fields,
nothing is safe. Thank God no other war has been fought in the
United States.

COUNTY

Darlington has a Country Club. It's on a creek too – a different creek, bigger, almost like a river: Black Creek.

The Darlington County Club is down the Cashua Street hill, round the bend, across a railroad track, and off to the right. It's on the town side of Black Creek, so turn before you get to the bridge.

We're not members. Daddy grinned and raised his eyebrows when I was asked him if we were going to join. I know what he meant. We don't have that extra money, and even if we did, some snooty people probly wouldn't think the electrical repairman, who does his work in coveralls, ought to be in a club with them.

But sometimes I get invited, and I go. Not just to a party somebody from St John's is giving, but in between times, with Marion. Locals aren't s'pose to, unless they're members, but Marion and her mother and sisters are Lifetime Members because Mrs Coggeshall (or maybe Mr Coggeshall before he died young) donated their off-side frontage on Black Creek to the DCC. That's like being Super Members. Nobody tells them they can't invite whoever they want to, which is how I got to kind of know the Club.

The DCC'll probly never need to build a swimming pool, because now it's put up a little bathing-suit-changing house at the edge of the Creek, above the wooden dock to sit on or dive from or push each other off of. The Creek's long; there's other places to swim in it, and other rather rich people have places that border it. Dr Willcox's cabin's kind of on Black Creek, where Mac has parties sometimes. You can't see the creek from their cabin, but walk a ways through the viney trees and you'll hear the turtles.

Dr Mac's a collector of arrow heads and other ancient artifacts. He has them in display cases in his cabin. He tries not to disturb the woods other than to pull wisteria vines off the smaller trees. (Did you notice the book's cover? That's wisteria.)

Wisteria is beautiful and strong and thrives here. Everybody knows wisteria vines are all out for themselves. They're slow growing, but one wisteria vine will crush a tree if you let it stay there long – squeeze it until it dies. Meanwhile,

33

tree branches will be dying and snapping off. I've seen wisteria with a trunk bigger than the tree it's climbing on.

The current all along Black Creek is tricky, plus you need to watch out for big branches snapped off by vines and for snakes.

Miss Illy gives swimming lessons at the Club. She tells her pupils, "Just swim on by if you meet one. Snakes are no more interested in getting close to you than you are to them."

I don't think that's quite right, considering some snakes I've known. I'd never contradict Miss Illy, of course. She's one of our best friends in town, mine and Mother's and Daddy's. But you have to watch.

Kathy's little sister Laura took lessons from Miss Illy, and met a moccasin one day while she was swimming across. Nobody wants to meet a cotton-mouth moccasin; they're scary looking, poisonous, and unpredictable. That one kept on its way and she kept on hers, but she remembers it real clear.

Nobody's drowned at the Country Club yet. The concrete pool at the Darlington-Florence county line on 52 didn't last long at all as a public pool. There was a drowning not long after they got it built, and it didn't stay open.

Florence has some pools if you want to drive that far, but there's always people in them – specially the big one at Timrod Park. Which means you don't know what's in the water along with the chlorine. Sometimes the chlorine smell almost knocks you out, but the city has to put it in because little kids pee in pools. They stay in too long or they get excited and can't help it. Everybody knows that because we did it too.

Plenty of swimming holes've been here all along and don't charge fees nor memberships either one -- natural places, like along Black Creek. Or the pool below Mineral Springs in the coldest water around, if the branches and leaves don't fill it up.

If you're tubing along on the current on Black Creek or a river, you're not likely to be bothered by wildlife and they won't be bothered much by you. If you're going down for a swim in a creek or a natural pool, don't go quiet; you don't want to corner a snake. Make some noise when you get close – sing out or develop a cough or drag a stick along the tree trunks. Before you get there, the woods sounds'll get quiet and you might hear turtles plopping down off logs into the water. Any snakes should disappear by time you get to the banks. 'Cept moccasins. Moccasins run from *nothing*.

One thing you know: in moving water, the current takes away contamination. No manmade pool can make that claim.

When the <u>News and Courier</u> wrote about Darlington County in 1889, newspapers had a flowing style with more commas. Some of their writers saw the world as beautiful, even poetic. These days we'd edit out the poetry part; it's not *in*.

IN THIS FINE REGION THE YELLOW PINE AND OTHER VALUABLE WOODS ABOUND, AND BROAD COTTON FIELDS, AS LEVEL AS A PRAIRIE, STRETCH FROM RIVER TO RIVER, ALONG WHOSE BANKS THE FERTILE BOTTOMS LIE, WHERE, IN FAVORABLE SEASONS, THE BURGEONING CORN UPLIFTS A THOUSAND BRISTLING BLADES--THE BAYONETS OF PEACE.

[Bayonets of peace! And did you notice that's *all one sentence*? It's true that corn grows huge when it's planted on river land that's been flooded in the spring rains. Newspapers back then could publish features that sounded like hymns of praise.]

HERE, NESTLING BENEATH THE EMBOWERING OAKS,

[South Carolina loves its embowering oaks. The most famous is the Angel Oak at John's Island. Some of its biggest branches are propped up, but the tree stands. Right here in our town we've got the original Darlington Oak. It's in front of the Armory on the hill at the Mill end of Orange Street.]

THE LITTLE CITY OF DARLINGTON, LIKE A COY BEAUTY, HIDES HER MODEST HEAD. BUT NO DREAMER SHE! THE DRUMMERS, THOSE HUSTLING "HARBINGERS OF TRADE," WHO PERIODICALLY VISIT DARLINGTON, PLAY NO PRINCE CHARMING ROLE, BUT FIND HER VERY WIDE AWAKE AND ALIVE TO BUSINESS.

COUNTY

[Everybody knows about Sleeping Beauty, but Prince Charming might be from a different story. Charming might be the family name for fairy-tale princes.]

A VERY PRETTY LITTLE CITY IT IS, TOO, WITH WIDE, DEEPLY SHADED STREETS AND MANY BEAUTIFUL AND EXTENSIVE FLOWER GARDENS AND SHRUBBERIES. SWIFT CREEK, A CLEAR STREAM, FLOWS ALONG THE BASE OF THE SLIGHT ELEVATION UPON WHICH THE TOWN IS BUILT AND AFFORDS A CHANNEL FOR THE DRAINAGE, WHICH IS EXCELLENT.

[The drainage *is mostly* excellent, I guess. Or it *was* before all the roads got paved and water couldn't soak into the ground as easy. Just don't get over into the middle of town today after a good hard rain and try to pass between the Masonic Temple and First Baptist.

But people like pavement a lot better than they like mud.]

Swift Creek is the very stream that passes by at the bottom of our lot here on Warley Street. You remember: I was sitting in my tree house when the "clear stream" took the huge vine under.

CARS

The main thing on Darlington's mind in 1950 when we first moved to town was Mr Harold Brasington's race track. Out on 151 he was building the biggest racetrack most of us had ever seen. After Pearl Street passes over the Atlantic Coast Line RR at the Cotton Mill, and dips and rises up again outside town, he'd soon have himself the first big-time stock-car raceway in the world.

The last thing Darlington was expecting at the end of the '40s was for the most important event ever to hit car racing to happen right here just outside of town.

Don't be surprised it was a Darlington boy who changed automobile racing into a big-time, nationwide sport. In the Pee Dee we know cars from the get-go. As kids we could identify make and year of any car we saw on the road.

In fact, that's the secret behind Darlington's suddenly getting crowned the nation's (or even the *world's*) car-racing capital: any car *on the road.*

Cap's 1st C'n Monroe Spears (we say MONroe, not MonROE) owned the first car in Darlington. People were always wheedling at him to let 'em drive it, so he took to renting it out. There's photographs of young ladies driving it around, sitting up just as proud and dressy, all smiling.

Out in the country, boys and most girls grew up knowing cars like they knew animals. You started out riding a mule and then maybe a horse, and the next thing's a pickup truck or an old car. The family wouldn't necessarily own a car -- a truck's more useful -- but whenever either one passes on the road, folks in the fields'll stand up and look till it's gone. About the age when we got up on tractors -- at 7 or 8 -- we'd be driving whatever car was around. The grownups'd be busy and need something from the store and maybe send us.

Not many cars pass on farm-to-market roads, so farmers don't worry about wrecks. Too, nobody's out there checking to see who's got a driver's license. Lots of grownups drive without licenses.

When Daddy was 11 or 12 he was driving a logging truck for Cap. That was after Cap lost his rural mail carrier job because he got the Spanish Flu so bad he had to spend a long time in McLeod's Infirmary. He nearly died, which was what everybody that went into a hospital in 1918 expected to do, but he didn't. With his mail carrying job gone, he went back to the family land and started being a full-time farmer, which he'd never meant to happen. The Depression started down here in 1926. Nobody in the North knew it yet.

From 1930 on, you were s'posed to get a license. What you did to get a license in the '30s, 'cording to my Uncle Hart, was go to Columbia and pay the money and pick it up; no driving test nor rigmarole like now. He thinks Colon King was the first patrolman around here, maybe the only one for a while, and Officer King didn't have time to waste on giving tests. Patrolmen were busy doing things like keeping Governor Olin D. Johnston from taking over the highway department. The Legislature got so disgusted it took away the Governor's right to name highway commissioners. C'n Ben Sawyer (he was the Highway Commissioner) won that round.

Columbia use to be the quickest -- and maybe only -- place to get a South Carolina driving license in the '30s. Soon as Cap's youngest boy Hart turned 12, Cap took all his young'uns across the big swamp to Columbia for their licenses. He picked a good dry day. No sense getting half way there and having to turn around because the road's under water.

Mules were mostly going out and tractors were coming in – little gray Fords (that's what we had) and big green John Deeres and red Farmalls and International Harvesters. Once you had a tractor, it stands to reason you had to keep it running or all that outlay was not worth a dead leaf. Farm boys -- and farm girls without older brothers -- grew up helping to fix whatever broke, including the car if there *was* one. Mechanicking comes with farming.

Even if it's just a mule in harness and a plow, things break down, so a farm tries to grow its own shade-tree mechanic along with the crops. In toddlerhood Daddy was the one in his family already set on knowing how motors and everything electrical works. Mile for mile, it's possible there's no place in the world where a larger proportion of the population has actually torn down an engine than here in the upper coastal plain of South Carolina.

Mineral Springs Road was like most other country communities: the first cars were a curiosity and an entertainment to all. They were always needing something fixed or tinkered with, and whoever was doing the tinkering or fixing was use to having a bunch of onlookers and unofficial overseers hanging around. We've got plenty of Pee Dee shade-tree mechanics. With a winch, a wrench and a screwdriver, they can put 'most anything on wheels to running the road again.

One of the onlooking boys was Harold Brasington. He'd go join in the wrenching at Mr Frank Drake's garage, a 1-man (sometimes 2-man, plus some curious teenagers most of the time), 1- or 2-car operation a block south of the post office. Space is precious at Drake's; the place spills over with tools. Inside looks like inside the cabinets on the sides of Daddy's work truck that use to have *Southern Bell* on both doors but you can barely see the words now.

Drake's Garage was one of the first corrugated sheet metal business buildings I was ever in -- it and Joe's Electric & Motor at 5 Points near Florence. Now Daddy trusts me to drive to Joe's to pick up Daddy's rewound appliance motors. I'm proud to do it. It's like being part of the family business.

To a country boy, cars are a lot less complicated than dancing and courting. So he'll save up 'til he can get some ol' scrap of a car, anything to work on and make go faster. Plus there've always been dirt tracks to race on, out in the county. First it was horses, and now it's cars. There's quite a few local drivers with winners' reputations in dirt-track racing.

The part-time job most esteemed by boys, specially country boys, is -- you guessed it -- working at a filling station that has a service bay.

Once he'd earned enough money in Rowesville to buy his own car, my brother Russell talked our grandfather (we call him Papa) into letting him look for an after-school job in Orangeburg. He got one in a gas station with a double bay. Pretty soon he had a job at Mr Horne's Ford dealership's garage.   Whenever he'd come to the Pee Dee in his shiny, sharp-fronted black Ford convertible ('way sleeker looking than the new ones), he was a teen sensation.   He washed and polished that car every week and wiped it all over every day. I never saw a speck of dust on it as long as he owned it.

You're bound to remember that car from when he'd visit us on Mineral Springs Road, specially the night he took us to the basketball game at St John's.   That was the one.

You might be picturing a lot of cars at my high school, but it's people, not cars.   Parents, neighbors, and highway-yellow buses bring us to school.   Other than some students with jobs too far from school to walk it, we're not car owners.   A few puddle jumpers and souped-up jalopies, but that's about it.

Oh, wait: there's Betty Jean.

A St John's *student* actually showed up in September of our Junior year in her own new car -- Betty Jean Goodson, a Senior.   One of *us,* almost. Mr Bob had bought her a brand new '55 Chevy, blue and white.   Not a Bel Air, but *new*.   I remember almost not believing her luck.

Some whole families don't have cars.   Uncle Clarence Gasque in Florence that's married to Aunt Tee – they've got no car because they live upstairs behind his hotel job.   My Gasque cousins get picked up by a neighbor or walk to school.

I mentioned Harold Brasington kind of casually, like I mentioned Russell.   But Harold Brasington's the center of this story of the new kind of racing.   He was already a dirt-track driver of good standing when he decided to go in the direction of a plan he'd had tickling inside his head from when he was in his early 20s.

Mr Brasington's sisters were already teenagers when he was born.   It was natural that as a boy he'd form a close friendship with his nephew from Conway, the one who left Wofford College to fly in the Army Air Corps and came out of the War a 1st Lt.   The nephew stayed on the ground long as he could and then went to flying again.

They were both of them daredevils, young at heart no matter what came -- the kind who if they're good and smart, can go out on a limb and accomplish something big.   It didn't hurt that they were tall, really tall, and slim.   I've noticed that other men tend

40

to do what tall men say, specially tall men with deep voices. Mr Brasington could play a cowboy and look right at home, 'cept probly be taller than the other actors. He's got the drawl and all.

Hard work's no problem for Harold Brasington; he relishes it. Along with earning a living and raising a family, he'd raced dirt tracks up 'til 1948 and started a business that would let him build tracks himself: Brasington's Sand and Gravel.

In 1933, the same year he got married to Miss Mildred, Mr Harold got with Jack Kirven and some others and traveled to Indiana to see the only big race there was. That must've been the place he received the vision.

He stored it in one side of his head and set the rest of his brain to converting the vision into truckloads and man hours. No matter how long it took him (he was 24; he'd finally make it happen when he was 40), he meant for him and his crew to build a paved super speedway.

They did it, too, starting at the very end of 1949 and working right up 'til paying customers were standing at the gate in September. Passersby on the highway would see him out there after everybody else was off work. He'd be driving his big machines, moving dirt, feeling his way, shaping the slope to match the vision.

He wanted an oval, but Mr Ramsey said not if that means bothering my fishing pond out behind there. Later on, NASCAR people who thought they were being cute got to calling it a minnow pond, but it was always more than that. It's a nice size, with shade trees.

If you're tired of reading "Mr Brasington" every whipstitch, you can imagine how tired I am of writing it, and this story's not finished. So I'm going to do something my parents and both my grandmothers would be ashamed of me for doing: I'm going to call a grown man by his first name, or try to, from here on. Just for the story, you understand. I have better upbringing than to call him that to his face.

The story they tell is, ~~Mr Brasington~~ Harold was playing in a gin rummy game one evening and Mr Ramsey was there. Some say it was poker, which would have been all right too. Perfectly respectable men around here play poker. My Uncle Bob Spears attends Central Methodist Church in Florence every

Sunday, including a Sunday School class, and plays poker with friends every other week reglar.

Anyhow, Harold said,

"Sherman, why don't we build a racetrack on that sorry piece of land you've got out there on the Hartsville road?" Mr Ramsey might've been grumbling about the soil; farmers do that a lot. Cap sure did.

By the end of the evening, Mr Ramsey said something Mr Brasington took to be a yes.

Then Mr Ramsey left town for awhile on business.

When Mr Ramsey got back, Mr Brasington, who's a doer not a talker, had a bulldozer and dirt-haulers out there starting to build the track.

RACETRACK

So Mr Ramsey, who's more for paperwork than for handshakes (all Ramseys are Scottish), set up a corporation. He and Harold got up $50,000 or so in cash and equity, and they took in another partner too -- Mr Bob Colvin, to contribute money and be the treasurer. The newspapers called Mr Colvin a "prosperous peanut broker." Funny the things you don't know just from knowing the person.

Mr Brasington had to borrow some of his part; he's not rich like the Ramseys. They're rich because Mrs. Ramsey was a Colt, of the Colt Firearms Company. Like both my grandmothers, she doesn't care whether she's in with uppity people; I don't get the impression she even knows which ones they are. She has high spiritual standards and she lives by them.

Mr Paul Psillos came in early too, almost as early as Sherman Ramsey. In December of '49, he says, "Harold approached me about attending a meeting in the McFall Hotel to make plans for construction of a 1.25-mile asphalt paved, banked race track with seating for 10,000 fans." 1.25 is exactly half the size of the Indianapolis track, which is probly where that idea came from.

The numbers changed after that, plus by the time Mr Psillos told about it, he'd forgot that the hotel's name had changed after Mr McFall died, but they organized is the point. Mr Brasington needed Mr Psillos, who runs Darlington Construction Company and the Builders Supply *and* is a civil engineer -- academically certified. Harold's engineering comes natural.

Here's who was at the meeting that formed the Racetrack:
1. Fred Stem. He owns a tobacco warehouse and use to be the Mayor. He and his family live in the Welling house. Mr Welling had the house built just before the Wall Street crash; he was a banker and you think he'd've known better, having

43

seen the cotton market go bust in '26. There's dark-stained white-pine panelling everywhere inside, a Spanish-tile roof like in Beverly Hills, Cal., and a whole room just for playing billiards. It's the nicest 2-bedroom, 1 ½-bath house you ever saw. (Mr Welling didn't want any overnight visitors. He sent them to the McFall.)

2. Floyd Young -- an insurance man, Mr Psillos says.

3. J C Stone that the men call Rock. He's the Coca-Cola bottler and Jimmy Stone's daddy.

4. A "public relations promoter from New York" name of Whitty. Mr Psillos didn't catch his first name, so don't ask me what it is either; I grew up not knowing anybody from New York.

And of course 5. Mr Sherman Ramsey,

               6. Mr Psillos, and

               7. Harold.

Mr Colvin was out of town making a living.

At that meeting they decided to build concrete stands instead of wood. (Mr Psillos also owns the Ready-Mix Concrete Co.) Whether Harold had counted on that much up-front outlay or not, he was determined to get the track built. After that, he'd do the best he could.

The Board chose Labor Day for the first race, figuring people could get here on the long weekend and watch the competitors trying the track ahead of the race, and then watch the race and hurry home for work on Tuesday. There'd be no racing on Sunday; Sundays are for church. Visitors in town would be more than welcome to join us in worship services.

The other reason they chose Labor Day was that Harold, who relished a challenge, said he could have the track up and ready by September.

Mr Psillos agreed to "design" the track if he could have "a topography of the land" pronto.

Harold said, "Sure."

The next day he had Mr Psillos himself out there working the instruments while Harold held the level rod and went "pacing off 100-foot intervals." They finished the measuring before dark.

Mr Psillos wrote later: "So I drew the plans, completing them after four days and three sleepless nights on New Years' Eve.... Work had to start immediately in order to finish by the 1950 Labor Day race." He was in a sweat, you can tell, but by then he was a believer.

Paul Psillos claims to be the man who told Harold how to work around Mr Ramsey's demand that the track not bother his fishing hole: they'd get out of the pond's way by changing the curve radius at the west end of the track.

In other words, they'd mash Harold's dream oval into an egg.

When you think about it, that egg shape probly had as much to do as anything with making Darlington Raceway "the track too tough to tame." No telling how many race drivers've cussed that decision since, without even knowing where it came from.

Harold worked hard to drum up support. No talker by nature, he had to be all the time going to groups and clubs to talk up the track and the whole idea. Daddy got involved from the first. Not with money; he didn't have money; what he has is knowhow. Daddy was hired as the track electrician.

Daddy's friends in town include Loomis and Bob Colvin and Harold, besides being as good as any Electrician the U S Navy can turn out. Bob was named Secretary of the new raceway's Board of Directors. Harold was (of course) President.

So the Racetrack got built, with a grandstand big enough to hold Darlington's entire population, plus it had tall sides to keep cars from flying right off the oval. From the highway you couldn't see the pond any more, nor even the trees around it.

Ramsey's Pond was instantly transformed into a popular romantic dating scene for teenagers and a few older patrons hoping not to be observed. I wasn't a teenager yet so we might talk about that later. Or not.

The main difference between Darlington and Indianapolis didn't show up yet -- not 'til the cars came to race. The cars are what made the Darlington track unique in the world -- the kind of cars people own and drive on actual streets and roads: Big-time stock-car racing started at Darlington. *Harold* started it.

Our track wouldn't be like the one in Indiana with drivers named things like Andretti and cars that look like oversized painted-up bullets hanging up there between 4 wheels. That's from their pictures, of course; I've never seen one in person.

Stock cars, though, we already *know*. We *drive* stock cars. Darlington's got dealerships for Ford (Sisk Motor Co), Chevrolet (Southway), and DeSoto/Plymouth (Evans Motors). You can buy a Pontiac in Lamar (from Daddy's buddy J G Woods) and Florence (Sam Neill) and a Chrysler, Plymouth, or Dodge from Cox Motors. There's Lincolns, Nashes, Oldsmobiles, Willyses, Packards, slick-looking low Studebakers around -- all *actual automobiles*, not fancied-up, stripped-down things you couldn't run on a real road. And believe it or not, suddenly almost all makers of cars were looking to make a national reputation at Darlington, the first place to provide that chance. I mean, a Henry J would enter in '52; a Henry *J*!

The Darlington track would get the attention of every American who ever owned or hoped to own a car. It's already starting to be copied all over the nation, especially on the coasts. Indianapolis can have the made-for-racing cars; Darlington's the place for the kinds of cars you drive.

You can bet Russell and every other car lover who could wangle a ticket and get here was crowding the narrow gateway on Labor Day 1950 for the first-ever big-time *stock car* race: the Southern 500. Russell's never missed one since.

500 *miles*, that was, around and around the first big-time stock car track, a mile and 3/8 circuit. I'd like to be exact, but some say 1.336 miles and others 1.366. You can see that Harold's 1.25 plan was exceeded, probly because of that (so to speak) ever-lovin' pond.

Seems like everybody had a say about what was going to happen.

How long would it take for the fastest stock car to do those 500 miles?

"Forget it," said the "experts" out there in Indianapolis, and even some officials of the National Association of Stock Car Racing. (Up until Harold built Darlington Raceway, NASCAR had nothing but dirt-track races to oversee. Harold knew who Bill France was -- they'd raced against each other on the strand at Daytona Beach -- but we didn't.) "No car built for the open road will last 500 miles at race speed," some opined. Whatever race speed might turn out to be. They didn't really know.

COUNTY

If Harold bothered to answer the doubters, I never heard it. As I said, he was a doer; he was busy doing. He left the talking to the talkers.

There was plenty of it.

Arguments kept popping up between friends and semi-friends and use-to-be friends, mostly about what car was the best car. Ford? Chevy? Oldsmobile? *Cadillac?*

The world and we were about to see.

One thing we saw was Darlington filling up with people we'd never seen before, who'd never seen us. It began to be an education.

So that's how the first big change in our shared lives came from a dreamer with a powerful dream -- a vision, it was, an unselfish one, and it's turning out to the good. It could end up helping a million people, or anyhow entertaining them. Right away it put Darlington on the national map, brought in celebrities every year, and helped us and the rest of the Pee Dee get more prosperous -- for awhile, anyhow.

A lot of silliness came along with it; people always want to crowd into the dream. Right away, almost, we had a big parade every year, a beauty contest, and tv stars, different every September. Some of the people were helping Darlington, I guess. Some just wanted their piece of the publicity and the action.

That's the way with dreams --they can run away with you. Or from you.

GENTLEMEN, START YOUR ENGINES

The track's first customers rolled into town at the end of August. And rolled in. And kept rolling in.

That grandstand was built to hold 8,000 reasonable-sized bottoms, hoping for even 10,000, figuring to put the overflow in the infield of the track. 10 *thousand* people -- more than the whole population of Darlington. Harold expected maybe 15,000, but after awhile he got tired of being looked at funny and stopped saying so.

That summer, some who lived close to the track got to thinking business in ways they'd never thought business before. Factory workers, store clerks, barbers, mechanics, whoever had a little piece of land around their houses or room inside, they got ideas. Farmers were suddenly not the Pee Dee's most numerous Capitalists.

Where would customers spend the night? Even now in 1957, that problem's not solved. The first year, it was met head on by locals, with every fan for him (or her) self. A whole lot of residents of the southeastern states must've been use to taking the family for an outing at the local dirt track on Friday or Saturday nights, so now they packed 'em up and came to Darlington.

The Park Terrace Hotel was booked solid, maybe for the first time since it stopped being the McFall. So were the Gasque and the Colonial Hotels in Florence, plus the few motels out and around.

But fret not: Southerners are neighborly, and don't mind making space in their houses and even on their porches (mosquitoes can't get at you through screen, but not all porches have screens) and down their front and back steps and out in their yards in a sleeping bag. Hardware stores sold out of sleeping bags.

By now, most of us were realizing there'd be a next-year's race.

COUNTY

That first race, people in the know said a few rabid fans of racing might come all the way from outside the Carolinas and Georgia, but they expected most people who came would be close enough to sleep at home Monday night.

Instead of 10,000, between 25,000 and 35,000 turned up; it was hard to tell.

Quite a few couldn't get tickets but hung around here and yonder anyway; the race was on the radio, and they were here. Some who came from a long, long way, no telling how far, they looked surprised at everything they saw, including us. Some were from so far away they didn't sound a bit like us when they talked. Quite a few of the Northern ladies sounded to us like parrots. Meaning no offense, naturally; tell the truth and shame the Devil.

Sudden signs went up in people's front yards for a good 20 miles around, offering rooms in houses you wouldn't think had a room to spare. Not the big houses; the little ones. I heard a man from Mont Clare talking out in front of Bonnoitt's Grocery, there in the vestibule by the snow-cone machine:

"Yeh, we haulin' the chirren over t'Lynchburg t'Mama's, so we c'n have us 2 spare rooms for the weekend. Man's offerin' $25 a room a night. $25 a *night*! Said 'e's use to payin' that much when he stays t' Virginia Beach, an' says a race'd be a heap better'n gettin' sunburnt at the beach; they c'd get sunburnt hyinh just as good and get some 'citement too. If they race again next year, we thinkin' 'bout rentin' the whole house out. We c'n ALL stay nights w' Mama over t'Lynchburg."

But Lynchburg filled up too, thanks to fans getting out maps ahead of time and knowing how to get a telephone operator to connect them with another phone customer on this end, "name of Bubba I-forget-what but YOU know, he's out on 76, be glad to hear from ol' Roscoe I know. Yeah, THAT might be the one, ring 'im please ma'm."

Effingham, Coles Crossroads, Kelleytown -- every little community you can name, as far out as Andrews, over to Lydia and Elon, up toward Loris and over as far as Marion and even Mullins and Dillon, Harold's dream fulfilled brings once-a-year prosperity, some of it going to people who scarcely ever thought about car racing. The Track's been running races for 6, 7 years now -- not just on Labor Day but some springs and mid-summers, and we don't see signs of stopping.

The track's made race fans of 'most everybody except Mother and some of the other ladies. They don't like the way the town kind of vibrates from the drone of tires right after the starting flag 'til the last car rolls into the pits. Even during Time Trials the town takes on a kind of hum. Too, you want to remember not to be out on the roads when the fans head home. Yankees are in a hurry, coming and going both.

The whole Labor Day weekend, people living any place close by the track turn their yards into close-quarters parking lots. From first light, they've got their kids standing roadside holding cardboard placards with TURN HERE or PARKING or just a big arrow. They might be yawning big as frogs but they're waving cars in.

Once they've wedged in all the cars there's room for, they get into their home-built stand selling watermelon chunks or drinks or Squirrel Nut Zippers or sandwiches or just water, which is what's left once they run out of ice and can't get any more.

The ice house on Broad Street -- it'll sell out time after time. The men are waiting around on the platform from about 10 in the morning for the next huge blocks to come in on a flatbed. You'll see the huge tongs leaning against the wall, waiting too.

Property owners across from the track who don't care to be in business themselves might rent a little square spot in their front yard. The renter hauls in his own stand and wares. A little wooden booth set up to sell Co' Colas from Mr Stone's Bottling Plant right here in town could've made a girl like me wealthy beyond my ability to imagine. If we'd built on 151 instead of Warley Street, I might have got in on the ground floor, so to speak, and become a businesswoman instead of being caged in my peach-colored strapless dance dress with the big net skirts, waving and throwing wrapped candy from anybody's float in the race-weekend parade.

Meanwhile, Harold became our local hero. Some outsider sports writers said 'way afterward that people laughed at him and called the track "Harold's Folly," but it's not true. I never heard any such of a thing, let alone that anybody threw tomatoes at him on his bulldozer. Who'd be stupid enough to throw anything to hit a man 'way over 6 feet tall with long legs? He could run 'em down in a minute if he took a mind to and then stretch out an arm and pick 'em up by the scruff of their necks. That's if he'd needed to, which he didn't because *they* didn't.

It's a libel on Darlingtonians, is what it is. Nobody here ever thought of doing such. It's just outsiders "projecting" -- saying what they'd've done if somebody built something new in their towns.

So Harold turned a low-producing 75-acre field (usually cotton, with grain planted after the pickers were through) into a crowd-drawing business that's put Darlington on the map and started people in other states to building copy-cat tracks. I expect by now Mr Ramsey thinks he was pretty smart.

I've never met Mr Ramsey, even though my C'n Monroe K Spears (it's the K that keeps him from being a Jr) is a close friend of the Ramseys' son, Jack. Could be the whole story about Mr Ramsey making his pond an obstacle is just a local myth -- except the track *is* shaped like an egg.

Mrs Ramsey herself, being Christian Science, knows about being different and going ahead with what you believe. She paid for their Reading Room to be built, right here on Warley Street. Probly she understands Harold better than most of us could.

I call Harold a genius, myself. A creative genius.

That first big stock-car race was a learning experience for everybody concerned 'cept Mr Paul Psillos. He says he knew it all along; says he expected 25,000 fans. On opening day he was still in that sweat he'd started out in because he'd spent almost a year knowing what was coming: "I and several of my employees worked to finish putting up the flagpole and raised the Star Spangled Banner just before the gun sounded to start the race."

But he gave Harold credit for knowing too, and for putting it together: "Harold was able to get local subcontractors including grading contractors, plumbers, electricians, and other tradesmen; and work proceeded on schedule." Daddy of course being one of the "tradesmen." Harold does what we call real work, so he knows people who can do it too.

That first race took almost 6 hours, every hour (as they say) action-packed. In the stands, you'd just be getting settled on the pillow you'd placed between you and the concrete, and next thing everybody's surging up craning to see what's going on down there in the straightaway or in whichever turn. In the infield, from your folding chair set up in your long-bed, you'd be whipping your head around following everybody else's. Or up on the roofs of buildings nearby, you'd be trying to focus your

binoculars before it -- whatever it was -- all got over with. (That's before people started throwing up viewing stands outside the fences and selling seats on 'em, which happened at the very next race. Right off, there was talk of outlawing it before somebody'd fall off or a stand would collapse.)

Quite a bit of the action in the '50 race had to do with tires. Every few laps somebody-or-other's tire would blow. Then all the cars'd get to running good again and BANG! another tire. No company had thought up 'til then there'd be a market for stock-car racing tires.

As I said, most of us learned a lot, and plenty folks had to eat crow.

For one thing, the winning driver was from outside the South. Here we were, knowing so much about engines and what makes them go, and lo and behold, a man comes 3000 miles from a town in California nobody remembers nor wants to (Long Beach, wherever that is), and shows us all how it's done. Not one of our Carolina dirt-track heroes either but a man none of us 'cept Harold ever heard of. He'd raced and done okay in Indianapolis (7th recently), but who around here paid any attention to that? Probly Harold was the only person in Darlington who'd ever met him, and he'd met him by racing against him.

Main thing was, the kind of car he drove to win our race was not a Ford nor even anything made by General Motors.

The South is full of Ford fans and Chevrolet fans and a handful of Cadillac admirers, including my brother. Engine-savvy arguments, bets, and sometimes fist fights erupted months ahead of September. Not involving Russell; Russell's got a quick temper but he never fights. He just stands there and *knows*.

One thing we all knew by time the race started was, it wouldn't be a Chevy. The bitter fact was, nobody had picked a Chevy to drive. Made you wonder were Chevys up to snuff.

Okay, practicly the whole world knows anyhow, so I'll stop teasing and tell you:

What won the race was a Plymouth. A *Plymouth*.

Plenty people own a Plymouth and drive it every day, but nobody I know thought of it as a racing car. It looks anything but fast; it looks slow, like a beetle. But that paticlar round-back beetle up and outflew the high-dollar birds.

Well, maybe not flew; more like bumbled on around the track like beetles do, but it won.

They *say* the winning car was bought 10 miles from here the Friday before the Monday race -- bought by Johnny Mantz, the driver who came across country without a car to race in. They say when he got to the Pee Dee, he went over to Cox-Fitz Motors and picked one out. I'm just telling you what we hear here in Darlington; if it's a lie, somebody else told it. They don't say whether Cox-Fitz was the only place he looked, and whether he tried the DeSoto and maybe the Chrysler at Cox too, or went there knowing he wanted the car he got. They just say he bought the Plymouth and came to race.

They say something else, too: that the reason West Coast Johnny Mantz won the race was, he knew tires. To him, whether stock cars could race 500 miles was not the question. It was how long would their tires last while they were doing it.

COUNTY

So Mantz didn't use tires made for cars. He used tires made for trucks -- *pickup trucks*.

All day those cars ran that blistering hot track on a hot day – and it's always hot days, end of August, first of September. And dry -- dry as a shriveled tree in a sand-dune desert. Asphalt -- black asphalt -- you can't walk on it barefooted in late summer even with calloused feet; you got to *run*.

Every car in that first race but Johnny Mantz's ol' slow Plymouth was running tires made for road travel, not farm work. Johnny's wore out too. Then his picked-up crew would haul-heels out there with another full set of truck tires, slap 'em onto the Plymouth, and he'd put it out there again.

He made just 3 pit stops and finished *6 laps* ahead. He held the lead from 49 all the way through the 400th, and got $3,520 lap money plus the grand prize of $7,000 – BIG payday.

Everybody who didn't get to the race (and most didn't have the price of a ticket) expected to get all the facts from the main daily newspaper anybody much gets in Darlington -- the <u>Florence Morning News</u>.

What a let-down.

The paper was interested in Mantz, as expected, since he was the winner as everybody had already heard. It said Mantz started from the 35th position after qualifying with one of the slowest trial runs. So far, good reporting. But then the <u>Flo Mo News</u> covered the race the way Indianapolis results get reported: they published the whole list under drivers' names *without the makes of their cars*. Indianapolis race cars aren't any kind you can name.

Right: the paper left out what everybody wanted to know: what make of car finished where. The only one identified was the winner: Johnny Mantz's Plymouth.

We couldn't believe we'd wasted our money buying a paper we don't even subscribe to. (We take <u>The State</u> so Mother can get news from Orangeburg County if there is any.)

Even now it's hard to find out just what kind of car finished how in the very first big-time stock car race, but thank goodness there's plenty around who remember and might never forget.

Once it got settled in everybody's mind nobody was likely to catch and pass Mantz, the crowd watched Red Byron and

Glenn "Fireball" Roberts battle for 2nd. (Roberts got his nickname from pitching baseball; nothing to do with racing.)

The Cadillac ran the most frustrating race of all. Everybody figured it would have the best engine. What they didn't think about was how much what the ads call luxury cars weigh. They'd watch that Cadillac race to the front. After while they'd watch it limp into pit row, get new tires, merge in someplace back in the pack, surge forward again, maybe blow a tire or two, pit, and merge. The story of its race was pit and merge.

The whole crowd learned some lessons about Cadillacs that day: They're more powerful than Plymouths, they weigh more than Plymouths, they use up tires faster than Plymouths, and they don't win races. So far, we don't see any reason to question those facts.

Johnny Mantz ran his brand new store-bought, mostly-unmessed-with car on the apron the whole race. Down there out of faster cars' way, he settled in and kept turning left.

There's a legend that Johnny Mantz's slow Plymouth started the race in last place. That's a fiction like the made-up story saying Darlington kids were throwing ripe tomatoes at Harold while he was building the raceway. Darlington County's children have better manners and better sense.

What matters is that Johnny Mantz crossed the finish line in 1st Place and took the first checkered flag at what drivers would soon nickname the Track Too Tough To Tame.

Winning speed: 76 mph *plus*.

That's the way big-time stock-car racing began, right here in Darlington.

I kid you not.

A Quiet Courthouse Town

I'm fixing to show you Darlington.

Well why do that, you might be thinking; *I know what a courthouse town looks like; they're all pretty much alike: Court House in the middle of its own square block with stores all around it and streets leading off that join with roads to everywhere else.*

And you're right. But look at what's changed since the old people in town were our age. Where would you park your horses or your mule and wagon today when you came in to be measured by a tailor for a bridesmaid's dress or a Sunday suit, and where's your tailor shop? (Dressmakers and corset makers came to the house, they say, or you sewed for yourself.) And the town pump's gone, so where would you water your animals? Would there be any place to eat and get ice cream or would you pack a lunch?

In the family stories our grandparents told us, they were showing us history. That's where we all live: in history. It's important to know that, and where in history we are -- like now, right after a World War that was never supposed to happen, and couldn't have, if nobody had ever invented boats, jeeps, and then airplanes. And now big bombs.

You could call our time in history the time of the big bomb.

When we moved in from the Sand Hill in 1950, Darlington was a thriving town centered on a really nice Courthouse Square. Even knowing about the race track, from just looking at Darlington you wouldn't think it's changed much in the 7 years since.

You'd be wrong.

Like most towns built around a Court House, Darlington's conveniently arranged. Cashua Street leaves the Square going east, mostly toward houses; Main runs along the west side of the Square north / south, and 2 short streets leave its eastern corners – Exchange runs south for a block, and the jailhouse

56

street runs north. Pearl and Orange both head west from Main at the western corners of the Square.

(This is not as easy as I thought it'd be. I'm bound to get some of it wrong, and it's not going to be action packed, not by a long shot. So if you're sure you understand '50s towns that are older than towns without real centers – like the towns that railroads built (Florence, Timmonsville, Mayesville and so on) --, you might just as well to skip this chapter. But it's got to be here for the reasons I just said.)

Darlington grew up around a wooden Court House before it built our red-brick one with white-painted trim. It's Greek classical, like lots of important public buildings in the South. The stores around the Public Square all look important too, and ready. Everything fits.

County business gets done not just in the Court House. The jail's down that short street from the Square with what use to be covered parking for carriages, so there's a gracious plenty of space back there for cars. The highway department's out past the Cotton Mill. It's a good plan -- keeps people from having to crowd into the Square every whipstitch. You hear some people saying the Court House's not big enough, but the stupidest thing any town could do, now that there's so many cars around, is put too much county comings and goings in the Public Square and not leave enough parking space for customers. I hope they realize that, whoever "they" are.

Most of the shopping stores are on the Square, all in easy walking distance from one another. Once you're downtown, walking's how to go.

The streets and sidewalks are wide and paved, and you've got all the stores on the Square you could want. There's 3 hardwares – Farmers', Barringer-McKeel, and Carolina. There's 4 drugstores -- Central, Darlington, Willcox's, and Davis's. All the hardwares and drugstores carry gifts, too, and all the drugstores have fountains. There's 3 dime stores: Rose's, McLellan's, and Woods 5 & 10.

Davis's Drugstore is on the Main Street side not far from the County Library. You want to go there for the best Cherry Cokes -- plenty of cherry syrup.

COUNTY

Miz Davis was my teacher in 2nd Grade and I was 'most always in dutch with her that year. She kept her eye on me, which was easy for her, me being the tallest girl in her room. I must have been the most obnoxious too, judging by how much trouble I was use to being in, so far in my school experience.

No need holding anything against Miz Davis right on, but there's no sense either in being conspicuous when I'm in her store and she's behind the fountain. Not that she'd put poison in my Cherry Coke, but I don't see any sense in ruffling past feathers.

Funny how much more I like her since she quit being a teacher. Back then I couldn't even see how pretty she is. Miz Davis had 42 pupils that year, and never had taught at St John's before. I'd've cut and run if I'd been her. Whenever I go in with Kathy and Joyce Anne or whoever, Miz Davis and I kind of smile at each other.

I never want to be a teacher, even if Mother's so sure that's what I'm s'pose to be. It can spoil the nicest disposition. Mine's not the nicest anyhow, as Mother lets me know all the time, so I can't risk it.

To me the Public Library use to be the most important place in town 'cept for church. The libry's just past the hotel, before Park Street comes into Main at Central Baptist Church. (Park Street twists around past the front of Central, past Mrs Coker's and Miss Myrtle Jeffords's to the front of St John's and goes on to St John's Grammar School.) Get past Central Baptist on Main and you're at the back of St John's High, the J C Daniels Auditorium and the gym plus Shop and some other classrooms. By then you've fallen down the big hill that leads out of town past the Muldrows and the Colvins and the Conders, toward the farm and Dovesville and Society Hill, where you take either the Cheraw or the Bennettsville road and go right on to North Carolina.

From Mineral Springs Road, just about every time I got downtown I went to the Darlington County Library. One day Mrs Yates the Librarian, a nice lady shaped like a grandmother, asked me whether my parents knew what books I was reading. I told her I didn't know whether they did or not. No matter what I said, I figured she'd tell Daddy pretty soon. (She never sees

58

Mother.) She did, too -- told him I'd checked out practicly the whole shelf of Zane Grey novels and even <u>Tarzan</u> by Edgar Rice Burroughs – books that with me being 7 or 8 I shouldn't even know all the words in, let alone understand the "implications."

Daddy thanked her very much, and told me she was concerned. But he didn't fuss at me.

Next time we were with Uncle Bob, Daddy bragged a little bit. They both turned around and smiled at me.

I have some great family.

There's plenty places to get your hair cut, mostly in a little add-on room of somebody's house, but our biggest barber shop is on the Square. You know it by its striped pole. The barbers are Mr Prevatte and his son Otis. Customers wait in chairs along inside the front window, facing the other way. You walk past and see the backs of their heads.

The Sansbury twins were reglar customers of the Prevattes from the time they were little things. The Sansbury twins' daddy farms and runs Sansbury Tractor Company out where the road comes up again from where the railroad track crosses Pearl. It's the biggest Ford Tractor dealership in the whole USA, with awards hanging on the wall.

The Prevattes put a special board across the barber chair for short customers like Marilyn or Carolyn to perch on and be swathed in a cloth shop cape. They'd always get giggly when the long powdery bristles brushed away clippings. They'd climb down, take Mis Arah their mama's hand, and prance out in their Little Beaver cuts.

Around the corner on South Main is City Barber Shop, belonging to Mr Arthur Hammonds, one of Darlington's Negro businessmen. He and his barbers specialize in Whites' hair; it's what they're trained for. J C Washington started out as a boy sweeping cuttings off the floor, and now he's back from hair-cutting school in Columbia. His nephews let him cut their hair once, but now they run off at the first sight of him with his barbering scissors. He laughs about them not wanting their hair cut White.

COUNTY

W D Coggeshall's department store is owned by Marion's cousin Albert, so W D must be for his father or grandfather. Mother bought a new frock there from Hattie Maude this past week. Robert Spivey runs the Men's Department, right in front, and the other half of the front is the china and gifts. You can tell from the display windows which front door you want. It's a long store, and there's a back entrance from city parking. It leads through the children's department, run by Mrs Jeffords, wife of Jeff of Bonnoitt's grocery. They're the parents of Adair Jeffords, who finished St John's in, I think, 1953. Mother calls Mrs Jeffords Irene, which probly means she's from Lamar. Mother went to high school in Lamar while Papa was preaching there.

B C Moore's is next to the Town Hall, and Belk-Simpson takes up from the jail street to where Cashua Street leaves the Square heading toward Mechanicsville. B C Moore's is all dry goods and shoes-- men's, children's, and shoes downstairs, and upstairs, women's coats and frocks and the office.

For women's clothes there's Julia's, and for men's we've got McLeod's, Witcover's, and Kermit's -- all locally owned, maybe, 'cept I've never met Mr Witcover.

Mr and Mrs McLeod go to our church. He's a tall gentleman and handsome, and she's short and plump and pretty and knits tiny crib afghans to give new babies. Mine's the size of a small towel; white with shades of blue. They're both as friendly as can be, with wonderful smiles.

There's not room for what they're calling "chain" grocery stores to be on the Public Square, so they're out round and about. There's the Dixie Home (but it's been bought out by an even bigger chain and renamed Winn Dixie), the A&P, and the new one that came in from Columbia: Edens'.

Colin Jordan (he left for Texas in July to join the Air Force) worked for Mr Marcus Joyner at the A&P the whole time he was in school, soon as he could get his own car. (He lives in Leavensworth, a suburb of Dovesville. (Suburb is a new word.) Last year they got a handsome Assistant Manager. Marion and I would go in and buy a 5-cent pack of Wrigley's Spearmint or 6-cent Coke or NuGrape and sometimes a carton of drinks (25 cents) and I'd talk with Colin while she looked at the Assistant Manager.

Give me a minute and I might think of his name.

COUNTY

Carolina Furniture that Clyde Spivey manages for Mr Linton Boykin is on the Public Square at the corner that leads to the County Jail. Plus there's another furniture store -- H & S – and the flower shops. There's none on the Square but they're around.

Mr Boykin use to be Secretary to Mr Bernard Baruch down near Georgetown. Mr Boykin is very important and use to date my Aunt Marie but she married William Sterling Bowie who came from England with his parents. The Bowies live in Florence now, and Uncle Bill drives a train: the Savannah run for the Atlantic Coast Line.

It's possible the Boykins had something to do with the Boykin Spaniel, our South Carolina State Dog.

How do people get that kind of information? Do we have State Cat? A State Rat? Everybody knows the State Wildflower (the Yellow Jessamine), the State Tree (the Palmetto), and the State Bird (the Carolina Wren), but the rest is murky. Who decides? The Legislature maybe, with a lot of people telling them what to pick. I doubt our Senators've picked a State Snake. Did, people would laugh and say, Right, *they'd* know.

Right off the Square on Pearl, once you pass the bank corner there's a furniture store, the Darlington Theatre, and the News & Press. The problem with having a store facing Pearl Street near the Square is that it's not wide enough for any parking 'cept parallel. A newspaper office won't need drive-up customers, so it does okay, and the Post Office is on a corner with marked parking spaces at both entrances.

Mrs Coffee, the Publisher, runs the N&P with her son Guy. They write practicly the whole paper, 'cept for the socials that Ruth Ward gathers by phone and writes up, and the clubs and other news that community writers send on from out in the County, and the state historical-places articles that come from Columbia with a picture. Even most of the advertising, the Coffees write over the phone and the staff designs, plus they drum up ad business by announcing Customer Appreciation Days and Sidewalk Sale Days and such. The paper comes out on Thursdays.

COUNTY

In early 1952, Mr Watts' law office was on that same block of Pearl.

Visitors don't ordinarily ride into town on horseback anymore, but if they did, the Livery Stable's still there where Exchange Street ends at Hampton. It's a gathering place for local men. When I was little, Daddy would take me in with him, which is how I know the front room has a pot-belly stove and smells like leather and looks how Daddy says things use to look before cars got everywhere.

Joe Sweeney (he's Bessie and Laura's brother; they all grew up on Mineral Springs Road on their own land) runs it. He worked for Mr Albert James who raises Guernseys, and he's good with horses and smithing. Uncle Bob's Florence Stock Market partner Bill Howard and Bill's brother Mr Jolly own the Livery Stable. Daddy says the Howards've told Joe the Livery Stable'll be there long as he wants to work.

Before you get to the Livery Stable, there's some small offices and Yarborough's Grocery and the A&P. On the other side of the street it's all offices – insurance and that.

The Liberty Theatre's in the auditorium part of the Town Hall that Mrs McFall says they use to call the Opera House. Traveling shows perform there too. We use to go to some.

I'm pasting in the picture the architect submitted in 1900. The building looks just like his drawing 'cept the city just recently removed the Victorian trim. I don't know what that was about; there's nice Victorian store fronts all around the Square. Could be the bits'd got broken and they couldn't find anybody local who knew how to make new.

There's lots of space in the back where actors can rehearse or change costumes and be there while they're not on stage. The fancier part beside the lobby is offices for Mayor Buchanan and other city officials.

You can see for yourself it's a "handsome edifice."

The street you see beside it is Main, heading north and about to fall down the hill to the back of St John's High School. The hotel is across where you can't see it – on your left. It was built at almost the same time as the Town Hall: turn of the century. Heading north from there on Main Street, you pass between the Hotel and the Lunch Box. You can't see it in the picture either.

CITY HALL & THEATRE
DARLINGTON . S.C.
FRANK P. MILBURN Architect.
COLUMBIA S.C.

Belk-Simpson is cattycorner from the Town Hall. It carries dry goods – cloth, clothes, shoes – and it's put in furniture and appliances. In the shoe department there's a machine that lets you see clear through your foot, bones and all. Children can't wait to stick both feet into that machine. You'll see 'em stand and gaze and gaze at their own foot skeletons. When that machine came, I went and did it myself. Eerie.

Samuels' is the only remaining tailor shop on the Public Square. (C'n Lillian said there use to be 4.) It's down from the Town Hall, near the corner that leads to the jailhouse. You'll see TAILOR UPSTAIRS with a bent-upward arrow. You can get a whole suit made there, the way you always could before store-bought clothes got available. Daddy goes up those stairs when store-bought jackets don't feel right. Daddy's shoulders and arms are strong and wide, but ever since the Navy, his back can't bend.

At the Cashua corner is Willcox's Drug Store, then the Phillipses' Farmer's Hardware, a jewelry store (I don't go in those, but Johnny Wells's father has Wells Jewelers on the Main Street side of the Square; he's on the town council too), and Bonnoitt's Grocery.

There's several local-owner grocery stores around and about. Blackmon's, Yarborough's, and Redfearn's are all in walking distance, and Mr Jimmy Brown the meat cutter's store and Bonnoitt's are right on the Square.

Bonnoitt's Feed and Seed is alongside and kind of behind Bonnoitt's Grocery, giving you room to drive your pickup to the double opening and load up. Hammond Bacote that grew up by us on Mineral Springs Road (Bessie's son, Joe's nephew) runs that part. He's married now, to Mattie, Dr Willcox's nurse. She's tiny and really pretty. They started keeping comp'ny while we were still living at the Sand Hill.

That's the tower of the Town Hall you see in the bottom right-hand corner of the next picture I'm pasting in. That's Main Street on the right, going straight through. You'll be looking south from above the top of the Town Hall because you're facing the opposite way from the picture you just saw. In this one you see the Court House dome and all, from far up.

I didn't take this picture; it belongs to the Darlington Historical Commission. I don't know whether whoever took it was an expert acrobat on a high wire like Mr Earl Gandy says Colin's grandfather Jordan was, or in an airplane or what.

The Lunch Box might not sound like much from the name, but believe me, it is. It's where "the elite meet to eat" in town. 'Course they don't say that, but you kind of dress up to eat there or else you're out of place. The Edwards sisters own it and run it, and they're always dressed up, including Miss Annie in her long voile dresses and button-up shoes of yesteryear.

The Edwardses are Darlington's eminent businesswomen, along with Mrs Olive Davis of Davis Electric, the gift shop where brides register their patterns. Davis Electric faces the Court House on the side away from you – the side with the

COUNTY

Confederate Monument. You can see it across there with a drugstore, Mr Prevattes' barber shop, and Barringer's hardware. Metropol's is the store at the Main Street corner.

I eat at the Lunch Box mostly when the Coggeshalls invite me. They're cousins or something of the Edwardses. Customers tend to flit from table to table chatting. I'd say most of the customers are "old Darlington." I plan to be out and gone before that happens to me.

Daddy keeps the Lunch Box equipment running, plus he has to stay between the Edwardses and OSHA. OSHA's one of those government organizations set up to cause trouble for ordinary people who're trying to be in business. It's bad when the Inspector's new; he's just as likely to contradict the Inspector he's replacing as not.

Like this:

One year, a new Inspector came from the Government and told the Edwards ladies they had to relocate their septic tank. You can imagine the consternation, them being such ladies, even having to discuss such a topic. So Daddy got it moved, which took a lot of trouble and some money. The next year, the *real* Inspector was there again. He told them it's in the wrong place *now* and they've got to move it *back to where it was*.

The Edwards sisters got Daddy to meet with the Inspector, who hemmed and hawed but ended up admitting that the first inspector couldn't've known what he was doing so they shouldn't've listened to him.

Daddy came home fit to be tied about no-'count government bureaucracies. He says the only real service government can do is deal with crime, maintain the military, and keep up traffic lights. Other than that, government's a burden and an intrusion. If we didn't have bad people, aggressive nations, and motorized road traffic, we could do without government entirely. He agrees with Henry David Thoreau in "Civil Disobedience": "Government is best when it governs least." (And they didn't even have OSHA back then.) Thoreau was what we'd call a Radical Conservative. I might get to be one myself; I'm not sure yet.

The newest place to eat in town is Joe's Grill. In January 1952, Joe's opened with an actual Grand Opening, like a hotel or something. "Beer, wine, and champagne cocktails [were] served" from 5 p m straight through 'til *2 a m*. I wasn't there; I was 12. Not that I better be anyplace but home *now* at 2 a m.

Joe's has really *great* spicy-hot barbecue sandwiches. Phil Payne introduced me to 'em. (I'm pretty sure it was Phil.) There's no curb service like there is at the Southernaire across from the PO, beside Trinity Methodist, so at Joe's your date goes in and orders and brings the food out to the car.

To get to Joe's, take Cashua from the Square and turn right onto Russell Street at Mr Hugh Sprott's Service Station before you cross the tracks. You'll pass between the old train depot and shipping warehouse and H & S Furniture. Joe's Grill's on your right, corner of Siskron and Russell. If you pass between Garland's Garage and a tobacco warehouse, you'll end up at Hampton Street, a block past Joe's. Sometimes Joe's will do lunch, but it's mostly open at night. It's not what parents call a juke joint, though. It's a family place, run by Joe and Ruth both.

If you get lost in Darlington, find a filling station. They always know where stuff is. I don't think they let people who *don't* know, work at filling stations.

66

Mr Hugh Sprott that goes to our church runs the Cashua Street Station, just a block from the Square. Marshall Medlin's Gulf Station is out Pearl; he's Joyce Anne's father; Ms Ruby Medlin keeps the station for him if he has to go out on a call. There're filling stations on Main, too, close to the Square. One's owner parks his huge chromed-up motorcycle out front. It's kind of a wonder to see.

Mr Kilgo's Oil Company and station are across from the PO and our church. He sends an oil truck and buys direct from the ships in harbor at Charleston. Daddy says that's where most stations get their oil, whether they've got a truck of their own to send for it or whether a tanker truck hauls it to the station. The only stations different are Amoco's; their gasoline is white. Unless you got to have Amoco white gas in your car, you might as well save by buying local-owner instead of Gulf, Esso, Atlantic, or Texaco.

Bonnoitt's Grocery faces the Square on the east side. Mr Jeff works there, and Mr Frank use to. In the open front vestibule, there's always some kind of machine making delicious stuff. In summer it's snow cones -- whatever color flavor you want. They're glad to come out and make one for you. In fall, it's a peanut parcher. Nothing smells better than peanuts parching, not even strawberry snow cones.

Either one use to cost a nickel when Mr Frank was there.

Mr Frank is Frank Bonnoitt, one of Daddy's very best friends, John and Jerry's father. He was born at Darlington but grew up in Epworth Orphanage. He saved his money in the Coast Guard and started a business, married Miss Myrtle Kyzer, and brought his brothers Harry and Esmond home. He gave them a start, plus bought land west of town and offered them whatever they needed to build on. Mr Harry married Miss Myrtle's sister, so Harry who's our age is double 1st cousin to the twins and Jenny.

Then Mr Frank got sick, really sick.

I use to go out with Daddy on some of his visits up the slanted lane. Mr Frank would be sitting out back in the sunny garden in his chair. Miss Myrtle would bring out a pitcher of something cold with upside-down Dixie Cups and crackers on a tray.

COUNTY

After we had something to drink, if the twins were anywhere around she'd say in her quick warm voice, "JohnJerry, make your guest welcome. Think of a nice game to play."

Seems like parents are always saying things like that, painting people into a corner. Take Mother; she'd say "Go play" with a person you've never laid eyes on before.

So the twins'd look confused and I'd look confused, and stand there digging the toes of our shoes (if it was winter and we had shoes on) into the gravel along the path.

We didn't really play that I remember, because they're boys, but they tried to be nice. (They *are* nice. We're friends at St John's.) Back then we'd kind of stare at each other and then play tag a little bit or swing on the tire swing, but mostly I liked roaming around through the flowers. Miss Myrtle keeps a beautiful garden in front of their vegetables -- day lilies and roses and a lantana bed -- plus gardenia and camellia bushes up at the house.

Miss Myrtle would head away into the house (it's lovely; real wood painted white) so Daddy and Mr Frank could have their time together. One afternoon she said, "Frank prefers you over any other visitor he has, George, even the preacher."

"*Especially* the preacher," Mr Frank said. (The preacher was Mr Garrison, before he got to be District Superintendent and Mr Pope came.)

"Why?" Daddy asked him.

"Because you don't expect anything for coming; you just come. The preacher costs me money," Mr Frank said.

Miss Myrtle stopped in her tracks halfway to the house. "Why, Frank, I've never heard him ask you for money."

"Doesn't ask. Just *expects*."

No wonder Mr Frank liked sitting there; it's a beautiful place. And he felt cold, he said, when he was indoors.

He was thin -- tall and thin and just the nicest man, with a twinkle and a smile always.

I miss him.

A Shower of Silver Dollars

We Spearses, we're farm people. I say that with pride and gratitude. In my humble opinion, the best people *are* farm people. You're probly getting tired of hearing that, so I'll try to tone it down. Daddy says he knows a man who started worrying about the national debt and ended up on Bull Street. Meaning there's things you can't do anything about, so don't go crazy trying.

Darlington's in probly the farmingest portion of South Carolina -- the Pee Dee, named for the Great Pee Dee River, which is named for the Indian tribe. You already know from how much I've said about waterways that it makes sense for us to be called by a river name.

Where Broad Street crosses Main just at the railroad to Dixie Cup stand 2 of our 3 tobacco warehouses. Come on east on Broad and you'll get to the W B Lewis warehouse, a huge brick building that must once've been the handsomest tobacco warehouse anywhere. East Broad is a mix of small houses and big businesses -- Bonnoitt's Seed Mill, the ice house, Diamond Hill Plywood, and the W B Lewis.

Darlington's the busiest tobacco market in South Carolina, but the present Mr Lewis has moved on to become Vice-President of Liggett & Myers Tobacco Company. That means he's also Jack Benny's boss.

An actress played Mrs Lewis on <u>The Jack Benny Show</u> not long ago. She had to make believe Mr Benny gave her a necklace – a dimestore one; he's famous for cheap -- and that she didn't want him to know her maid was wearing it.

The real Mrs Buck Lewis is Mrs Coggeshall's and Frank Williamson's sister, which makes her Marion's aunt and Edwin Williamson's both. She grew up here. Buck and Mrs Lewis have to live someplace else now, New York I think, but they use the Williamson beach house at Pawley's Island and they come back to visit. The tobacco industry's funny like that; the tobacco's here, but the cigar and cigarette offices of Liggett and Myers, and I guess of Brown & Willliamson and Phillip Morris are up North.

COUNTY

The South's where the tobacco sales happen. Farmers bring it in, and all the big cigarette and cigar companies send buyers. When I go with Marion and Mrs Coggeshall to where the auctioneers and the buyers and the farmers walk among the opened-up bundles of cured tobacco just in from the barns, it takes me a little while to get use to the strange dusty smell. Marion says it's the smell of money.

Tobacco's not all.

Thomas Sansbury and our Henry Stokes of Mineral Springs Road are both involved in cucumbers and cucumber futures.

Peanuts, too. We all grew peanuts on our farms. I love peanuts, specially boiled, which you can do right after you pull the ripe plants out of the ground. Every root'll be loaded with "green" peanuts. You pull 'em off, wash 'em good, and put 'em in to boil with just enough salt to suit you. Remember what Bob Colvin use to do? Right: he brokered peanuts.

And 'course there's cotton, and soybeans, and pecans. A big pecan processor is T B Young & Co, on 52 this side of Florence that his son Givens Young came home from WWII to help run. Our grove usually gave us a good crop of pecans at the Sand Hill. I made good money from picking up pecans.

Daddy and his brothers are all involved in the livestock business. Daddy's only in it on Thursdays, when he keeps books for the Darlington Auction Market, but Uncle Bob's with Union Stockyards in Chicago as their local buyer here, and Uncle Hart raises hogs and cattle and is a full-time farmer. Darlington Auction Market, at the end of Spring Street, belongs to Daddy's good friend Mr Earl Gandy of Dovesville.

The **News & Press** carries plenty of agricultural news. There'll be an article by Wilda Gray the County Agent giving the latest advice from Clemson College on how to farm better. There'll be articles for the farm wife like how to make a little bag that slides along the clothes line and holds clothespins so you won't have to toss 'em into the laundry basket or leave 'em on the line to turn gray. It's no accident that Sansbury Tractor Company in Darlington is the busiest Ford Tractor dealership in the nation. Darlington started out long ago as an agricultural center.

Towns don't grow much, though, without factories. Darlington's got 3 big factories and some smaller industry too.

COUNTY

The Southern Cotton Oil Company, on the Atlantic Coast Line Railroad where the road starts toward Timmonsville, makes the whole neighborhood smell like peanuts parching. Its buildings are some of the tallest in town. Our round feed house was made out of corrugated, but SCOCo's corrugateds are huge.

Kathy's daddy is the Manager of SCOCo: Mr Lawrence E. Graham. The Grahams moved here for him to run SCOCo. They took a year to get loose from Sumter, with Mr Graham driving back and forth, an 80-mile round trip. Kathy got up early every morning and came in the car with Mr Graham. Pat was already in nurse's training, and Laura stayed in school that year in Sumter.

Making friends here at St John's right off wasn't so easy for Kathy because she's so beautiful -- tall, blonde, with totally smooth skin that I bet never experienced a pimple, and the longest eyelashes you ever saw. All the boys went sappy over her. It was sickening.

Now we're all use to each other and she's one of my very best friends for always, but she certainly is pretty. Her smile is wonderful, and when she's sad she looks even more gorgeous, with all those eyelashes drooping down. When we're together and meet some new boy, I am *nowhere*.

The Individual Drinking Cup Company has its own railroad spur that crosses Main just before the Broad Street jog. Everybody calls it Dixie Cup because of its famous original product, but today it makes paper into lots of shapes for drinks and food both.

Now and again, with so many orders to fill and so many different designs to set up, somebody on the Dixie Cup line makes a mistake, or maybe after so many, the printing just goes cattywampus. They set that run aside for the next give-away day. That's when everybody working at Dixie Cup can come pick from the rejects. They hold food and drinks just fine.

Daddy brings home a fair number of off-printed plates and bowls too, eventually, because Dixie people share with their friends. The Dixie's misprints show up at our weenie roasts, peanut boilings -- any gathering where there's food. So many companies order from Dixie Cup, no telling whose advertisement you'll get from how far away. It's an education in far-flung industry.

No telling how much bigger Dixie Cup'll get. I think Darlington's probly its main factory, but Easton, Penn., is its head office.

Our biggest employer is Darlington Manufacturing Company -- the Cotton Mill. It's built on high ground that we call the Mill Hill, and has its own village of houses. They're on both sides of the railroad and within walking distance of the Mill. The Cokers -- the same Cokers that built up Hartsville, the second biggest town in the county – put up most of the houses when they built the Mill in the 1880s.

More Darlingtonians work at the Mill than anywhere else. 100s of families depend on it, and it's 1/3 of the town's economy. The Millikens of Deering-Milliken own the business -- they're the big textile chain -- but South Carolina stockholders own the Mill itself. Roger Milliken, President of Deering-Milliken since his father died, has more stock in the Darlington Mill than anybody else, and he lives up in Spartanburg -- moved there a couple years ago because he loves South Carolina. Writes about textiles; we see his articles in the N&P. He says one reason textiles moved South (other than the reason everybody knows: to get away from Unionization) is that textiles aren't respected as an industry in New England any more, so in the South, textiles attract better workers and managers than in New England. I never thought of it that way: the more respected an industry is in the area, the more qualified its employees.

You won't pass by Darlington Manufacturing Company accidentally, but if you head west from the Square on Pearl and turn right before it dips and crosses the tracks, you'll come to it. Major Coker put it there because of the railroad -- the Atlantic Coast Line track that use to be the Cheraw & Darlington. It's been right there for 100 years, which shows that Darlington tried hard to share in railroad prosperity.

Florence got to be the rail center before Florence was even a *town*. That's because the port of Wilmington built a railroad to the Pee Dee, and then the line from Charleston came rushing in to keep Wilmington from getting the Pee Dee's produce, which caused Cheraw and Darlington farmers to get money together

COUNTY

to build their own line to meet the other 2. The South's prosperity from its own railroads lasted about a decade, until War came. After the War, all our railroads got taken over by Yankees and renamed the Atlantic Coast Line.

The Mill's location was nice for the Major when he came in from Hartsville in his buggy or on horseback. It's on his side of town.

LESTON, S. C., WEDNESDAY MORNING, APRIL 24, 1889

The Cotton Mill at Darlington.

HE PRIDE OF THE PEE-DEE.

HISTORY AND RESOURCES OF THE CITY OF DARLINGTON.

The very year it opened, the Mill doubled Darlington's size from under 1000 people to 2000.

In 1889 Charleston's paper, the <u>News and Courier</u>, published that essay praising Darlington as a fine town and praising the Mill too. I figure the sanitation problem must've been taken care of by then.

Sanitation was quite a problem for the original workers who flocked here for the Mill jobs because they weren't *from* here; they were new and there were a lot of 'em. Cousin H D Fraser (the same one that had to shut down some burial grounds because they polluted drinking wells) was head of the Darlington County Board of Health, so he had considerable to worry over. In his 1885 report he asked for help in making reglar inspections of the 100s of new households and in cleaning the ones that needed it: "The factory people have suffered since the Spring of the year. This is doubtless due to the fact that they are strangers and not acclimated to this section, together with their mode of living, which necessarily renders them more liable to its influences."

What he meant was what I told you: they weren't *from* here.

They're from here now, for sure; they're *us*. Darlington has 3 generations descended from those early workers. Some are our neighbors on Warley Street.

The Mill has its own newsletter, but the rest of us don't see that newsletter. What we see and hear are mostly the unusual events. A death soon after Christmas, 1924, made the front page of the Darlington News. (C'n Monroe was editor of the News. After he died, it was folded into the News & Press.)

The news story: A young husband and wife were in the spinning room right after lunch. "In placing a band upon a pulley," his sleeve was caught, "drawing him into the machinery with fearful velocity."

"With fearful velocity" -- hard to forget that description of a man's body being drawn in by a machine.

The next afternoon at 4, Robert Wilson was laid to rest in Grove Hill Cemetery. His father came from Rockingham and sat with the widow and the baby boy 4 months old.

In farming country, we know machines -- big machines. We know that every combine, reaper, and tractor increases efficiency but can kill quickly and with fearful strength.

The usual Mill news is good, though, like awards. Not long ago a lady and her husband got awards from Manager James Oeland at the same time -- Mr J H Boan for 35 years and Lola L Boan for 30 years of service.

I could picture them meeting and falling in love the very first day she came to work. Probly it didn't happen like that; probly they grew up together. Either way, I like imagining his eyes one day lighting upon Miss Lola and seeing the beginnings of love.

On payday December 1st, 1950, the Mill gave the whole town a surprise: it paid out in silver dollars. *28 thousand silver dollars*. Mr Milliken and Mr Nicholson must've planned it. How do you smuggle in that much heavy money in secret? A plain-wrapper armored truck, maybe more than one, with guards inside? Maybe even an 18-wheeler? How big *is* $28,000 in silver?

Our *house and lot* cost Daddy $3,000. An egg salad sandwich at Edwin Turner's Chicken Basket on Irby Street in Florence, as fancy a restaurant as I know of 'cept maybe the Sanborn Hotel, costs 25 cents, and the broiled red snapper dinner is $1.75. On holidays, turkey and dressing dinner at the VFW is $1. Just ordinary days, it's 50 cents.

Suddenly silver dollars were all over town and all over the county, into the Chicken Basket and beyond.

For months Daddy got silver dollars for working on people's appliances. He was use to putting money into his pant pockets. After a pocket ripped and spilled out on the ground, he got a Citizens Bank bag to keep beside him on the truck seat so Mother wouldn't have to keep sewing in new pockets.

Mr Davis got silver dollars for plumbing. Mrs Olive Davis of Davis Electric got 'em in exchange for wedding gifts. Moody's Grocery and Miz Warr at the bottom of Cashua Street got cash-registerfuls. Julia's raked 'em in for dresses and costume jewelry. Mr Albert James Jr got 'em for drawing up Wills. Silver dollars kept turning up all the way into spring planting. Banks must've had bags full, because businesses had to take 'em somewhere.

Some who could afford not to spend their money as soon as they got it said they were holding onto them to remember the occasion when the Mill showered the town with silver. I wonder how many still have those shiny dollars.

The year after, the N&P carried a story about mills selling off their housing to the mill workers that live in them. With gas less than 50 cents a gallon, a person with a car can live miles away from work on their own piece of land. All over the South, mill houses are being offered to the families at a good price. Some are turning them over at a profit or starting a business at home, like car repair or woodworking. The mill village scene's been changing, but mills are what keep their people going.

At the start of that same year, the President of the American Cotton Manufacturing Institute, a man named William Sibley, had an article in the N&P. Sibley said he was encouraged about the prospects for textiles in the US because the "international outlook" favors "a widening of the free markets." He said we all "can look to 1953 with new assurance. The outlook for textiles as with industry in general, is no longer clouded by the fog of inflation, fears of higher taxes, and anxiety for our nation's solvency."

He sounded happy that "the United States Delegation won [international] conference acceptance of a policy to expand the consumption of textiles through long-range promotional efforts based on the principles of free competition."

Daddy and Uncle Bob talked it over later. What that optimism didn't take into consideration, Uncle Bob said, is what free competition from low-wage nations will mean: "Sibley's thinking 'more markets.' Japan's thinking 'let's build factories.' "

Sibley wrote that the US push for international "free competition" might "prove to have been a milestone in textile history."

It is proving to be a milestone – just not the kind he wanted.

Darlington's a normal town, not all farming and not all factories. Lots of people work in stores, and a few build their own livings, like barbers and plumbers and druggists and mechanics and Daddy. But if not for farms and local factories, people wouldn't gather here and need stores, electricians, mailmen, insurance men, lawyers, dry cleaners, café cooks, carpenters, filling stations, and deputy sheriffs.

Looking at the bigger picture changes things in your head. Towns depend on people earning money and wanting to live close in. Railroads planted quite a few towns around here -- Florence, Timmonsville, Branchville -- but farms and then factories made towns before that. Too, railroads sometimes pull up tracks, leaving their smaller towns to languish. Look at Mayesville, and now Timmonsville. Railroads leave and factories can close. Farm communities never grow so big, but they might last the longest. People will always need what farms produce, and farms can adjust and produce what people need -- so long as people have the heart and the gumption not to give up on farming.

They tell us the '50s are becoming the good times, now that the Office of Price Stability has shut down. Daddy says if President Truman hadn't been determined to keep Roosevelt's wartime price controls, mills would've ramped up manufacturing sooner.

1951 and '52 were slow times in textiles. Price controls made people afraid the factories wouldn't make enough cloth, so they hoarded. This led "the mill men" to make more cloth, and people snatched it up. Too much supply clogged the system, and manufacturing slowed to a crawl.

Then General Eisenhower got elected and closed the OPS.

Uncle Bob worried -- he worries a lot, maybe 'cause he's the oldest brother and not married – that supply-and-demand might not work well after years on price controls. Prices might go 'way up in a free market.

Turned out he needn't've worried. Customers – ladies who sew at home, makers of store-bought clothes, factories that use cloth in products -- started feeling better about being able to get all the cloth they wanted. Business was back.

In 1952 and 1953, the Darlington Manufacturing Company was hiring.

Essie Jackson Weatherford, Eltas Jean's mama, was one who went to work there. I don't remember Mrs Weatherford ever having a job away from their farm when we were their next-farm neighbor on Mineral Springs Road.

Can farm people leave the country every day for town and not be changed from who they use to be?

GRANDMOTHER LEAVES

Early one morning soon after we moved into the house Daddy built, a phone call hurried us out of bed and over to Florence. An ambulance had taken Grandmother to McLeod's Infirmary.

When we walked into the front hall, Uncle Bob met us. He took Daddy by the arm and said, "Gone."

Grandmother was dead in the hospital.

Dead, like the people in Grove Hill Cemetery. *Grandmother.*

I was 11. I didn't know what to do. I was in Grandmother's house on Cheves Street, but strange people were sitting in living room and dining room chairs and walking around the halls and the kitchen. Even people I knew looked like strangers.

Weenie couldn't talk. Tears ran all down her face. She went to her bedroom and stayed there a long time -- the only time I ever saw her leave guests to wander the house.

Everybody's eyes were red -- Uncle Bob's, Daddy's, Uncle Hart's. Sister and Ellison and Aunt Tee hadn't got there yet, and of course Saidee.

The people in Grandmother's house that I didn't know must've been from St John's Episcopal church; Weenie and Grandmother go there. Whoever they were, I didn't know them and didn't want to meet them. A lady came up while I was in the back hall and held me by the arm and looked into my face, explaining what didn't need explaining.

I interrupted her. "I'm looking for Mother," I said.

"Mother has gone to heaven, where ...."

Who is this woman? She thinks I mean Grandmother. I pulled away. She stood up and left. I wasn't playing the role she wanted played.

I could count on Mother not to be weeping but I couldn't find her. I didn't want Daddy, because if he cried I didn't know what I'd do, and besides, he was probly gone to Irby Street to get Aunt Tee. Grandmother was the only one I wanted to be

78

with, and that's when it started to sink in: *she's not here and she won't be here ever again.*

She'd not long got back from visiting Saidee and Uncle Win and Washington D C. I'd missed her a lot, so far away. Now she was gone even farther away than that.

Grandmother's heart had stopped beating.

Grandmother was a lady. A musician, the mainstay of her children, a Christian, and a lady. Mother called her "a Saint in this world." She loved us all, all equally, which was quite a feat now that I think about it, with 7 offspring and 5 of 'em married. Besides, Mother said, Grandmother put up with Cap and his sharp tongue and selfish ways and still treated him with courtesy and honor whenever he'd visit her (rented) home after their grown children took her and moved to Florence. That by itself proved to her that Grandmother is sanctified forever.

The family has a letter she wrote to all of us from that one trip with Saidee and Win (he's stationed at the Pentagon), the only vacation I ever remember her taking. She wrote something special to each of us, like being so happy for George and Mary and me moving into our new house in Darlington; so proud of George for somehow building it. For just me, she was bringing mementoes of the coronation of the young Queen Elizabeth II in London and of the celebration in Washington.

I never got the coronation mementoes; maybe my aunt Weenie kept them for herself. But that letter is a one-of-a-kind treasure: it was the only time in my life she'd been far enough from us to need to write.

Grandmother was not the kind of lady that joked and took on, much. After the funeral, there wouldn't be any laughing about her funny sayings and about what a card she was. Whatever a card's s'posed to be, she wasn't one. Maybe that's why I remember the funniest thing I ever heard her say. It's this:

Grandmother was sitting in her chair in the living room, her hands busy as usual. Also as usual, my cousin Linda Hart was present. She and her mother had lived there in Grandmother's house before Uncle Hart got out of the Army and moved them into a tenant house out on Uncle Bob's farm at Claussen. Even

79

after they didn't live at Grandmother's any more, it seemed like they were there almost every time I was.

I don't know why, but I up and asked, "How old are you, Grandmother?"

She said, "I'm 68."

Linda Hart said, "I thought you were 65."

Grandmother kept looking through her spectacles at what she was crocheting (a tiny dress for a kitchen bottle, I think), kind of raised her eyebrows, and said, "I *was*, 3 years ago."

I laughed right out loud. And a tiny smile even came to the ends of Grandmother's mouth.

Once she said about Saidee's baby Dick (they use to call him Fat Face) that he had such a short little nose they'd have to be careful to rush him into the house if it came on to rain. Mother chooses that one as the funniest, but I couldn't tell whether Grandmother meant it to be funny or not.

I don't remember the funeral. What I do remember is walking into Waters Funeral Home and then on into a little room toward the back, and there she was, lying in white satin within a casket. The bottom half was closed.

Her coffin.

Her hair looked just so, in finger waves like always, and she looked rested and calm, the way she usually did. She had on her little spectacles with the thin gold rims and one of her voile dresses and her corset; I could see the outline of the stays.

That was nice; she would have wanted that.

I never saw her leave the house without being done up nicely and wearing a soft, swingy dress in a pastel blue or maybe navy with tiny white dots in the cloth, and usually her single strand of pearls and Sunday lace-up shoes, navy blue or black. They had chunky heels that went *clp, clp* when she'd come out onto the wide front porch. She'd be adjusting her gloves and giving her hair's close and careful finger waves a last pat. (At night in bed she'd wear a little net over them.)

I was looking at her lying in her coffin when all of a sudden, without knowing it was going to happen, I broke out crying. Not little sniffling crying, either: loud sobs. I couldn't get a breath hardly in between. They probly heard me rooms away.

Russell was in the coffin room too. He'd brought C'n Mary; they'd just got married and she'd soon graduate from Columbia College in math with a teaching certificate. He put his arm around me when I started crying, but when I couldn't stop, he walked off. Then I was there alone. I was crying so, I couldn't've seen anybody else anyhow.

I felt deserted, but I couldn't blame Russell. We share just one grandmother: Mama, in Orangeburg County. His other grandmother Sue Carter Mims was probly sitting in the center room of her house in Lamar that very minute, I had almost no doubt. She's blind, and she sits right there every time we visit. Etna lives at home, does art paintings and collages, gardens, arranging flowers, and takes care of Miss Sue. (The daughter who doesn't marry is the expected caretaker in every family.) Daddy makes sure we pay our visit because Miss Sue is blind and Etna was his and Mother's friend in Lamar High School. He never forgets friends. And Miss Sue is Mother's dead husband's mother.

So this wasn't Russell's grandmother lying in that coffin. He loved her, though. Nobody could help loving or at least admiring her. I've thought since then about him leaving me there alone. I think it's this: he might've been about to cry too.

Mother and Daddy weren't in that coffin room; they let me wander in there alone. I guess they didn't know how much I was *not* ready to see Grandmother dead.

I don't remember the burial. Maybe they didn't take me and that's why I don't recall the grave flowers and her preacher's remarks. They may've been ashamed of the way I was acting. Mother dislikes crying in public, hugging, kissing in public and all sorts of "demonstrations." On the Spears side, there's lots of "demonstrations"; my aunt Weenie sometimes leaves the table in tears just if she thinks somebody doesn't like something she's cooked. So the Spearses cry and kiss and hug in public, but not most of our Boones and Dukeses -- anyhow not Mother.

Cheves Street is not the same since Waters Funeral Home took Grandmother's body to Mount Hope. Mrs Douglas is still there in the stately brick house next door, and Chase Park with its slide and swings and jungle jim is across the street behind the Masonic building, but I don't ask to go to Cheves the way I use to.

I still like the back-corner fig tree and the hydrangea bushes, and I'll always love Mrs Douglas, moving through her lush dark-wood rooms surrounded by wonderful books.

But the park playground's no use to me now except as a place to go out of the house -- Grandmother's rented house that's so different without her. I never knew until she went away what a difference she made. She kept things -- well, *nice*. People just acted nice *around* her. You couldn't *imagine* acting picky and whiny or grownups talking in sharp voices around Meade Hawley Spears.

Lately it's like other people have claimed her, like she belonged to them and not to me at all. Being the oldest, I knew her 4 years longer than any of the other grandchildren did, but one of the aunts -- I won't call her name -- acts like I never really knew Grandmother, nor she me. Like this:

Soon afterward, that aunt gave me a card she said Grandmother had bought in Washington especially for me. And maybe that was true, but somebody else had signed it. I knew because it said "Granny."

Sister, the eldest aunt, is smart and pays attention. She saw my face when I opened the card. She asked to see it. I handed it to her, and she looked up at the others.

"She never called Mama 'Granny.' She was "Grandmother."" Sister knew.

I left the card at Cheves Street. I don't care what they did with it. Let them give it to one of the other grandchildren; they called her Granny – the ones who could talk by then.

Since I couldn't feel right any more about mentioning her in her own house, I started talking *to* her. Grandmother is the first person I ever knew well who lives in heaven. For awhile after she died, I prayed to her the way Roman Catholics pray to the Virgin Mary. I thought about getting a rosary, but I don't know how to say the beads. Besides, I didn't have any problem talking with Grandmother in my own words.

I figure Grandmother knows Jesus and God and a good number of her fellow angels already, and I know she loved me on earth, so I reckoned then that she could easily explain me to them if needed.

After while I didn't pray to her any more. She has a right to enjoy heaven without having to worry about our problems, is what I think now. And I'm not the same little girl she knew so well. She could be distressed to hear sad things that've happened since she left.

Cap came to Grandmother's funeral but wouldn't sit on the front row, they said, and I guess they didn't want him to. The other grandchildren don't even know him, really, except from seeing him at the head of the table on some holidays.

He left as soon as he could, Mother said, and went back to the country. Cap's my grandfather who use to be married to Grandmother. Still is, but not really.

After the funeral week, I told Daddy, "I got to go out to St Paul's and see Cap."

He took me that Sunday. Daddy's good that way. Lots of ways, actually. He specially believes in visiting the sick and the maybe lonely. Cap would never say he's lonely; you couldn't expect him to; it wouldn't be Cap.

Sometimes he lives in the Gubmint house and sometimes in one of the cinderblock houses sprinkled around on the old Spears place where Great-Grandmother Phoebe Wright Spears brought them up and added acreage after their father died. Sometimes he spends awhile in the house his sister Salina (Aunt Liny) lives in. She's the sister that never married but as far as I know never had anybody to take care of. Long ago she studied piano at Welsh Neck Female Academy. Now it's called Coker College. She never learned to drive, but one of the Tolson boys was hired to chauffeur her over to Hartsville and wait for her classes to be over and bring her home.

We found Cap that day at Aunt Liny's. He didn't have much to say, but he kind of brightened up. He lets me hug him, and he hugs me back. Nobody else in the family gets to touch him much, unless it's for picture taking with the little ones.

Aunt Liny's happy when Cap's there. She thinks her baby brother is wonderful.

Trouble is, they neither one cook, so Cap takes Lassie and they ride around to country stores at like Cartersville and Lydia.

COUNTY

That's where he eats, which is not a new plan in his life. He seems just as satisfied to eat vi-ena sausages and drink bottled drinks in freedom as to sit down to a good fried chicken dinner with sliced tomatoes, rice, butter beans, and sweet tea.

Aunt Liny, though, she always looks glad when we bring her cooked food.

We're careful, though, not to let one food touch any other kind of food, or she won't eat it. The string beans shouldn't touch the rice-and-tomato-gravy which shouldn't touch the baked side legs. (Side legs are Aunt Liny's favorite piece of chicken because they're dark *and* light meat.) And *nothing* should touch the banana pudding; that goes without saying. So everything's in its own bowl or bag or cup, and although she won't eat until we leave, I actually suspect Aunt Liny finishes each kind of food before she starts on the next. 5-course meals, so to speak.

In between our visits, I s'pose she eats whatever Cap brings from a crossroads filling station store -- Cheese Nabs, Moonpies, apples, baked bacon rind, dill pickles out of a barrel, Bit o' Honey, Squirrel Nut Zippers, a wedge of cheese from a wheel, and loaf bread – Holsom or Merita. (They've got Sunbeam now, without any holes, but Daddy says bread without holes is too refined to be good for us.)

And Spam -- certainly Spam.

That day Aunt Liny said some specially nice things about Grandmother -- Meade, as she calls her. Aunt Liny didn't come to visitation nor the funeral; she hardly ever goes anywhere. She says if she leaves the house, thieves might "break through and steal," like the Bible says.

Mother says (but not to Aunt Liny), "Wonder what it is she thinks they'd want?"

Our closest Spears cousins in the County are mostly over near where Aunt Liny and Cap are living, on the old family farmland at St Paul's and in Lamar. I might know more about the Spearses in St Paul's Cemetery than I know about the Spearses in Lamar today.

Robert L (Hot Shot) Spears wears glasses and runs an appliance store. When I met him, from his nickname I was expecting something different. Maybe he was an athlete in high school.

C'n Sambo is on the Lamar school board. When Darlington plays Lamar and the school board members cross the football field at halftime, C'n Sambo's the tallest and widest. You can't miss him. It's like he's a ship and the other board members are being swept along in his wake.

The Reynoldses whose mother's a Spears have left Lamar, but they're interesting to think about. C'n Genevieve turned her back on getting married so she could travel and have a famous career, and now she's a newspaper reporter in Washington DC. Her brother Buck's someplace in Texas, selling insurance to politicians. One of his customers is Lyndon Baines Johnson, Speaker of the House.

Cap's sisters are our closest-kin Spearses in and around Lamar. Their brothers, all but Cap, died fairly young. Great-Aunt Ida Mims lives alone now in the Spears house between the abandoned Presbyterian church and the taken-up railroad tracks. Great-Aunt Liny out in the little house at St Paul's. Great-Aunt Betty Young was widowed early like Ida – so early I never knew their husbands. She farms the old Spears place at St Paul's; it's hers now. She's the only sister with a living child -- her son Charlie. She sent him through law school. He's a big shot in North Carolina, with a nickname – Cy, like the ball player. He bought Senator Maybank's big stone house in Flat Rock after the Senator died there.

And Cap, of course, their only living brother and my grandfather.

Cap sits there most days in the house we all call the Gubmint house -- the one the US Government built free on their land during the Depression. He'll sit 'til he takes a notion to drive off to a store or somewhere, just him and Lassie.

ST JOHN'S

Consolidation kicked in about the time we finished grammar school. It means country schools will disappear soon. Town schools will get all those pupils – all.

The way it's always been is that most country schools run through 6th or 7th Grade, and pupils transfer into town for Jr High and High School. Consolidation means they'll come in earlier and earlier, a lower grade every year, and country schools will close down grade by grade. Pretty soon the only schools left will be town schools; that's in the plan. Some places, other states, they've already Consolidated.

There won't be a chance to learn in a small school where everybody knows everybody any more.

Is that good? You tell me; I never had that chance. I was in a town school from the start because we didn't live far enough out. I was glad to get to school so I could learn to read, but town schools and I didn't gee-haw right off. I saw the light after being kept in so much in 1st Grade and being regarded as such a pill in 2nd.

Town *kids*, though -- I adjusted pretty early to town kids. There's a lot they don't know about the natural world -- the earth around us and the creatures -- but it's not their fault.

I think it's good our class missed being Consolidated. It's hard enough to come into a big school in 8th Grade, let alone earlier than that when you're a little kid. Some came to our class already use to being the smartest in their grammar schools. It took them a while to realize they wouldn't be stars at St John's. It was kind of embarrassing to watch, or fun, depending on how underdeveloped your sense of mercy was. It had to hurt.

I can imagine myself in their place. Probly not a single one of us out in the country ('cept Wayne that lived in town back then) was ever in such of a thing as a Kindergarten, but kids in country schools get to really know their teachers and get more encouragement. They're maybe 12 in a class, and here we start out in classrooms with 3 or 4 times that many, of course with just one teacher. You're on your own more often than not. You learn quick not to ask many questions because you might ask a stupid one, and what's she going to think of you?

Pretty soon the new students coming into our 8th Grade at St John's got the picture and stopped raising their hands to be called on. The last thing you want to be is a hand waver when practicly everybody in school knows the answers. St John's is that kind of school. If you don't know what you need to, you hit the books. That's what we're here for and we know it, plus your parents'll take the school's side against you every time. That's when you start learning to stand on your own, no favors asked.

Darlington has one kindergarten, Miss Frances Edwards's. The townies that went to it learned how to sit still and be quiet. Townies are not smarter than us, they're just stiller. There's so many of 'em, there's less room per person to be stirring around. Stillness is contagious. After years and years around 'em, it's happened to me too. Years ago Sister -- Aunt Ferebe -- took me to Charleston with her to a Welfare Department conference in the Francis Marion Hotel where she was giving a speech, and I sat through the whole thing without the foggiest notion why she wanted me there. But I learned what a conference is like, and I found out the use of patience.

With town schools getting bigger, you might not be able even to know everybody in your grade. *That* can't be good. The Class of '57 is small – the smallest in several years they say – and yet even 72 is too many people to really know as friends, and Graduation's not even 2 months away.

But since I had to be in a big school from 1st Grade on, I was lucky: it's a good school, the best anywhere in the Pee Dee, maybe the toughest school anywhere. I know that now. Standards -- that's what St John's 's got. *Standards.*

From the name, you might think St John's is a private school, but it's not. I know just 2 people my age who don't go to public school: a boy from here and one from Florence. Their families sent them to military schools. Phil's father's dead, his mother has the twins to raise, and she rents out part of the house into an apartment. Jack's parents are divorced and rich; she drives a white Cadillac convertible and him a black one. Jack and I saw his daddy at the drive-in picture show with a date one night. That was spooky. Jack said the show wasn't all that good anyhow, so we left.

I'm friends with Phil and Jack both, but I feel sorry for them because they're not in public school and so neither one knows anybody else much our age here. I keep introducing Phil and Jack around. Going to school in your home town *matters*. People get to be friends; you do stuff for each other.

In 9th Grade Clyde Lane carved me a wooden rabbit in Shop. It's got no whiskers, but I bet if I asked Clyde to make it some, he would. Or use to would; he's going with Sylvia Willliamson now. Mother says the rabbit looks kind of blocky to her but I think it's a remarkable likeness. And how many other girls at St John's've got a work of original art sitting on their bookcase bed?

When I was taking Typing, it was my worst class. New skills are hard for me. I'm better in English and whatever else gets graded by how well you read and understand and discuss and write about it, like Mrs McIver's class in government. Aptitude Tests say I should be good in math, but I'm not, to speak of.

Daddy says don't avoid stuff just because you don't like it. He says math's good mental training, and schooling's all about training the mind to work. Anyhow, I can't *avoid* math – not the way things work at St John's. I went into Advanced Algebra and I didn't even like *normal* algebra.

He also says I'll profit by growing up without luxuries, knowing I have a living to earn. I'll try not to lose these opportunities, but I hope I don't get worn out first by having to learn everything. I've already got astigmatism and near-sightedness.

Mother blames my eye problems on reading in bed after she tells me to cut off the light and go to sleep. She might be right. It could even be a punishment, a cross to bear. Plus I think teachers think because I wear glasses to see what's on the board, I must know a lot.

My eyesight went weird in grammar school. I kept copying some numbers off the board wrong without knowing it. The school was kind of slow to figure out what was wrong and so was I, but Miss Audrey Reno caught on and sent a note home saying my problems were done right but that they weren't the

COUNTY

right problems. She said I needed to go to an eye doctor. It was expensive, but he put glasses on me, little round ones in light-brown plastic frames to kind of match my hair. I don't wear glasses all the time; just when I need to see the board.

St John's offers 3 foreign languages: French, Latin, and Spanish. I had French 2 years and now I'm in Latin. Hubie sits in front of me and is all the time turning around saying something ridiculous.

Latest: Hubie says he's running off to Cuba to help Castro defeat Batista.   Hubie says it's time for Batista to go -- something about finding bags of fingernails. He expects when he gets to Cuba there'll be hardly any freedom fighters there that still have fingernails.

I told him Daddy was in the Navy in the '30s when Batista took over. His ship the *Wyoming* anchored in Guantanamo Bay to keep other nations from interfering in our hemisphere.

Batista got in power the same way Castro wants to -- by knocking the top guy off the top.

Batista's bad now that he's in power, but let Castro in, would he be any better? Different's not the same as better.

Hubie's the tallest in the Class of '58 (his parents wouldn't let him skip 4th grade with Nancy and me, remember), but what does he know about fighting in jungles and swamps?   He sunburns awful, and mosquitoes go after him like 40.

Living here in Darlington County, though, no wonder Hubie thinks people in power for a long time need to be moved out. If there's ever a revolt here, I expect Hubie'll jump right in the middle. But we don't revolt here. People here just vote, usually for the same people over and over again.

What I think is, Hubie won't go any place. He'll still be in Latin class talking, mostly to me. Some days his head's very pink. That's when he starts talking ridiculous, like, I purloined this stuff out of Mac's daddy's bag. (He likes Edgar Allan Poe.)

Huh. Pish tosh. My foot. I know there's no drugs at St John's. Besides, whoever heard of belladonna?

Mr Cain calls me down if I answer Hubie (I don't think he hears deep voices as clear as he hears girls'), but sometimes the stuff Hubie says out the corner of his mouth is too ridiculous not to answer out loud. I'm better at keeping out of trouble now than when I was being kept in after school practicly every day in

COUNTY

grammar school, but I forget sometimes. Still, I know perfectly well I need to listen to Mr Cain in class and not to Hubie.

We love Mr Holley (he's the Superintendent now) but we're all kind of nervous around Mr Cain. Some of the boys call him (not to his face) "Killer" Cain. When he gets mad, his eyes bulge and his voice gets loud and shrill and he calls us "BUNNIES!" Really he says "bonnies"; he's from Charleston.

He says it like bunnies are kin to lice.

MR. CAIN CROWNING ANNE WEAVER

Anne Weaver Crowned
Homecoming Queen

Here's a picture (sorry I cut it out wrong) that of course shows Mr Cain in his gray suit. You get to see Anne Weaver too. She's the Class of '57's Queen – Homecoming and May Queen both. She's not just beautiful and popular, she's a star on the basketball team.

COUNTY

Mr Cain's not just the Latin teacher, he's also Principal of St John's High. He's tall, bony, and knows a lot. Latin is the course taught by any school's smartest teacher. In Orangeburg County, that's Mother's oldest sister Rosa. She's whiplash smart. St John's Latin teacher is Mr Cain.

Mr Cain appears to own a closetful of gray suits that all look alike. He darts around corners so quick, his coat-tails sail out behind him. You can tell he's thinking, thinking all the time. He'll stop cold when you least expect it and then head off in the exact opposite direction. Could be that's why he's also a state champion tennis player -- instant maneuverability, like the kind of a car they say turns on a nickel and stops on a dime.

It was kind of a shock when once I was invited to Saturday lunch at the Country Club and walked by him in action on the court when he was *wearing tennis shorts*. But he's a wonderful player. When he's swooping after long shots and smashing overheads, his bony knees are just a blur.

Latin's tricky; to me it seems unnatural. All that inflection, and besides, nobody alive knows how Latin ought to sound. I feel silly reading *aloud* in a language so dead. How do we know a Roman in Jesus's day wouldn't laugh himself silly if he heard us?

French, that's different. We know how it's spoken in France and some other places because Miss Louise Douglas plays us records. The trick is to <u>do</u> it that way, which I really am not good at. Tell the truth, Miss Douglas's French is not much like those records either; maybe she speaks Southern French. Joyce Anne Medlin, though, she *gets* French. Her French words sound really French.

Jane Johnson -- she was a Junior in French I with us – she pronounced French words in English. *Avocat* (Ah-Voh-CAH) is French for lawyer. Jane said AV-o-cat. I mean, not that it wasn't *cute*. You couldn't help but laugh when she read aloud; none of us could, even with her being an upperclassman and all.

Jane's pretty, with a sprinkle of freckles all across her nose and smooth, turned-under shoulder-length brown hair, so she didn't care; French couldn't embarrass *her*. A few snickers from

COUNTY
a bunch of underclassmen meant much of nothing, water off a duck's back.

Mr Cain got me to take Latin the same way he got me to take Physics, 'cept he didn't erase any courses; he just *put* me in Latin, extra.

Mr Cain's the reason I got to this final year needing only one course credit to graduate. He made sure I never got to have a normal 12-credit year; I took 15. And here I still am.

Here's what St John's High School looks like from the auditorium side. The picture's not where I wanted it, but I'm not great at layout.

Mr Cain is also why I've been working my head harder than I meant to. I meant to kind of coast *some* of the time anyhow, and have more of that fun my parents and other older people had in high school. Mother couldn't've sweated a single course and still played basketball (she's just 5' 3", so she was a guard) and had all the social life at Lamar High they tell about having. Going through St John's is not like that at all.

Well, maybe a little. Sometimes.

Think, though -- would I deliberately choose courses that bring down my grade average, when I'm going to need scholarship money for college? No siree I would not. But Mr Cain -- does he care? Foot, no. He says I've got too good a mind to frivol away. He calls the whole class of '57 exceptional.

I have to admit, in Columbia at the State Mental Contests, St John's High of Darlington cleans up, specially the Class of '57. We *shine*.

COUNTY

Mr Cain's been saying all along to just wait 'til the Class of '57 gets the results from the new National Merit Exams.

I don't know of any school with tougher grading than ours. To graduate from St John's, you've got to average 3 or better in at least 16 year-long courses. Grades go from 1 (the highest) down to 5, and the teachers average the percentages out to the nearest number. (*Your* school might use A to F.) The widest part of our scale is 3 (80 to 89). If we make worse than 3 on some courses, we can't graduate without making better than 3 in at least as many.

The grading system is printed on our report cards:

1   95 to 100
2   90 to 94
3   80 to 89
4   75 to 79
5   Below 75 (below passing)

You can see just from that, St John's is not a school to slide through. These teachers don't mind sticking a *minus* sign after your grade, either. If you're at the low end of the grade, they let you know it. You might get a *plus*, once in a blue moon. But a *plus* makes you feel worse – it means you just missed the next grade up. 1-plus, though, is phenomenal. It won't help your average, but it's something to remember.

One of the teachers says the school is kind to say *Below Passing* instead of calling it *Failing.* There's no actual difference, but it might make some people feel better. Not that our good feelings seem to be a faculty goal here.

At the end of last year, one of my best friends turned out not to have enough grade-quality points. She talked about transferring to Florence, where the schools are easier. They don't compete on a state level the way St John's does.

My friend's still here. She decided she rather buckle down this year than leave St John's. Besides, she'll surely pull a 2 at least in the only crip course for seniors -- Better Family Living.

With the newspaper to run and being kind of curious, I signed up for BFL. But am I in it? I am *not*. Mr Cain punctured that plan the first day of classes. That's when he called me in and told I'm in Physics, not BFL.

COUNTY

"No sir, I don't know anything about Physics. I signed up for BFL. There's been a mistake."

Mr Cain didn't even look up from where he was erasing and brushing off rubber bits from a card, fixing to write new stuff in its place.

"Yesss, you're correct, quite correct. There *has been* a mistake. The mistake was, you signed up for Better Family Living. You could not have *meant* to do that, and naturally I've corrected the mistake."

By then I was thinking *I got to get home and tell my side before he gets to my parents*.

Mr Cain reads minds, so he cut that off at the pass. "Your parents understand perfectly. They want you in Physics."

Then he *looked* at me.

Mr Cain has a nose that works *with* a look -- sharpens it up. Cap's nose does that too. Mr Cain's eyes are right *there*, prominent, not hooded and mysterious like Cap's, but Mr Cain does a lot with his eyebrows to make up for it.

I knew he could make it stick. If I argued, pretty soon I'd hear "Bunny!" in a sharp Charleston accent.

So I'm in Physics, like it or not, with a bunch of boys. The only other girl's a Junior. I didn't know her; she might've moved here from someplace. When Mr Patrick calls on her, she looks like a deer facing a bowhunter. I don't see how she can last long in the class. The lever principle almost did her in; the internal combustion engine we're taking up next is bound to finish her off.

Tell the truth, though, I'm actually liking Physics. When I have to rebuild an engine someday -- grind crud off the pistons and like that – I'll be prepared, and won't Daddy or whoever be surprised. I'm even beginning to be sorry I never took Chemistry, because I might really've liked it. Daddy did.

Seniors

I almost didn't have a senior year, even though one credit was all I needed to graduate in summer school and finish in July '56.

One reason is money. We need to have more put aside for me to start college.

Another reason is, something amazing happened in May: I was elected Editor-in-Chief of St John's newspaper without running for it. I've secretly wanted that job ever since 8th Grade, when Miss Jones chose me to be Bugsy Bookworm for the library. So how could I not stay for another year? I couldn't not, is what.

So I'm Editor-in-Chief, backed up by the best Business Manager there's probly ever been in the history of St John's High -- Vivian Booth. There's no problem getting sports and the news stories written and in on time, plus I've got people standing 'round begging to write features. Best of all, when ads start filling up the paper we get an extra page, sometimes an extra fold, thanks to Vivian and her staff. More ads mean more pages for more stuff, more writers, more articles.

Viv's one of my closest friends, but who ever expected her to be so great at picking and managing a go-getter staff to sell ad space? Not me. And to be such a great saleswoman herself?

Think "Vivian Booth," and you think nice disposition, wonderful attitude, contagious smile. If she's had a motto up 'til now, I'd swear it was "Let's party" -- let's get together and have a good time. She knows how.

She throws fine parties at their house on Pocket Road. Nobody has better peanut boilings. You drive up (it's maybe 8 miles out) after the big iron pot's been boiling for hours over a wood fire in her backyard. You know she been getting things lined up all that day, but here she comes strolling out, arms open for a hug, looking like she's done nothing all day long.

95

COUNTY

Sure, her brothers help (she's the only girl) and her parents too maybe, but she always manages to look like she's just revving up.

If I didn't know better, I'd say she lets a party give itself. I can see her now, smiling and sliding out her right hand palm down like she's about to start dancing: "Pahty, Pahty, y'all!" I've been hearing her say it for years: "Let's have a PAHty."

So when you think you know somebody, look out.

Turns out Vivian Booth's a born businesswoman. Thanks to that hidden Vivian, the one who knows how to buckle down and achieve goals, the Bulletin'll break a school record before we graduate. It's lost money every year in living memory, but we're sure enough in the black this year.

I'm planning to throw the staff a big party on some of the profit. Party time for the whole staff, just Vivian's style. Can't tell them yet, but it's our money, right?

"In the black." Before I got to be Editor-in-Chief, I don't think I'd ever heard "in the black." I'm coming right along.

Nancy that skipped 4th Grade with me, she's not here for Senior Year. They moved to Columbia because Mr L A Rogerson got transferred by the Liberty Life Insurance Company. He must be good to be in charge of an office in the State Capitol.

Seems odd without Nancy. She and I've been in the same grade ever since 1st, when she climbed the cloakroom wall and made such a fuss, the rest of us in Detention all got out early. Except for Eltas Jean Weatherford that I grew up with on Mineral Springs Road, Nancy's the one I've been with the longest in Darlington, during school and after at her house. She lived right across the schoolyard all those years.

In high school, Nancy wasn't as interested in socializing as I was, so we weren't as close. If they hadn't moved away, she'd probly have the 2nd best grades in the class after Mac. She might've beat him. Even after she'd been in Columbia for months, St John's was just before hearing from Nancy – or rather about Nancy – again.

I don't know who's 3rd in the class but it's not me. Not after what I made in Home Ec that I never would 've taken if Mother hadn't made me. And typing. I am definitely not a typing talent.

96

COUNTY

Miss Jac Douglas said I'd 've gotten my accuracy up higher if I hadn't flung my hands around like the typewriter was a grand piano.

Most of us at St John's've either been here all along or came in in 8th grade or (a few) moved from out of the county, but we're all use to each other now. We know each other's kin -- which ones moonshine, which are on the county payroll, which ones work at factories or clerk in stores or do service work like Daddy, and which ones are lazy or enjoy poor health, like the "hunter" who shot himself in the leg and got rich on insurance.

We're pretty tolerant, though. Jesus says for us to be perfect; that's the goal. Although I don't know anybody my age who actually *is*. Well okay, *one* – Anne Weaver -- but she's the exception that proves the rule.

We're all close, the Class of '57; we're tight. We care about our families, our school, each other, paid work if we've got it, and music. Even the few who've got strangers for parents (but maybe not so few as I use to think) can get into music.

Not all of us dance, specially some country boys that I wish *would*, but we all like some kind of music. We even sing. I'll talk about our music later. Can't leave that out.

We have house parties, usually at the beach. The ocean's only an hour or so away. You just take the road east through either Pamplico or Marion.

I'd say our class started out normal for our age -- kind of loud, strange, and uncertain -- silly, some say. Sometimes with your closest friends you squabble about nothing and make up almost without remembering why you got mad in the 1st place.

I'm wondering, now that we're about to graduate, how many of the people in the Class of '57 are ones I'd have enjoyed knowing better than some I knew, specially boys.

Its beginning to feel like it's too soon to leave. Maybe when we have reunions....but oh my gosh, we'll be out and different then.

Anne Weaver and Martha Boyette, the 2 prettiest girls in the class probly -- I don't know either one as well as I'd like to. I shouldn't be this busy, maybe.

Phila (say FIE-la), Anne's stepmother, works for Southern Bell, and Mr Weaver has a rural mail route like Cap ran when

COUNTY
Daddy was little. I know all that, plus that her younger brother's named Danny.

And what do I know about Anne herself? Only that she's kind to everybody, and everybody likes her and voted her Homecoming Queen and May Queen both. She's got beautiful teeth, but even if she didn't, you'd still feel honored somehow when she smiles at you. Oh, and she's on the basketball team.

Martha Boyette's younger brother Joe works afternoons and Saturdays at a worm farm out on the Leavenworth Road: he told me about it just last week. (Joe's in the underclassman study hall Mr Cain assigned me to keep; just came and got me out of my own study hour and told me I'm in charge of these little kids for the rest of the year. But I can't say they're not interesting.) Joe says when loud motorcycles come by, the earthworms stampede to the other end of the enclosure. He has to get out of the way or they'll run over his feet.

How many 9th graders have a hilariously strange job like after-school foreman of an earthworm farm?

And take Anna Jeffords, one of my favorite people, who all I use to know about her was that she's blond with cute freckles and a wonderful grin, and that we both took piano from Mrs Childs and she came out to the Sand Hill to practice our recital duet.

When we were Juniors, Anna invited Sally Hyer, Kathy Graham, Joyce Anne Medlin, and me to spend a Friday night at her house. Her mother and step-father (the George Gedras) were away.

That house party made us friends.

Not only was Anna a good hostess but interesting things kept happening, things you'd never wish on anybody, but after it's all over, they're imprinted on your mind.

Right after supper (toasted ham-tomato-mayonnaise sandwiches, potato chips, dill pickles and RC Colas), the toilet stopped up. We had to keep using it anyhow. If we'd been in the country, no problem, because no matter whether there's a toilet in the house or not, you've always got a privy or anyhow privacy. But you can't just *go* right there on a corner of Main Street, and houses in town don't have outside toilets hardly ever.

Needless to say, as time marched on, the situation and the smell went from bad to worse.

So Kathy took charge. She stuck a cigarette between her lips and lit it so she wouldn't gag, and she cleaned out the toilet. Then she got the plumber's friend and broke the clog. Then she even helped mop the bathroom linoleum.

That woman, when you think about it, is a hero.

Then for some reason, somebody locked Joyce Anne out in the front yard in her underwear. What Joyce was doing outside in her underwear in the 1st place, I missed that. Maybe she was pushed. But after Joyce hollered through the door what all she was going to do to us if nobody unlocked the front door, we unlocked the front door.

It's not as bad as it sounds; there's bushes close up to the house.

It was probly Sally that locked the door. To look at Sally Hyer, you'd think butter wouldn't melt in her mouth. Neat, shiny brown hair – sort of a chestnut – in a smooth shoulder-length pageboy. Freckles across her nose and nowhere else on her face. And a chuckle you join in with, even before you know why she's chuckling.

But impish? I'll say she is. When Sally gets a glint in her eye and laughs that husky laugh of hers, watch out.

Bad Scenes

Growing up on Mineral Springs Road, I use to get malaria every summer from mosquitos. Malaria's nothing much; Dr Willcox gives you quinine. Quinine makes you swimmy headed and cures you.

Then after we moved to town I went out for tennis and got hepatitis. Not saying tennis made me sick; I liked it. But I had to quit because hepatitis lasts for maybe months and you're weak as dishwater. I could still go to school but had to give up on becoming an athlete. I'd never been on a court before; we didn't have such things as tennis out on Mineral Springs Road. Who knows, though; I might not've been any good at it anyhow.

To get me well Dr Willcox gave me -- was it called hemoglobin? – and prescribed lots of rest. I never turned very yellow I don't think; only the whites of my eyes.

In Africa and other places with a lot of mosquitoes like we have, you hear that people die from malaria all the time. They haven't developed medically like the United States. The only African countries with good hospitals and doctors like ours are Rhodesia and South Africa. Even in America, men digging the Panama Canal died from malaria not all that long ago.

By time I didn't have hepatitis, the rest of the team had got good at tennis, and I try not to do stuff I'm not any good at. I hate looking pitiful, maybe 'cause in grammar school I use to get picked last for softball. Once, but only once, I fooled everybody by hitting a ball out really far and making a home run. Next time I came up to bat, all the fielders moved way back, just in case. That was fun, but just that once.

Jerry Cox told me how he got Infantile Paralysis. I didn't ask him; I know better than to do that; he just wanted to say it.

One really hot day, he'd got all sweaty playing outside and came in for a bath. He started cramping up in the tub, he says – seemed like as soon as he got into the water. He couldn't understand what was happening. Nobody could. He was just a little kid.

Infantile Paralysis could have killed him but didn't. He's slender right on, and not able to walk the same as he use to because one of his legs got different, and one of his arms.

The changes didn't stop Jerry Cox from being nice looking, with intense dark eyes, and it didn't stop him from being determined to do school. I'm not in his grade any more so I don't see him a lot, but I expect Jerry will do well in life. They say what doesn't kill you can make you stronger. He's that kind of strong.

There was a pretty little girl named Suzy who was there when we started school, but when 3rd Grade started, she didn't come. Somebody said Suzy had Infantile Paralysis.

I never saw her again.

When I was little, nothing was more feared than Infantile Paralysis, unless it was the Atomic Bomb. For the whole US, Infantile Paralysis was the Plague.

On a hill outside Florence, on the Timmonsville Highway, is a big white frame building everybody calls the Crippled Children's Home. Dr Julian Price started it in the '40s. He somehow got the WPA to build it, and he managed to furnish it with "iron lungs" and good nurses and all the known treatments for children brought in with serious afflictions. Betsy Eaddy works with him, and so do other professionals dedicated to bringing afflicted children as far back from the effects of polio as possible. They don't claim to perform miracles, but every child that goes there leaves after a few months stronger and more fortunate than when they went in.

Dr Price has a big heart for children and a multitude of admirers. He was my doctor when I was little. He always drew me a funny picture to take home with me – a doctor with a long nose, maybe, or a little person with "Grumpy" written under. Mother's sister Marie Dukes Bowie, Floor Supervisor at McLeod's Infirmary, sings his praises. If I'm still here and have children, Dr Price is the doctor I want for them.

Polio is what they're calling it now, not Infantile Paralysis. For years everybody would turn on the porch lights for the March of Dimes, meaning they were ready with a donation to hand the volunteer for the National Foundation for Infantile Paralysis. In the awful year of 1952, the US had 58,000 cases. 3,145 died and 21,269 were left paralyzed. In *one year.*

Then in our Sophomore year, something wonderful finally happened: Jonas Salk and his research team he'd picked, who'd been working for years on the disease, announced they had a vaccine ready. The whole country kind of held its breath and prayed. Then the nation waited.

20,000 doctors and public health workers, 64,000 teachers, an army of volunteers, and 180,000 children took part in the trial run.

Our prayers were answered. The vaccine worked!

On April 12, 1955, Dr Salk announced it was a success. Now never again will parents have to fear the coming of summer, the season of polio.

Why that day is not a national or world holiday, I'll never understand. There's not even a Jonas Salk Day. Who's done more for children and the future? WHO???

We pass the Crippled Children's Home every time we visit Uncle Bill and Aunt Marie. It's a graceful, beautiful place, like a mansion. But even passing by sends chills up my back, remembering how scary things were until Dr Salk beat polio. To me it's a symbol of terror and hope both.

We all ought to be thankful to Dr Salk and the thousands involved in the cure and the testing. So many little kids died, and so many victims live in crippled bodies. May God give them the strength not to be overwhelmed by whatever comes next.

In between the not-so-bad illnesses and the most dreaded illness, there's rheumatic fever.

Rheumatic fever lasts a whole year. Judy Slaughter that graduated last year had it. When I visited her, she was lying propped up on pretty pillows in a big bed in a front room of their big, high house on Hampton Street. I didn't know what to say. Other people were there – people in her grade, acting like it was a party. I think they were trying to keep her from feeling left out, but it had to be hard on her, being sick for so long.

Betsy Banks had rheumatic fever before Judy, all the way back in 8th Grade. When Betsy finally could get out of bed, she was still in our grade. She must've worked hard or be really smart.

Being sick didn't stop Betsy from having her reglar sense of humor -- almost too much of one. Soon as she got well, she was back joking and kidding around and being fun to be with.

Betsy lives on South Warley like me. The Banks house is almost at Cashua, but that's just 3 blocks away from Grove Hill Cemetery. One day 3 of us were sitting up in my treehouse, and a new little boy named Stephen Dore meandered over from the Davises'. He was scratching around in the dirt with one toe and looking shy, but he kept looking up at us. We were looking down and feeling important because we were older -- probly 9th grade then -- and up in a tree.

So Betsy asked him what his daddy does for a living, and he said Mr Davis is not his daddy, he's his uncle, and Betsy said well what does your uncle do for a living.

Stephen answered right up. He said, "He's a plumber."

So Betsy said, "What does he plumb?"

Stephen said, "Toilets."

Which was a perfectly reasonable answer but it struck Betsy so funny she almost fell out of my treehouse laughing and got the rest of us laughing too.

Stephen, who we didn't know before that day, went back in the Davises' house and didn't come out any more until we climbed down and went in my house for Kool-Aid.

We weren't laughing at Stephen and the toilets, I don't think; we were laughing because Betsy was laughing so she like to fell out. I hope if Stephen ever reads this, he'll know.

Betsy's main thing is practical jokes like short-sheeting beds and phoning people to ask if their refrigerator's running and then asking them hadn't they better go catch it.

Wrecks are nothing to laugh about, we all know. They say that if we die in our teens, wrecks are what's most likely to kill us. My cousin Betty Anne Turkett that lives upstate didn't die in the wreck they had when her granddaddy was driving (she was beside him in the front seat), but she was in the hospital a long, long time. Now Betty Anne's fine, but they couldn't save one of her eyes.

103

COUNTY

The wreck I remember most, though, happened to my Eltas Jean from Mineral Springs Road.

In May of 1953, I was at home getting ready for 2 exams in one day. Eltas Jean, thinking she was lucky to be through with her exams early, decided to treat herself to a picture show that same afternoon. J L had his own car by then and said he'd take her into Darlington.

I was studying for Mr Harper's English exam when Daddy came home in a rush. He parked his truck in the backyard instead of leaving it in the driveway like normal on a work day. He came in through the kitchen looking for me.

"Jean's been in a wreck, Bood." (Sometimes he calls me Bood or Boodle, sort of like he's thinking I'm still a little kid. That day, though, he was expecting me to be a grown up.) "Get in the car. They've taken her to McLeod's."

I don't remember anything we said going over, not in so many words, but he told me there'd been a wreck -- Eltas Jean and J L in his convertible.

Instead of stopping at Hampton Street, another car went across and hit J L's car. Both front windshields were smashed, Daddy said. There was blood from where Jean's face hit.

The passenger door was wide open and so bent up it couldn't be shut.

Daddy came up on the wreck just happen-so: he was driving on Woods Street heading to fix the McCauleys' refrigerator. Course he spotted J L's car right off, the one J L had then. (It was a convertible painted chartreuse with red upholstery. A Mercury, sort of.) Daddy was just in time to watch the ambulance leave for Florence. Jean was alone inside it 'cept for medical people.

The policemen told Daddy the drivers of both cars ought to be all right. Dr Willcox came right after the ambulance and was sending them to his office to be patched up.

But they said "the girl" -- my friend from Mineral Springs Road that I explored the world with when I was Gene Autry and she was Roy Rogers and we rode tobacco stick horses -- I have to stop or I'll cry again --

She was too hurt for Dr Willcox to fix.

104

COUNTY

She'd got thrown onto the pavement when J L's car smashed against the wide oak tree after the other car hit J L's at the corner between Jimmy Willcox's and Judy Slaughter's.

On our way to McLeod's, I realized more about how Daddy thinks: we're supposed to forget about ourselves if somebody we love needs us. He didn't say it in those words. He just said that Jean was bad hurt and would need to see a friend if she could, and that we had to do what we could for her and whoever was with her.

At the hospital, the doctor or whoever the man was didn't want to let us see Jean, once he found out we're no kin.

Daddy insisted. "We've been friends of the Weatherfords for years. All these girls' lives."

"*You* want to see her?" the man asked me. He was tall; he had to look down.

"I'm her *best* friend," I said, unsure and shaky. The only time I remembered being in a hospital before, I was 7 and they were taking my tonsils out, and I couldn't have water, only ice, and I was dying of thirst. *Maybe we've got no right to be here*, I was thinking. *What good can we do? But Daddy thinks we can do some good, and he'd know.*

The man told us to wait there. He disappeared through a door but left it open a crack. I heard Mrs Weatherford's voice asking, "Who is it?"

"She says she's her 'best friend' and has been all their lives." He sounded sort of amused but kind, like he was remembering what a best friend is.

"Oh," Mrs Weatherford said; "The Spearses. They can come in, can't they, Jean. For a little while."

Jean must have answered but I couldn't hear her.

When I saw Eltas Jean lying there on that hard-looking gurney, looking so miserable, I didn't feel like crying; this was too serious. What I felt was stunned, like I'd run hard into a big rock.

She was broken.

Her legs were in some kind of troughs so she wouldn't move them.

She hadn't had much attention yet, you could tell, and nobody was there helping her now. Looking back, I guess they

105

had her on pain killer and were waiting for it to take hold. Maybe they were waiting for the real doctor to come.

Somebody had tried to wash her face, but dark blood was still there, some of it in her earlobes (she has tiny, pretty ears) and some by her nose and her eyes. There were cuts, too many cuts.

It hurt her to breathe, you could see that. Her mouth would open and her nice front teeth (not small like mine) were gone. Her lips were swollen and blood was still oozing from the cuts that must've got there when her face broke the windshield. Her nose, her little turned-up nose, looked so pitiful, so hurt.

Eltas Jean moved her eyes toward me and said "Hey." It was so weak, that hey, but I heard it.

"Hey back."

She tried to say something else, but you could see how it hurt her. Anyhow her mama was talking, and Daddy talked some. I was afraid to hold her hand or touch her almost any place, so I put my fingers just barely on the hand I saw moving, the one on the arm that didn't break.

Then we left. On the way home it was okay to cry.

"She'll be all right, Bood. It'll take some time, but she's strong and young. Broken bones mend."

"But she's so hurt, so broke up."

He kept his eyes on the road. It was over for now; we'd done all we could. "She could have died. She didn't. Thank God for that."

I do thank God Eltas Jean didn't die.

Just a year earlier, one of Daddy's friends from his Sunday School class died in a car, but not from a wreck. That summer too, one of Russell's cousins in Lamar died in a car that wrecked. Maybe the wreck killed him; maybe not. Between those, another man died, but not in a car.

Daddy says there's more than one dark secret left lying over Darlington County from 1952.

It's horrible to think, much as you can suffer when nobody wants to hurt you, that there's those who set out to cause suffering because they're too selfish or too stupid to care.

COUNTY

Eltas Jean's almost as good as new now. Her front teeth look like the ones she use to have even though they're not them, and her smile is just as pretty. She's got scars various places, but scars are nothing really, she says. They go away or they don't.

Eltas Jean knows about scars.

She still has a place from when she was little and putting washed clothes through the wringer on top of their washing machine and it grabbed her arm. The scar runs all the way from her wrist to her elbow on the tender inside, as clear as when we were little.

She never thinks about it, far as I can tell. Probly no more than I think about the tiny splinter scar all the way through my eyelid from when I fell into the dead bush playing tag, 'cept that I can't see mine without taking a handmirror and really looking.

Things happen.

Bomb Shelters at the County Fair

When the weather starts getting nippy in the evenings, we know the Fair's coming.

The State Fair's in Columbia, 'way out Assembly Street just before you get to Carolina Stadium. Mother and Daddy and I always like the agricultural exhibits -- the horse riding and the cattle and hog judging, the unusual rabbits and the exotic bantams and pigeons (somebody named Plato McWhorter wins for pigeons every year), turkeys and fancy hens and roosters, and 'course we go inside the ag barn to see the ducklings go down the water slide.

The art competition, we can't miss that, because Russell's Aunt Etna Mims and Aunt Ehrline Mims Harper both enter paintings or collages and generally win ribbons. You wouldn't believe how much talent's displayed there. There's intricate paintings of broke-down pickups rusting in tall grass, and glass-cased collages of dainty lace handkerchiefs and a tiny glove beside just a corner tip of stationery in a penny-stamped envelope with a faded address --- enough to break your heart. (Etna does those). And lots of others that mostly confuse me but for all I know are the work of great artists coming along.

Daddy's up for anything, but Mother never wants to stay as long in the Art Exhibit as I do. She likes wandering around in the building opposite, just inside the stadium-side gate. Big-city florists build indoor displays that imitate gorgeous gardens. In Florence it's mostly just flower arrangements judged for beauty or inventiveness (and some of them certainly are inventive), or bottles of water with single blooms to be judged for beauty. I guess it takes being in the State Capital to inspire florists to put together whole gardens that they know perfectly well'll have to be taken apart in 2 weeks.

And 'course the rides -- I like the rides. The Bump Cars are fun if you're not prone to headaches from getting rammed into. And watching the little kids go round and in and out sitting in their slowly revolving suspended cars takes you back. We've got pictures of me gliding along in some of those. You'd think I was under arrest: not a smile in a mile.

There's nothing like the Ferris wheel, the big State Fair one. Up there on the highest seat, waiting for the sudden lurch that starts you rocking just enough to grab the bar, you can look down on the whole Fair -- on its shape that's new and temporary both, and outlined in bright lights, all here just for us this very evening in South Carolina.

Mother and Daddy use to wait for me on the ground below. I'd look down and they'd be grinning at each other. Fairs just make you feel good.

Florence County's fair is the Southeastern. Most everybody goes. Dating to a Fair is expensive, so we usually ride over in a bunch, go dutch and chip in for gas.

You know not to hang around the games at Fairs; they've got to be rigged. 'D'you ever try to slide a coin onto a saucer way yonder and make it stay? It must take days or years of practice and some kind of finger and wrist twist to make a coin not slip on off the other side. I like those frilly gold and green Fair dishes, but I never won any. Once the man up and *gave* me a saucer. I've got it under a violet on our kitchen windowsill where it gets good sun. Mother's good at violets.

The yellow plastic ducks you pick up from the water flowing by in the little trough in front of all those great looking stuffed animals and other prizes -- that's a gyp sure enough. Even if you pick up a winner, the man'll look at whatever code's on its bottom and hand you a pencil or something not worth calling a prize.

You've seen a guy walking around smiling and lugging a huge stuffed teddy bear or alligator or Tweetie Bird near as big as him, that looks like it came from one of the game booths? Well, I hear those people are with the show. They've got to give those big prizes *back*.

Still, it's fun just to *be* at a Fair. You know not to wear anything good; it'll be dirty by time you get home. Your best bet's dungarees.

Fair food's not too tempting to me. Cotton candy looks like fun, a swirly pastel cloud on a stick, but after a few bites or rather a few plunges of my face into it I'm ready to hand mine to any passing child. Not only does it get to be a mess, but it's got no taste but sweet – a pink-and-white or a pale-green sweet.

It was at the State Fair that I had my 1st Italian sausage sandwich. I was hungry and it looked like just what I wanted, with greasy onions and green bell pepper slices hanging over the sides of the bun. I don't know that I'll ever want another one, but that was a sausage to remember.

Candy apples are probly my favorite Fair food. Even a Delicious isn't bad; mealy, but not bad. Best of all is when the hidden apple turns out to be sour, firm, and full of juice. The sweet red coating breaks under your teeth; you feel the sudden tart juice; all at once a riot of tastes and textures are in your mouth. Oh WHY are Fairs the only place with candy apples?

One part of Fairs I don't like is the Freak Show. Everybody's got different tastes, and okay it's a living for the freaks, but I feel strange about the ones they make stand in front of the curtain to lure the crowd. Usually it's the Fat Lady and the Thin Man and the Fire Eater.

How can anybody that fat be happy? And yet she laughs; they all laugh, the Fair Fat Ladies, and shake all over. I guess that's part of their job, but they must weigh . . . who *knows* how much they weigh.   They look older than tv's been around, so they couldn't've got that fat from watching tv, like people might get to be a generation or so from now. It's bad enough tv makes you sit, so thank goodness tv ads are mostly about soap, toothpaste, shampoo, new cars and other things you can't get fat on, not about food. Your normal restaurant can't afford ads on tv, thank goodness; let's hope they don't get together and start putting food pictures on the screen.

And where do the Fat Ladies stay after Fair season? You *never* see anybody that big out on the street. Mother says an affliction like "a gland problem" could make a person overweight like that. We should have compassion for the afflicted; they shouldn't be for laughing at.

The Fair Thin Man -- could he be afflicted too, to be that thin? Worms, most likely. Like the lady in Rowesville that had goiter; she was thin, but they removed it. Removed it several times, I think. Most people here and in the rest of the world are what you could call "thin," but Fairs find *really* thin people.   I think Fairs must recruit a thin man that's above-average tall and then put him in floppy clothes with up-and-down stripes. He can't get prosperous and fat up; he has to stay skinny or lose his job.

I say "he" because it always is. To be skinny enough to look that different from reglar ladies, a woman'd have to almost starve, and there's nothing funny about daily hunger that lasts all spring after the only hog's butchered and eaten and the vegetables aren't up out of the ground yet. The Depression's not all that long ago. The pictures Miss Eudora Welty took down in Mississippi and Alabama for the WPA in the '30s show life in a way we don't ever want to live again.

The Fire Eater, no sense worrying about him. To be sure he could quit eating fire if he got tired of it. I don't see how he could be a fire addict or anything. A Fire Eater's looks don't give his habit away; I mean he doesn't look scorched or paticlarly red. A week after he quit you could see him on the street and not even know what he use to do.

I've never been inside a Freak Show. I don't want to see a 3-headed calf; I wouldn't believe it anyhow; they put it together I bet. I haven't been a townie *all* my life; I know calves. Besides, it's a $64 bet the Fair calf'll be in a jar, pickled in formaldehyde like the specimens in Biology, not living. The Fair banner up there makes you think the calf's alive, but no sensible farmer would raise a calf like that, poor thing. He'd put it out of its misery right off.

And I sure don't need to see a Wild Man eat a live chicken.

Growing up, I saw plenty 'nough chickens running around headless after their bodies got slung off their heads by Carrie, my grandmother Minnie's use-to-be cook before she went to New York City to live with her daughter. It looks eerie, makes your skin crawl. Besides, eating live chickens or any other live animal is a sin according to the Old Testament, and I can see why; think of the germs. I 'spect that applies to the chicken-eating Wild Man too, 'cause surely by now somebody told him he shouldn't be fooling with raw blood. Even without the Bible, I'd guess nobody around here ever thought of any such of a thing. We like our chickens fried. *Good* and fried. You don't want to even see blood at the *bone*.

111

COUNTY

Up in New York City, Carrie cooks full time -- you might say full time for 6 different families, a different family every weekday. She cooks enough that day to last the family the whole week. She had to educate them what to lay in for ingredients, like lard; they never use to buy lard; they're Crisco people. They think her lard biscuits are heavenly, and of course her peach cobbler, plus for Sundays they want vinegar-recipe roast beef. (Carrie marinates the roast 1st thing, puts it in the ColdSpot so it can absorb, then cooks it in the afternoon with the onions. Carrots are cooked semi-firm in another pot with some of the roast broth. Actually it's a recipe Papa concocted for venison, but it works for any red meat.)

When Carrie comes home to her grands and them for Thanksgiving in Orangeburg County, she tells Mama all about how the different ones of them live up there, how their children act and all. She mimics the way they talk and the things they say. You ought to hear her go on. Carrie and Mama sit together on the screen porch and just *laugh*.

Going back to the Fair: there's always a tall white scale at the Fair that's got HONEST WEIGHT printed on its round face and GUESS YOUR WEIGHT on a placard. There'll be a man standing there to holler out that if he can't guess your weight within 3 pounds, you get a prize. Or if you'll give him 5 pounds and *then* he's wrong, you'll get a better prize.

You get a nice prize only if he misses it a lot, otherwise you get nothing much, like at the plastic-duck trough. You have to step up on his scales and weigh, and everybody sees. Not that most people mind. You want to go home from the Fair with some kind of a prize, even if it's only from Guess Your Weight.

The Strong Man Scale has a big wooden hammer thing to test your strength. That's what the sign says: "Test Your Strength." Country boys, 'customed to real work, can't resist it. You'll see 'em swinging that mallet 'way up over their heads and coming down like 40. Whether many of 'em win anything, I don't know, but I've seen some send the line pretty far up.

Nobody can make it rise as far as the man who runs the scale, though. When he demonstrates how easy it is, he sends the line nearly to the top. And him such an unremarkable looking person, too. He had to grow up on a farm; I'd even bet on it.

The end of the War brought a new thing to Fairs: a Bomb Shelter Booth. It'll sometimes be in an exhibit building or maybe out on the fairway, with a man saying you ought to let his company sell you a plan to put one at your house.

The man at the Florence Fair made it sound like the Bomb might fall on us any day.

"How long will your shelter last without falling to pieces?" Daddy asked him. "What if we don't get bombed for a long, long time?"

The man got kind of surly. I could tell he didn't like Daddy's questions.

But his flyers and pictures made me think. After all, there's huge bombs now. Huge bombs with names like Big Boy. There didn't use to be huge bombs like these ones.

On the way home, I asked Daddy if we oughtn't to get a shelter.

"Well, Meb" -- he still uses nicknames for me; I never know which one he'll come out with next -- "Say we got one and our neighbors and our friends didn't, and say it worked, and a bomb came, and we were secure in there. And what if they begged to come in. What to do?

"Would we have enough food to last us, let alone enough for them, not knowing how long we had to stay in the shelter? And mightn't they be contaminated? Would we refuse to open the door? Would we just let them die?"

He stopped and looked at me hard and said, "I wouldn't want to have to decide to let our friends and neighbors die, would you?"

"But they could get a shelter too," I said. "We all of us could get bomb shelters."

"Well, I doubt we all could, but say we could and did. How long would we have to stay in ours, and how would we know when it was safe to come out? And if we came out too soon, we'd die, even if the dying took a long time. And if we waited long to come out, wouldn't we all be liable to be crazy by then? Or maybe just one of us would go crazy -- there's such a thing as stir crazy; I saw it in the Navy -- and do who knows what.

"Me, I just as soon not have a shelter in the first place, Meb. I'd rather take my chances a bomb won't be falling on the

Pee Dee in our lifetime. Even if one did, we wouldn't be any more killed than anybody else. The man's shelters just might fall to pieces first."

My daddy is a good man, a smart man. He's not always right, but near enough right as to make no difference. He always talks sense.

And I know what he'd do if somebody came to our bomb shelter. It'd be like when we were at Murrell's Inlet and been crabbing for hours and he gave all the crabs away to a hungry family without even asking us: he'd open the door and we'd all die together but our consciences would be clean.

THE MAD OCTOBER WIND

Most of this first part we found out afterward:

A tropical wave moved off the African coast in the early days of Autumn, 1954. A pilot spotted it 50 miles east of Grenada, 'way out in the ocean, already stirring things up. On October 5 a hurricane hunter went out (oh yes, we've got 'em now; no more being blindsided, we thought) and measured winds at 70 mph.

That's the beginning of a hurricane.

Hurricanes are named alphabetically, first come first served A to Z per season — and always for girls. In '54, we'd got through G. In our minds, it was over because the really hot months were gone. We're 75 miles into the coastal plain, so what did we have to worry about? Nothing. We weren't worried.

The name next in line was Hazel. Hazel's not a woman's name in the South so much as a man's, like Hazel Warr at the store at the bottom of the Cashua Street hill. There's a Hazel cartoon woman who every week puts Drano in every drain, so I guess up North it must be a name for females. Here, mostly we think of hazel as a color for eyes.

But male, female, or eye color, Hazel won't be the name of any more hurricanes. That one's been retired. Forever.

The Carolina coast knows everything there is to know about a hurricane. People with the most worries when a hurricane comes are the ones with a house at the beach. Practicly the whole coast of South Carolina is beaches — clean white-sand beaches.

People with beach houses, like Daddy's 1st Cousin Ola Ham that married Mr Haynesworth Van Epps in Lake City this very year (they own half of a block on Ocean Boulevard north of the Pavilion), they have to think, "Will our expensive property get flooded and ruined or squashed like a bug and fall into the ocean?"

Because it might.

Then there's others with beach property that're not a bit rich. The vacation lot and shackly trailer Uncle Hart bought at Garden City are okay in the summertime, 'cept that you know in your head the whole time you're there that a good-size tree limb could squash the trailer flat. Which wouldn't be much of a loss if it was vacant at the time. They could hitch it up and haul it away and put something else on the lot, which is only a few blocks from the water -- just a good brisk walk.

Normal people, though, we don't own a thing at the beach. We go down for a day or so at a time when somebody invites us. Uncle Hart's trailer is as comfortable as you'd need at the beach. You don't do anything in it but sleep and eat, and it's good for that. I hope nothing bad happens to it.

Even if a hurricane came all the way to Warley Street, there's not a house on our block with an upstairs to get blown off, let alone stilts underneath that give wind a good chance for a purchase. Winds from Africa don't blow this far inland.

Anyhow, that was the thinking 'til Hazel showed up.

Maybe if we'd known about the big North Sea storm that flooded Holland in January '53, and then about the huge Midwestern tornado, both in the year before Hazel, we'd've been paying more attention. Maybe.

The '53 North Sea storm is the one that shocked Holland into reshaping itself. That's when they started their massive project of dikes; they're still building them in 1957, putting their whole nation up behind walls. A sea storm that huge can't really happen here, but it's the *timing* – the timing that makes you think, *Do terrible storms come in clusters? Do they spawn each other?*

The most violent tornado the US ever saw came in the summer of that same year, 1953. It hit Michigan, tore through Flint, slammed the auto industry, and killed 116 people. It earned a terrible name for itself: *the worst tornado on record.*

The summers of '53 and '54 were hot, really hot, but 'way weirder was the warm winter that followed Hazel. Instead of a coat, warm socks, and boots, on Christmas Eve I strolled around the Square buying gifts wearing a white cotton strawberry-print blouse, my gored hip-stitched skirt, and ballet-style flats. Not even a sweater. I remember exactly because on that very day I *knew* how strange that seemed. It could be that Hazel was what taught me to be aware of weather and what it might be saying.

Hazel was weather to learn from.

Hazel came west for 4 whole days without striking any land at all. She rolled over the open ocean until she was just north of South America. By then she was what we call a Cat 2. (Cat, for Category.) She kept on going west. Some high peaks along Venezuela's coast slowed her down a little, but the experts all kept their eyes on Hazel. They said she'd likely hit Jamaica when she finally turned northward.

But she didn't.

Hazel never did do much she was expected to do.

Jamaica was ready, or as ready as an island can get for a hurricane. Small craft got out of the way, and large craft too.

Hazel made a hard right. On October 11, she blew through the Windward Passage between Cuba and Haiti.

Haiti is French -- a colony of France -- and the poorest country in our half of the world. Plus it has "poor communications infrastructure." Warnings don't get to them, somehow. Surely somebody there could learn English, and build a ham radio to get the warnings, but they don't -- or not often enough to do them any good.

Hazel killed 1,000 Haitians. Most of those drowned.

She moved on northward from there at 17 mph and struck the southeastern Bahamas. They were ready.

By then Hazel was getting attention here at home. Not from us at St John's High School, though. We had our own lives to live.

We'd been 10th Graders more than a month before we heard the name Hurricane Hazel. Who even knew hurricanes started as a tropical wave on a hot plain in Africa? Where if they'd just plant some trees to interfere with those early waves -- but Daddy says you can't tell another continent what to do, even to save 1000 lives.

117

COUNTY

The whole time, Hazel was heading northward on a line curving into the coast. Now that she was over open water with nothing between her and us, she gained strength again. That's the way it works in summer, but this wasn't summer.

The ocean must have been warmer that fall than anybody took notice of, because the usual thing is for north-heading hurricanes to lose power after they leave Florida and pass over cooler waters.

Not Hazel. She not only got stronger, she got faster.

On the eastern coast of the United States you've got Florida at the bottom, then Georgia and the Carolinas. Georgia's tucked in pretty nicely; it's not a big hurricane target. From Beaufort SC up, though, you see the coast slanting out into the ocean more and more until you're past North Carolina's Outer Banks. When hurricanes move up through the islands below Florida, quite a few seem to aim for the Carolinas. It's not unusual to get a direct hit within 30 miles of where the Carolinas come together on the coast.

And we got it. The outer edge started in here late on Thursday October 14th. All through the night we had howling winds and lashing rains -- not just at the coast, but inland too. A howl, whether it's a dog doing it or a wolf or the wind, is a lonely sound.

Here in the inland Pee Dee counties, no houses blew down, but plenty of outbuildings did. So did some huge trees and an incredible number of thick branches and sturdy limbs. Streets were blocked in towns all over the Pee Dee. Flooding was everywhere in Darlington, with water over the curbs. The deepest place is on Main Street in front of First Baptist Church -- Illy's church, where she teaches the littlest ones.

Illy and Mrs Cook, Parry's and Charles' and Peggy's mother, run a nursery school right here in the front room of the Cooks' house on Warley Street, but nobody could get to it that Friday the 15th. The water drained off down the hill at the end of Broad Street and behind the cemetery without bothering the graves, but too many limbs were down for any school to open, and the buses couldn't run their routes.

St John's High students are our bus drivers. They're as good as any, but they weren't any more anxious to spend that

118

tense day in classrooms than we were. Foot no. Any unexpected day off from school is good. Usually.

A vacation day during Hazel though, was different. Electricity everywhere was out or iffy.

Most of us had portable radios, but Myrtle Beach (WAVE, is it?) must've blown; it wouldn't come in. WJMX and WOLS in Florence and WPFD (We Pull For Darlington) told us as much as they knew about what was happening as it was called in. A hotshot radio crew got the bright idea of going out into the storm in the station car with the call letters on the side. We heard later that an oak limb broke off, smashed the hood and popped a tire. They had to run for it. I don't know whether they got fired or what. Maybe they just had to pay to have the car fixed.

The people who made it to work were most of them told to go back home. Nothing much was open. It's times like Hazel when you find out how important electricity is. People were calling Daddy, but he'd just try to talk sense to them and say to wait a bit, even if they couldn't cook now, it wouldn't last forever, probly not even till Saturday. He was right. Things were different at the beach: no power for I don't know *how* long.

People do miss a warm supper when they can't get one. Hominy grits and eggs or something meaty, you know. That night we made do with banana splits (that's banana halves with peanut butter and Dukes' Mayonnaise spread on, on a leaf of lettuce if you're fancy and got lettuce) and some left-over red macaroni (you cut up tomatoes and onions into it instead of milk and cheese, so it's just as good cold) and iced tea. We had plenty of iced tea made, and we kept the Frigidaire door closed so nothing would spoil. We drink iced tea all year long, and that October was warm anyhow.

But it was a strange warm, with all the wet in the air. You felt kind of shivery.

The ones who'd had television sets the longest and gotten use to depending on them, they seemed to suffer the most. Television didn't know much about Hazel, and plenty of people thought it ought to. Not only that, most of the aerials in town got so blown around, they couldn't catch a signal you could depend on. There were plenty that snapped and hung there, looking like spindly metal upside-down trees

COUNTY

Radio, though, battery radios did fine. We had time to think, to start paying attention to what-all Hazel had been doing in Haiti and out there before she got to the inland Pee Dee.

Dawn, October 15: After slamming and battering the coast and keeping us on edge with that howling wind and rain all Thursday night, Hazel hurtled into Myrtle Beach Friday as a Cat 4, as strong a hurricane as even Daddy remembered being in, in the Navy on the battleship.

Instead of slowing down over land, the way almost all hurricanes do, Hazel accelerated to a forward speed of 30 mph.

Raleigh (named for Sir Walter, friend of Queen Elizabeth I, Mrs Ervin says) is a good way from the coast. NC State's there, far inland; they don't put big universities at the beach. But Hazel swept Raleigh anyhow as a Category 3. Houses in Raleigh aren't built to stand up to a hurricane, let alone one with internal winds holding at 100 mph.

Seems impossible, but by nightfall that *same day* Hazel's center was over New York State and Pennsylvania.

Darkness during a killer storm can be a blessing. You can't see the worst of what's going on. Trees break and you hear mysterious sounds, but you don't *see* whether they make it to the ground or crash onto a house or your car. Listening in the darkness, you pray nothing comes through the roof.

We didn't worry that night about what might be going on in New York, Pennsylvania, Delaware and Maryland. We had no idea they were in 100 mph winds. Even if we had, the 50-mph winds in Darlington on the western *edge* of Hazel were taking up our attention. We weren't s'pose to *get* winds like that.

We didn't know yet how lucky we were.

I've been at the beach overnight when a hurricane hit. It's not fun, but it's not fatal. Thank God I was never there for a hurricane like Hazel. Thank God I was home in Darlington.

95 died in the United States. Then Hazel crossed the border into Canada.

Hazel didn't weaken near as fast as she was s'posed to, and she wasn't near through.

Moving fast along the ground, she hooked up with a front -- a cold front -- and hit the national border. Slashing rain fell, 8

120

inches and more, on Ontario. As a Cat 1 hurricane, Hazel smashed into Toronto -- 77 mph winds with gusts at 90.

Finally she passed over James Bay into northern Quebec.

81 people died in Ontario during Hazel. Just like in Haiti and the United States, most of them drowned.

In Quebec, Hazel stopped being a hurricane and got back to being only a storm. To the Quebecois it seemed plenty bad enough.

She wasn't a lady nor a man nor a color for eyes, but she was well named: Hazel was a witch. She took her gigantic broom and swept the North Carolina coast from our state line all the way to the top of the Outer Banks.

Jimmy MacInnis came home from the Citadel for the weekend and took me with him up to Holden Beach, up in Brunswick County. The weather was clear and beautiful, the way it usually is after a bad storm sweeps the air clean. We were talking and laughing all the way up -- 2 or 3 hours, counting turning off to Calabash for a tiny-fried-shrimp dinner. (You probly know Calabash; it's famous. Daddy sometimes drives us up for dinner from church if we get to missing the taste of ocean-creek-caught shrimp too bad.)

We went right at Shallotte from Highway 9 before turning north again on 17. He was on an errand for his mother to check on their house up there.

We couldn't find it.

Where it use to be was a sandy beach again -- no houses at all, only splintered boards lying against some stripped bushes -- maybe yaupon. The MacInnis cottage was gone. Not one of its boards nor pilings was standing nor even lying around.

Jimmy figured out which one of the level bare lots was theirs by what was left of the utility pole at what use to be their corner. It was still there -- jagged, ripped, and sticking 2, maybe 3 feet above the sand drift.

Jimmy didn't look excited or anything, the way I think I would 've if I couldn't find a house I'd grown up with. He looked more like life had slapped him and he was waiting for his ears to quit ringing.

"You not gon' get out of the car and walk 'round and look?"

"No use," he said.

COUNTY

I hushed. Jimmy's lots older than me (but it's okay; our parents knew each other when they were no older than we are now) and he thinks my friends are silly. He thinks I'm silly too but he's nice enough *most* of the time not to say so. So I try not to sound silly when I'm around him.

We drove around some, thinking he'd see something that came from the house, but no, nothing. No sign of boards nor fixtures nor cook stove nor colored coral from the little corner whatnot. No telling where they'd blown to.

I hope some nice little girl found some of the coral or a figurine not too broken and cherished it for her own. That can happen in a hurricane. Not everything breaks that blows away.

I don't remember us talking much after that, nor even any sounds except shore birds calling and normal-sized waves breaking and the tires of his mama's green '53 Mercury crunching along what use to be the beach road behind front-row houses. We didn't stay there long because there were almost sure to be nails and who-knows-what-all under the sand that covered everything.

Out on the beach, you could see little shore birds inspecting heaps of washed-up shells. A gracious plenty of shells; I don't think I ever saw so many before.

But we didn't stop.

I *almost* asked whether we had time for me to run out there in hopes of finding a perfect shell -- a conch, olives, sea biscuits, sand dollars -- but I kept quiet. Asking to pick up storm-washed shells on this day would probly be callous.

Silly even.

I was mostly quiet too while Jimmy looked for the Holden Beach he'd known. I knew and he did too that he wouldn't find it. *That* Holden Beach blew away while he was in his dormitory at The Citadel (Hazel mostly missed Charleston) and I was in Darlington.

On that October Friday, Holden Beach went back to being the place it was before people came and bought lots and built houses: low bushes and white drifts, busy birds, shells, and salt water rolling tiny sea life in slow waves onto the sand.

And driftwood.

Driftwood from ships that long ago met terrible storms at sea.

122

Boys

Wayne -- that same Wayne, the one I keep bringing up for some unknown reason -- is country like me, plus he says he can't remember all that much about when he was what he calls a city slicker in Kindergarten. That's probly because his family moved to the farm early enough that he went all through grammar school out at High Hill.

Wayne says Miss Cammie Jordan, their Principal, is a great lady. She's old and in good shape and says the secret to long life is to drink 2 glasses of water first thing every morning; that's what she and Mr Jordan both do. So Wayne does too, and there's nobody healthier than him, 'cept I wish he didn't smoke.

Blackmons are always good at football, but farming kept him off the team. The day he went out for it (and had to walk the last 5 miles home because he couldn't make practice and the bus both), Mr Blackmon met him at the door and blessed him out awful.

"You needn't to think you're gonna be out there practicing that game when I need you here to help me," his daddy said. And that was that.

Coach Welch was fit to be tied to lose Wayne after watching him block the big boys that 1st day. (Wayne learned how by playing against his cousins. Fudgie Blackmon was St John's biggest tackle. Wayne's more lanky than big, but Fudgie says it's better to try to run around Wayne than to meet him head on.)

So Coach Welch went out to High Hill and almost begged. He needn't to've wasted the time. Francis Blackmon is a stone wall.

He did let Wayne go out for band and sign up to drive a bus. Bus driving pays money, plus it gets him back and forth from High Hill and Lake Swamp to school in a reasonable time. All farmers know machinery; didn't and they'd be stuck out in the field with a broke-down tractor a good deal. If the bus

123

breaks down, like buses do a lot, Wayne won't have to wait for a transfer and a tow, not 'less he just wants to, to make a point.

Wayne plays the drum. Not the big one with St John's on it; a little drum. He says it's the instrument requiring the least talent. (He talks like that. Great syntax.) It gets him to the games free, plus having fun in the band room and on the band bus.

And he does. He's shy but likes to talk to girls and they like him. *I* like him, in case you hadn't noticed. He's got the Blackmon eyes -- wide side to side with black lashes, and blue as the deep sea.

I don't think he dates, actually. Not yet. But gosh, we'll be graduating in not much more than a month -- when's he planning to start?

Jimmy Galloway is probly Wayne's best friend.

Wayne's kind of a maverick. He knows how to get out of school when he wants to. Mr Blackmon gets Wayne excused pretty often to help out on the farm, see, and Wayne can sound just like his father on the phone. He does it from time to time.

One paticlar day, Wayne had got himself excused to go someplace. Jimmy wanted to go too.

Jimmy called the office, figuring Cora'd be the one answering; she'd answered Wayne's. So he (Jimmy, remember) said, "I need Jimmy to come home and help me disc a field today. Man had to go home, take his woman to the doctor."

But Cora fooled him. She said, "Wait a minute, Mr Galloway. Mr Cain's coming in the door right now." And he was, too; Johnny on the Spot's other name is Mr Cain.

Mr Cain's nickname among the boys is Killer Cain, too, remember. He's the last person Jimmy wanted on that phone.

Jimmy said again 'bout the man having to leave and needing Jimmy the rest of the day. But Jimmy was losing confidence. Worse, his voice range was wandering around.

Mr Cain's voice changed too -- kind of sharpened up. We all know what it means when Mr Cain's voice sharpens up.

"Who is this?"

Jimmy cleared his throat and said firmly, "This is my father."

While he was trying to get his hand on the hook to break the connection, Jimmy heard somebody in the office start to laugh.

Jimmy says he failed to see anything funny.

That afternoon Mr Galloway didn't laugh either.

At the time, Wayne thought it was hilarious. He was standing by Jimmy at the pay phone and heard the whole thing.

Turned out, though, Jimmy's not the only one sorry he made that phone call. Mr Cain's no fool. *Now* the only way Wayne gets excused from classes is if the person who asks really *is* Mr Blackmon.

I've just got to tell you this about a pair of Wayne's cousins. It's second hand like the Jimmy story, but it's too good to leave out.

Wayne's got a zillion cousins around here -- Blackmons, Rhodeses, Helmses, Lewises (including Judge Woodrow Lewis), and the Rawlses over by Columbia (his mother grew up in Eastover before they moved to Broad Street), and I don't know who-all -- but this story is about just the Rhodes boys that are our age at St John's.

They like to watch drag racing, Baxter and William do. If they don't have money for tickets, they park as close as they can and walk up and watch from outside the fence. Rather they *use* to, until one evening at the track out past the city limits toward Florence.

That paticlar night, they had got their old pickup parked so close to the track, they decided they could sit in it and watch.

They were feeling real smart alecky about it.

You know drag racing: 2 cars at a time start off side by side and go as fast as they can for a set distance and see which one beats to the finish line. Sort of like local horse matches, 'cept for horses you don't need to build a track.

Drag racing might sound kind of dull 'til you realize how many things can interfere with a car trying to go from no speed to top speed and only a little distance to do it in. Most likely, something blows out under the hood. Second most likely, something falls (or flies) off the car.

Unfortunately for the Rhodes boys, what flew off a contestant car that evening was a tire.

125

COUNTY

They looked up and here it came. "Both our mouths was open. Next thing, we was fighting to get out its way, him on his side and me out the door," William -- I think Wayne said it was William -- told him, using his elbows to act it out.

The tire landed -- no, wait, it didn't land yet; it bounced and went on a ways.

"God knows how far," they told Wayne; "Gret *Dow*, it was traveling" after it went *sprunngg* off the roof of their old pickup.

Bent it almost to the dashboard.

They both had to lie back on their spines all the way out to the farm. Whichever one drove home that night had to look at the road through his knees.

Next drag race, they bought tickets and parked a good way off.

While I'm talking about boys, this is the right time to mention the Smoking Area, since far as I know, boys are the only ones who smoke at St John's 'cept for some of the teachers.

Jimmie Perkins told me he skips lunch and eats out of machines in the Area so he'll have time to smoke, which he's planning to quit. He says the Smoking Area's behind the school, and that 20 boys at a time might be in it, "huffing and puffing away so, it's hard to even see who's there." Could be he just doesn't want to tell me who they are; afraid I'll put it in the *Bulletin* or something. I wouldn't if they didn't want me to, but are they ashamed of smoking? If they are, why don't they quit?

Maybe they will; Jimmie, for one. He says he figures he needs to stop smoking because he's got a huge crush on Mrs Moody that teaches him Bookkeeping. He's afraid if he keeps on smelling like cigarette smoke, she won't still tutor him after class.

Wonder if Mrs Moody knows she's got an admirer and not just somebody who asks for a lot of extra help.

Funny – I never thought of somebody getting a crush on a teacher. I mean, I know the girls think Mr Harper is handsome, and he is I guess, but he's family -- my half-brother Russell's 1st cousin, actually. I have to keep myself from calling him William at school, which is what the family calls him -- the Mimses and

126

the Harpers and us.) He and Mr Cain are tennis buddies, both with state-level ranking.

And there's something else: I never knew 'til now that there *were* machines on the school grounds vending honeybuns and sandwiches and carbonated drinks and whatall. None of the rest of us get to eat out of machines; we eat whatever's on the cafeteria lunch line.

Not that it's so bad. I really like those huge green butterbeans they call limas, and sometimes there's hotdogs, plus if you don't much like whatever else there is, you can fill up on milk and rolls and butter. Mrs Griggs and the ladies, they make their own rolls fresh every day -- big and doughy. Really good, actually. The lunchroom ladies take some home.

'Til Jimmy told me, I thought the closest food other than the cafeteria was the little stores at the bottom of the Main Street hill. Some of the boys go there during school, but not many, because from there they've got to run uphill like lightning to be in time for 5th Period. Nobody can run that fast but Jimmy Perkins and Lavon Kelly and them. I guess they go there just to show they can. Or if they run out of cigarettes.

The Newspaper Business

Mac Willcox ran the school newspaper last year when we were Juniors, so I went to his final staff meeting expecting Mac to be elected Head Honcho again.

If you haven't figured it out already, I'm not the easiest person to get along with, so I'm not what you'd call popular. My friends get elected to things but I don't. Which usually suits me, since I didn't want the offices and honors they get elected to anyhow. Except for one.

I wanted to be Editor-in-Chief of The Bulletin.

There was not a snowball's chance in Florida it would happen. Mac's in our class; he'd just get it again and that'd be all she wrote. I'd be maybe News Editor or Feature Editor, and that would be okay. Really, it would.

But wouldn't you think I'd've told somebody what job I'd be willing to work my heart out to do? Wouldn't you think I'd've somehow started working on getting there?

Not me; not Spears the Private Dreamer. I couldn't bother God about something so vain and just for myself. Also, I didn't want anybody to know after I tried for an elected office and (certainly) didn't get it, how miserable I'd probly be. So I kept my mouth shut and turned around and refused to glance in that direction, hoping if I pretended I didn't want it, if I didn't let Fate know I was thinking about it, Fate might get it for me.

And she did. Fate in the form of Edwin Williamson.

Edwin Williamson -- who's not even a friend, only a friend's cousin (Marion Coggeshall's) – all of a sudden nominated me for Editor-in-Chief. And I got it. Nobody even ran against me, not even Mac. Mac might've been tired of the job and he might just've wanted to be Sports Editor, which is what he ran for and got. He might've even fixed it up with Edwin to nominate me; who knows. Mac is a friend, I guess. We talk a lot.

But Edwin and I do have a couple things in common. Mainly, it's that he's from the country like me, although the B F Williamson place is an honest-to-goodness plantation named

COUNTY

Oaklyn (say Oak Lynn), miles out from Darlington and Florence both. It's not like any place I've lived, not even the main house at the Sand Hill -- the one the new owners tore down. Oaklyn is huge and white in a setting of ancient beauty. The trees in the yard so beautiful, I doubt caterpillars even drop on you when you walk underneath; they wouldn't dare.

But country's country and farms are farms, and that's a background important to have in common. You're country and you love it. The Willliamsons work every day at preserving the beauty of their property. You don't even see a piece of paper lying beside the old moss-hung stagecoach road that goes through their land. If we'd had some really rich families out on Mineral Springs Road, it might be preserved like their road. But that's daydreaming.

Most likely Edwin nominated me because he thinks I write okay. I've been on The Bulletin staff ever since Miss Martha Jones the Librarian appointed me Bugsy Bookworm in 8th grade, probly because she noticed I was usually reading in study hall instead of studying. She'd supply a book for Bugsy to write about every other week. Miss Jones' idea was, somebody might check out whatever book I wrote about and even read it. I don't know that anybody actually did, but I got into the Bugsy role. I'd pretend I was chewing through pages and sometimes comment on the book-of-the-week flavors.

I don't remember Miss Jones ever asking me for my opinion on what books I should write about; she just handed me the next one. That was okay; I didn't have much literary taste back then. She got somebody artistic (we don't have art classes) to draw a bookworm coming up out of a bitten book. It was nice to have a logo, and I don't ever remember her not liking anything I wrote. Which now that I think about it, is kind of strange. I mean, I was a *child*.

One day I got up nerve enough to hand Editor Patsy Sturgeon an article on something else -- something silly -- and in 10th grade I got to write features. More silly stuff, but I put in plenty of underclassmen's names. It's good to have names besides upperclassmen's in the paper. St John's High is big — 400 students plus. Lordly Seniors didn't know us lowly beings.

By then I knew I wanted to be Editor-in-Chief of the Bulletin. Nothing else at St John's; just that. Maybe if I were pretty or athletic, I'd've wanted to be other things, but I'm not pretty; I'm just okay. Also, every time I think I want to play a sport, I find out I don't. I never wanted to be a cheerleader like Joyce Anne either. I'm not that limber, I bruise easy, and anyhow I'm okay watching from the stands with buddies. The only thing I wanted out of St John's was to be run the newspaper – and I wouldn't tell anybody.

I've thought about it since. Russell's 10 years older, plus he grew up at Mama and Papa's in Orangeburg County, so I'm kind of an only child. I had neighbors and cousins, but nobody in the house. Maybe if I'd had brothers and sisters to compete with, I'd've had more confidence -- more *brass*.

As it was, if I could have gotten to be Editor-in-Chief without anybody having to vote on it, like by talent and grit and hard work, I'd've thought Y*eah, I'll make it happen*. But to ever get anything because other people voted to give it to me -- no. I don't run for stuff. It would hurt too bad to lose.

That's enough about weird me.

I've got a great staff.

Bobby James is Editor, which means he's 2nd in command.

Betty Charles Baxley is News Editor.

JoAnne DeWitt, Peggy Jean Melton, and Jimmy Willcox are the Make-Up Staff. Don't ask me why we call it Make Up instead of Lay Out; it's tradition, like the lame name Bulletin.

Anne Weaver is Exchange Editor. She doesn't have a lot to do, because we always have a full paper; we don't need columns and editorials from other schools. She's ready just in case, you might say.

Feature Editor is Betsy Banks. You already know about her sense of humor and she's got good ideas besides that.

Betty Lou Abbott, Marion Coggeshall, Joyce Anne Medlin and Rose Young are the columnists, all volunteers. Betsy and Betty Charles share them. We all like to write, so there's always extra copy ready to fill whatever last-minute space opens up between ads. It doesn't happen much, the Business Staff sells so many ads.

Quite a few issues even have extra pages because of the great work of Vivian Booth, Faye Byrd, and their hand-picked staff: Gloria Banks, Jean Blackman, Linda Boseman, Rosanne

COUNTY

Dargan, Mary Lou Finch, Mary Pearce, Margie Rhodes, Brenda Rogers, Sheila Sherrill, and Sylvia Williamson. They're the staff I've been bragging about. I listed them for you in alphabetical order instead of by class. I wanted to give credit to the best, but they're *all* so good I couldn't decide which names to put toward the top.

Mac Willcox picked Karl Dargan and Bright Williamson as his Sports staff. Their articles and photos are ready and handed in to Make Up as soon as the games are played or any other kind of athletic events happen. I don't have to worry with that part of the paper at all. Sports get a whole page -- more if we sell enough ads. All my writers have to be flexible and go ahead with articles knowing they might get squeezed out.

Billy Rhodes, a Senior 3 years ago and gorgeous, broke records for rushing, running right over the defense. At school he liked to lounge around the front entrance before classes started; you'd see him there a lot. Once morning he spoke right to me; called me "Woman." I turned red like a pure ninny and nearly fell up the steps. Talk about cool kats, I am definitely not one. That was back when Upperclassmen seemed so grand. Now we're them!

We've got real athletes in the class of "57 -- Lester Holley, Bobby Smith, Karl Dargan -- oh and Vorn Leon Bairefoot for sure. Bill Smith (Bobby's older brother) and Jimmie Dixon set standards pretty high. Bill took huge pride in his work. He even had an official motto: "Anyone Can Carry the Ball. It Takes a Man To Block." None of the backs seemed to want to challenge him on it, either.

The blocking didn't always work perfect, but fullback Ray Norwood could stay handsome all the time he was out there getting tackled. It use to be amazing to watch. Even with mud on his face and maybe some blood trickling down, all he had to do was smile and he looked fine. You can't beat glamour.

Ray and Wayne Norwood are active at church, too, and so is Mrs Norwood. She sometimes drives us to out-of-town activities.

In front of a carful of people one night coming home from Hartsville, Bea (she likes us to call her Bea) looked around toward me in the back seat and said, "I'm so glad you're not so shy any more, Dear. You've really come out."

131

COUNTY

How do you respond to a comment like that? I sat there like a knot on a log and couldn't think of a thing to say, which proved she was right when she wasn't. I was never shy; not in my own mind anyhow. Strange how adults think when you aren't talking you must be shy. I usually wait for older people to talk to *me*, don't you? Before you talk?

Anyhow Miss Bea's not shy a bit. She tosses her dark curls and laughs and is really nice to be around. Plus she's got sons that coaches salivate over.

Lester, Bobby, Charles Cook, Charles Bradshaw, and Vorn Leon Bairefoot were selected to play in the Tobacco Bowl this year. They were good, maybe even better than the players who've graduated. Still, it's not easy to hero worship somebody your own age, even after the hoopla of a Friday pep rally.

One paticlar Friday, the paper was late coming in from the N&P; they print it. It was slim that week, only 4 pages -- one big sheet. Folding it would be easy once it got to us. We like to furnish the Bulletin hot off the presses, even when it gets here late.

Everybody was still in Chapel. Which sounds religious, but Chapel's what we call the weekly whole-school meeting in the auditorium.

Vivian and a couple other staff were with me in the back row, planning to give out the paper in the lobby when Chapel let out, assuming it got there before everybody left. Otherwise it'd be Monday before anybody saw it, distracting everybody.

It showed up and we grabbed it. There was no time to fold the copies before Chapel got over, but nobody cared; they wanted theirs. We couldn't hand 'em out fast enough, and nobody wanted to leave without one.

So -- log jam.

Here came Mr Cain. He must've started from the stage and run all the way down the aisle.

He burst through the doors coat-tail flat out. The bunched-up people at my end of the lobby stumbled over each other letting him through.

"*What* .....?"

He didn't finish his sentence. When he saw what was causing the log jam, he knew who to yell at. And he did:

COUNTY

"You .... BONNY!"

He grabbed the papers that were still draped over my arm and headed up the hall, shouting over his shoulder "Spears, follow me!"

I did, but can't say I wanted to.

Seems I was creating a fire hazard, endangering people of getting pushed and jostled, and in general creating chaos. That all came out at the top of his lungs on ascending notes, ending in a forceful squeak.

Don't ask me how he makes a squeak sound forceful; he just does.

At the end of the tirade I slunk out. Vivian and the others had got all the papers handed out by then, 'cept for the ones I'd just gathered up from the floor of his office. I didn't notice him throwing them down, but they got there somehow.

Shows what a bunny I am. I just thought I was getting the paper to its readers on time.

SEX

This could turn out to be the shortest chapter in the book, because sex is not a big thing with the class of '57. After all, whether it happens is not up to the boys; it's up to the girls because we have the babies. We didn't need Biology class to tell us that.

Come to think of it, I don't remember babies even being mentioned in Biology.

We call having sex(ual intercourse) Going All the Way. The subject might not come up any time soon, but if it does, girls know the answer: No.

Sometimes it might be I *Do* Believe You Love Me But No. Or I Like You a Lot But No, or You're Really Nice But No. Sometimes it could be Are You Out of Your Mind NO. Whatever suits the situation and whoever's asking and answering.

Actually I've never been asked The Question; I may as well tell you that. I single date some but it's always – except for once – with nice boys. They're smart enough to figure out from how a girl acts what she'll answer if Going All the Way comes up, which it probly won't. Heavy breathing is about as far as it gets, and not even that unless the boy's a really good kisser, and then you go someplace for a hamburger and a PepsiCola around other people you both know.

It could actually be that boys our age don't really want to go all the way either, yet. Or anyhow not with girls they actually like and might want someday to marry.

Maybe I should've titled this chapter "Boy-Girl Relationships" the way church youth groups do, but I can't spend all day looking for a title. Sex'll have to do. Anyhow, here goes.

I'll start slow and early.

COUNTY

Schools have definite rules about Conduct. In Grammar School and Jr High, most rules apply to boys and girls both:

Respect each other's space. Don't hit or push each other, no fighting, no spitting, don't run with a gang, don't run into anybody at recess and if you accidentally do, pick the person up, apologize, and help them brush off if they'll let you.

Respect property. Don't spit on the playground, no gum chewing, take care of your desk and your belongings, and don't bother anybody else's stuff.

In other words, obey the Golden Rule.

There's one grammar-school rule that applies to the boy-girl relationship even before there *is* a boy-girl relationship: "Boys must not touch girls." Principal Susie Brunson was a legendary enforcer of the don't-touch rule. She might actually've invented it or anyhow got it on the books. She's retired now, but her rule's still around. Actually, I like it. I probly got that from Mother. Touching ought to be necessary and specific, like comforting pats or a hug if somebody's starting to cry, or pounding on the back if somebody's choking and turning color.

The not-touching-girls thing was probly easy for *little* boys. What real boy wanted to touch a silly ol' girl anyhow, they must've figured. Some of these conduct rules might sound silly, but I'm not sure they don't have a hold-over effect and make the whole scene better as we grow up.

In high school, the rules get seriously adult:

You can't be married and stay in school.
You can't be expecting a baby and stay in school.

Neither rule creates a problem here. Nobody at St John's has gotten p g that I know of, which must mean they don't have sex(ual intercourse) since we know that girls who have sex(ual intercourse) are pretty sure to *get* p g.

Being p g would mean no more beach parties and peanut boilings and sudden fun gatherings with people that show up at your house and y'all ride off together to somebody else's. The girl's time to be free would be over with -- shot. She'd be an adult with full time responsibilities unless she turns the baby over to somebody else to take care of, and if she does that and doesn't get to do the mothering, why get a baby?

135

COUNTY

And sure, school's not perfect but it's our life now. It's where our friends are. The p g girl would still be with friends at church, but she'd miss out on what happens at school. Education, for one thing.

Not that babies aren't cute and even precious, except when they're colicky. But they're for after we've got our own growing done, enough to figure out who we're turning out to be. If that seems selfish, it's really not. It's respecting nor only the potential mother but also the potential baby. Babies deserve grown up parents.

I could say "or at least that's what *we* think," but who with any sense wouldn't think the same?

This next part's going to be about boys.

I know what you're thinking if you're a boy: *You're not a boy, so how do you know.* Well, a paticlar boy -- a good friend who we can talk about 'most anything -- told me. Then some others told me yeah I guess that *is* it. Plus, nothing I've seen makes me think this is *not* the way things are. If you get to be really good friends with a boy, and he's thought a lot about girls and about how his buddies act, he'll tell you. Probly not in these words, but I"ll bet you what he says'll be something like it.

The paticlar boy who told me is not only more honest than most, he's also better with words. So now I know the words to use, and I'm fixing to tell you.

But wait just a minute:

I'm not asking you to lock your lips exactly, but you needn't spread what I'm saying here around to the wrong people. Even be careful if you say anything about this to adults, because thinking seems to change every generation or so, including the words used to describe relationships. And there's plenty folks our own age who don't know how to discuss sex. Those same people might tell really dirty jokes, I think they do that to avoid serious thinking. I don't know any dirty-joke tellers who'd dare discuss sex seriously. And what I'm fixing to tell you -- I promise you, it's serious.

It's the Sex Trophy System:

If you have sex(ual intercourse without being married or incredibly in love like in wartime, the girl loses and the boy wins.

136

It's that simple.

If you'd rather have complicated and psychological, I've read some of those books. I think I might even study Psychology in college, so okay, here's a semi-psychological explanation of what happens and doesn't happen when sex(ual intercourse) takes place between people who aren't married or even committed to each other. I know we don't have a Psychology course at St John's, plus I doubt the course would cover the Trophy System anyhow even if the teacher knew about it, so I'll go slow.

See, the boy's got what he wants -- or is s'posed to want, according to how human males think. If a boy doesn't want sex(ual intercourse), other boys think there's something wrong with him even if he's on a sports team and got muscles out to here.

But the girl -- sex(ual intercourse) is not what she primarily wants. There's something more important to her: *love*.

Having boys on her mind (which every girl does, probly) is not the same as having sex(ual intercourse) on her mind. The girl's more likely to be hoping the boy loves her or is about to love her.

But sex before you're grown up and understand yourself, who you are and all that, is *not about love*. It's a *contest*.

The Trophy System explains it:

Because the boy's got what he's s'posed to want when he gets sex, he's the winner. We can call what he's won a trophy. We could give it some other name -- a prize, an award, a blue ribbon to pin wherever he might decide to pin it. We don't have to get all that specific; just call it a trophy.

Boys don't get too specific either about whether the trophy is the sex(ual intercourse) or the girl he had it with. Probly it's the sex(ual intercourse), because he might not even want to keep the girl. Point is, he and his buddies consider him to be a trophy winner.

That's *if he tells*.

And he might. He even probly will; boys are like that, specially if they're a long way from grown up. (I'm not talking about age. It's maturity I mean. Some people will never get there.) Loose lips sink ships in the Navy, but this is a whole

137

'nother kind of contest. He's won a trophy and might not have much else to brag about, so he brags.

Does the girl win anything?

Nothing worth having, that we can figure out.

If she tells her friends, the friends might ask her all about it because they want to know, but they'll think she's a dope for doing it. If they're kind they won't call her a dope or a sap or say they're sorry for her, but they'll think it. And if her friends are nice people -- like at her church -- they'll know it's a *sin*, too.

For a while – maybe just until the next morning dawns – she might think she's won something: the boy's love. But sooner or later (depending on how smart she is), she'll wonder whether he really loves her and would have loved her without sex(ual intercourse), or if he just wanted to be what his guy-friends consider a winner.

So he's got a trophy, and the girl gets nothing.

Well, wait; she does get something. If he tells, just like that she's got a "reputation."

I hate using "reputation" this way to apply to girls, but that's how everybody means it. Boys can have reputations for lots of different reasons, but with girls it's just one reason. No girl wants "a reputation." Everybody'll know right away it's for being a pushover, a (pardon my French) skag. They might even call you hot to trot even if you're not; you did it for what you thought was love.

This is where the Trophy System comes in again:

Having sex with a girl with a "reputation" is not a real trophy. He can't win a trophy some other guy has claimed and bragged on. *

*Assuming the other guy's telling the truth, which he *might not be*. See next page.

Being a trophy can't be near as satisfying in the long run as being a reglar person, because a trophy is less than human -- not what God intended a girl to be. The Bible says God intended our bodies (guys' too) to be temples (not trophies).

Even if a girl thought having sex before marriage was okay from a moral standpoint -- which it's *not,* it's fornication -- who wants to be a loser?

COUNTY

For somebody to win a trophy, it stands to reason somebody else has to lose.

That took longer than I thought it would, explaining the Trophy System. People might *want* trophies, but why in creation would anybody with a brain in her head want to *be* one?

You can see it's not got a thing in this world to do with love.

Another thing that's got nothing to do with love is lying about sex(ual intercourse) -- saying things that people take as meaning a girl's been having it when she has not.

I know how that feels.

A boy I use to date before I had better sense said it about me. That's when I found out that not only can sticks and stones break your bones, but words can make you want to spit tacks.

I don't know now why I ever went out with him, 'cept that he was an "older man" a grade ahead of us in school. Plus he played baseball. Football too, but I really like baseball, ever since listening with Daddy to Dizzy Dean on the radio.

So one night at the Southernaire he gave me his ID bracelet.

I was just a Freshman and didn't know wearing a boy's ID bracelet meant anything much, and besides, he acted like he really wanted me to wear his bracelet and said he had never let any other girl wear it, so without thinking much I let him slip it on my arm. Now I know it was like asking me to wear his Class Ring, which of course he didn't have because he was just a Sophomore. I don't think my parents knew that code with, because they didn't say much about the bracelet.

That heavy silver chain felt strange on my arm, but it made a big sensation at school next day, and that was fun for a while.

We didn't go together long. To tell the truth, I don't remember us going anywhere there weren't a lot of other kids we knew, like at ball games. Not even a picture show, that I remember. We spent most of those weeks on the phone and at other people's houses fussing and breaking up and thinking of ways to test each other's loyalty. It made gatherings and what we called parties not near as much fun, because he'd be watching me like a hawk even if I was just talking to another girl,

139

like he was thinking I might be saying something he needed to hear. If another boy looked at me cross-eyed he said it meant I was tired of being his girlfriend. We didn't even kiss much because he was so bad at it. To show people he'd got his teeth knocked out playing football (he said; maybe somebody knocked 'em out for him; I can see how they might be tempted), he liked to push his tongue against the back of his false front teeth and stick them out.

Gross.

He wasn't gross enough to do that during a kiss, but somehow the picture of him sticking his false teeth out would pop up in my mind. Talk about a *mood* destroyer.

One day I forgot to wear the bracelet to school (I told you it was heavy) and he hit the ceiling. So I told him I'd bring it to school tomorrow or better yet I'd leave it on my front porch and he could come to my house and pick it up that same day, and if he was so inclined he could wear that bracelet all day and all night for the rest of his life for all I care.

So after that, he told the lie about me. I know he did because Jimmy Kilgo told me what he said, which was not exactly that we *did* it maybe -- he can't be *that* much of a liar -- but to Jimmy it sounded that way. Jimmy was just in 8th grade, and his daddy and my daddy are practicly best friends, so Jimmy asked me about it, mostly as a warning not to trust that guy.

I don't think girls believe it about each other, but boys (specially boys younger than the liar) kind of do, when they first hear it. I don't think Jimmy believes it now, not after what I said when he told me. And if any other boys believed it, then after dating me they must feel really confused.

All a girl can do to avoid having a "reputation" is not let anybody turn her into a trophy.

Picture Shows

Hollywood and tv are what's making some older ladies worry about their weight. Some actually come out and talk about being "on a diet," a phrase I never remember hearing when I was growing up, no more than I heard "pizza" and "ravioli." We ate spaghetti at home, but others came with WWII – I guess once our boys fought their way into Italy. And McDonald's: when we were growing up there was no such thing as fast-fixed food, and there's none in Darlington even now. Our hamburgers are *good,* with slow-cooked chili-and-onions right inside the bun with 'em.

It's a new thing, having more food than we need and lacking sense enough not to stuff ourselves. Maybe our parents drummed it into us too hard about the "starving children in China," but now we hate to waste food. We know perfectly well we're s'posed to eat everything we take on our plates, or else not take it in the 1st place.

A little fat's good on a cold morning, but come Spring and good outdoor weather, you naturally slim down again. On Mineral Springs Road, the only fat was on the pigs.

One year, a doctor put Mother on a plan to *gain* weight. She didn't gain any; maybe she gave up too quick on the milk-and-raw-egg mixture. Remember Huckleberry Finn wondering why Miss Watson couldn't "fat up"? Now they've got people thinking in the *other* direction: how to slim down?

A girl that was a Senior 3 years ago -- I don't know her but her father's a big customer of Daddy's -- had a dieting lady for a mother. Dieting and "exercising."

A friend of hers told at school about going home one day with the daughter -- unexpectedly I guess, or too early. They walked in the house and right away were hearing somebody going "oogh" and "uff," along with bumping sounds.

The friend wanted to go see what was wrong in the room it was coming from, to maybe save somebody, but the daughter said, "That's just Mama."

"But what's wrong? Is she moving furniture? Shouldn't we help her? What's she *doing*, for Pete's sake?"

"She's exercising! Just exercising. And she would *not* want us to go in there. When she knows we're here, she'll quit."

Turned out her mama rolls around on the bedroom floor when she thinks nobody's home, to smooth out her bulges.

Boggles the mind, right? Looks like it would hurt, bruise you up, and ruin your clothes, rolling on the floor. That lady can buy new, though; they own a store. Someday there could actually be clothes special made for fat rich people to wear while they're rolling around on the floor or going to exercise classes. Boggles is not a strong enough word for that thought.

Fat won't generally happen until you're a grandmother, if then. Grandmothers have free choice: to be skinny as rails or be chunky and wear corsets or just relax and look like pillows. They've got more sense than to worry about weight one way or the other. Grandmother was committed to corsets, whereas Mama (Mother's mother) is tall and comfortable. Either way, you hardly ever see a grandmother with a waistline. And do you think they care? Not a bit, far as I know or ever heard. They rise past it. They hardly ever go to picture shows.

People my age, we all go to the show -- indoor theatres on Saturday's starting from when we were little, and drive-in theatres now, mostly on dates,. There's the drive-in theatre at 5-Points, this side of Florence, and one out on 52, and others round about. You see your friends there and y'all wave and sometimes go sit in each other's cars and talk during the time they show popcorn and frosty Coke on the screen to get you to the refreshment stand. Some people get a little too romantic at drive-ins and don't see much of the show, which is a real waste of money. Maybe they don't know about Ramsey's Pond and the bluff at Black Creek up from the Country Club swimming hole.

Eltas Jean and I grew up coming into town for Saturday Westerns. There'd be the Main Attraction (the show you went to see), plus an action-adventure episode that took up from last week (that's the serial, the "cliff hanger"), plus the MovieTone News (some theatres carry Pathe' News) that covers the whole relevant world in maybe 4 minutes.

142

COUNTY

Television in homes has mostly killed News at theatres, but it use to be really good. You might see what you never expected.

One evening my Aunt Ferebe (the one we call Sister) went to the show (you can walk everywhere in Lamar) after she got through fixing hair at her and Aunt Tee's temporary teenage beauty shop business. (They were *entrepreneurs*; that's a good French word meaning "workers starting a business for themselves.") Sister was sitting there eating popcorn when *bam!* she was looking at Daddy on the screen. Daddy's ship, the battleship *USS Wyoming*, was anchored in Guantanamo Bay just in case some other country (Spain, maybe) tried to take advantage of the confusion during the take-over by Batista.

Sister stayed through the whole show of course, having paid good money, but then ran the 2 blocks home to tell.

The next day the whole family pooled its cash buy tickets to go to that same show for the chance to look at Daddy for 20 seconds or so. He and 5 shipmates were on the beach holding rifles and wearing tan shirts and britches -- maybe for camouflage. The camera came close up to Daddy's face. Sister said you couldn't've missed him anyhow, with his blonde wavy hair shining against the dark palmettos. The family hadn't even known where his ship was going.

Nothing that exciting ever happened to me watching MovieTone News, but it could have. I was on the alert.

Now, though, pretty much all you get besides the main show is Previews of Coming Attractions.

Jean's and my favorite stars were (probly still are) Roy Rogers and Dale Evans for her, and Gene Autry for me because of the singing and because he talks real, being from Oklahoma. Derrick likes Lash LaRue and Hopalong Cassidy, and we all like the Lone Ranger on the Great Horse Silver with the Faithful Tonto who saved his life and now rides by his side.

Maybe it's because I don't go to the picture show on Saturday afternoons anymore, but seems to me shows aren't as good as they use to be. Too many of 'em pretend to be about people falling in love, when it's just acting. You wouldn't believe how much kissing goes on between people who might not even like each other.

COUNTY

I'm beginning to think some people aren't smart enough to be allowed in theatres, judging by how they're beginning to copy and "put on."

Taking picture shows serious is daft.

Everybody with any sense should know we aren't looking at reality. Take the train wreck in <u>The Greatest Show on Earth</u>.

That picture show got the most up-front publicity I ever saw. Weeks before it came, the <u>News & Press</u> ran circus-y photos every week. I remember Betty Hutton in a tiny costume and net stockings sitting on a high-wire swing, and Jimmy Stewart in clown paint. The show is circus acts mixed with a muddle of personal conflicts because the circus people can't get along with each other to save their necks. Egos run wild.

Then comes the wreck – the most awful train wreck you can imagine. First you see huge metal passenger cars and animal cages speeding across the countryside by night. Suddenly there's the terrible squeal of metal wheels desperately sliding on metal rails, and then the horror of railroad cars piling up on each other amidst smoke and screaming.

The smoke gradually clears. Quiet descends.

Everybody climbs out, groaning. But don't worry. Not only does nobody on the train die, most of 'em don't even look bad hurt. Being troupers, they get up the next morning, put on a parade, and get back out there. The Show Must Go On.

I figure the whole train wreck is so Jimmy Stewart will have to reveal he's not a clown, he's a doctor. Turns out too he's a Wanted Man. In case you haven't seen it, I won't tell you what he was Wanted for. If you like circuses and drama, you'll like it. But does Hollywood think we all just fell off the turnip truck? In the real world, horrendous train wrecks kill people.

Not that all picture shows are a bunch of bull.

I liked <u>Paint Your Wagon</u>. It's a crazy show, but Lee Marvin's a drunk I can believe in and so is the music.

A lonely man wishes he'd never come out to the wilderness to be successful (and he is) but left his sweetheart behind, so he (Harve Presnell) gets to sing "They Call the Wind Maria." And Clint Eastwood, who has a real problem (the woman he loves has already married Lee Marvin the drunk), walks through virgin forest singing,

COUNTY

> *I talk to the trees*
> *But they don't listen to me*
> *I talk to the stars*
> *But they never hear me...*

Plus I like Doris Day / Rock Hudson "romantic comedies" and Esther Williams swimming shows and some musicals with interesting plots and foreign locations. <u>An American in Paris</u> was nice, but I'm not much on watching Gene Kelly or any other fellow singing and dancing in the streets in shined-up shoes beside rivers. Maybe they're use to that kind of thing in Paris.

The ones that seem like a waste of time are man-woman picture shows with older people coming on to each other with something in mind other than love -- looks, maybe, or trophies or games in general. People get to be Hollywood stars mostly on how they look or dance or sound and on how willing and able they are to act like somebody they're not.

Some actors and actresses don't act at all; they just play the same role in every show. It's called the Star System. If they're glamorous, they get glamorous roles, period. If they're villains, they're vile every time. Styles change, but if Rudolph Valentino hadn't swallowed a toothpick in a martini olive and died of a perforated intestine, he might still be the world's hair-oiled romantic heart-throb, idolized master of the smoldering silent gaze. And Tab Hunter and Rock Hudson might still be nobodies with their real names.

Except for cowboy shows and Tarzan and the serials, most are made for older people because older people pay higher ticket prices. The business of show business is making money, not showing a real world of actual people. If a show pretends to be real, it misleads us if we take it seriously.

Some girls in the class of '55 took picture shows to heart and actually came to school trying to look like Jane Russell or Marilyn Monroe. There had to be right uncomfortable padding involved. A wad of stuff fell out on the hall floor one morning, and most of us just looked away. A crass Upperclassman -- Julius Broadwell -- picked it up, looked around, and laughed.

Some of the boys like the busty look, I s'pose; I heard some comments (not too complimentary) and some snickering. Once

145

at the Race weekend beauty contest, I heard a man (notice I didn't call him a gentleman) say about one of the beauty queens, "They forgot to milk that one before they left home." Granted what he said was gross, but he did farm work and knew what had to be done before showing cattle. It just shows that looks are getting more and more talked about, with less and less courtesy.

Picture shows, tv commercials, and magazine ads might be what's making people think everybody's all the time s'pose to be on display — teeth, hair, hands, shape and all. Used to, smokers held a cigarette between their lips, squinted their eyes, and kept on working. Now you'e s'pose to hold 'em between two fingers and flop your wrist.

Until an actress lit up in a show, I never saw a woman smoke. Dip snuff and chew tobacco, but not smoke cigarettes. Now even some girls at St John's smoke, mostly on dates. Social smokers, you could call 'em. 'Course I had to try it myself, during a spell of stupid. To me, cigarettes are like beer: more trouble than they're worth.

They say smoking helps you lose weight. It could, too — all your weight, 'cause cigarettes can kill you. We've known that all my life and my parents' too. WWI soldiers called cigarettes "coffin nails." The match they used to light 'em was called a Lucifer, another name for the Devil. (Lucifer was an Angel of Light before he fell, but how many people read Milton? Not even me, all the way through.)

I took Home Ec in 9th Grade because Mother was so sure I needed it. That class was the beginning of me having to think about my looks, 'specially my shape. Miss Graham was all the time at us about how we look.

One day she had us all stand with our backs against a wall. Then she said, "Slide one hand between your waist and the wall."

'Course we all did it. She didn't say *try* to do it; she said *do* it. So we did, every one of us.

Then she told us we weren't s'pose to be able to get our hand through there; that it meant we're all swaybacked.

GOSH.

COUNTY

I tried to get my waist tight against the wall by flattening my bottom, but I'm not made so I can flatten out that much.

Then Miss Graham stood against the wall and showed us that her waist was as flat against it as the rest of her back. That's how Miss Graham proved she was the only one in the room shaped right.

Hmmm.

But swaybacked? Really? Everybody but her?

Okay, so I'm swaybacked. And my nose is shiny all day and one shoulder is higher than the other and I've got an inadequate arch in my right foot. Worrisome conditions blight my life, and plus I think a pimple's popping up on my nose.

I liked being unaware of my physical imperfections. I'm a total frump and never knew it. My small waist is nothing; only my unflat back counts.

But look: Probly no girl in the whole Senior Class (not just Home Ec) weighs over 130, 'cept maybe the tallest ones. (I'm not the tallest any more. Others caught up and passed me.) We average say 110, about equal to a couple good-sized sacks of feed from Bonnoitt's. But heck, even if you weighed 90, wouldn't you have a bottom *somewhere* back there?

Miss Graham's different in another way, too – she's rich. She didn't say so in those words. What she did was tell us *we* need to learn how to make a budget but that she never had to. (Her daddy's the Senator of Florence County.)

I don't think she teaches any more; not here anyhow. I think she's married somebody. Probly somebody rich like her, without a discernible bottom.

It's like this: most people are medium, and a few are thin or fat. People use to not think much about weight; they thought about food. During the Depression and a long time afterward, though, you didn't eat in public because somebody might see you who didn't have enough food. Not everybody did.

Even now, Mother says for me to finish the little box of Raisinets or Goobers before I leave the picture show or to keep it in my pocket until I'm in the car or someplace else private. Is anybody in Darlington hungry today? I doubt it; most everybody's got a garden, but you'd hate to eat in front of somebody who has no food. Did, you'd be glad to give the person your Raisinets, but how could you know?

147

COUNTY

For us Seniors about to graduate, weight's not really in it. We've got trouble enough figuring out who we are and where our lives are going.

We don't think much about clothes, since most of us know better than to plan on spending money we haven't got. We're okay with that. We grew up wearing clothes 'til they didn't fit and couldn't be made to fit any longer.

Boys' clothes are pretty simple, really: dungarees, khaki pants, dress pants, a narrow brown belt, a white shirts, plaid or small-checked shirts (a long sleeved and a short), 2 slip-over sweaters, a cardigan, a jacket for church, and a windbreaker. For us it's flared skirts (and a good crinoline), wide belts (maybe patent leather or black elastic cinch), blouses and slipover sweaters, cardigans, a nice jacket or a pea coat with anchor buttons, and a windbreaker. The ballfield stands are open, and the cold can make you really glad for a knit scarf.

Most of us wear brown penny loafers with cuffed-down white socks. With wide skirts we like low-cut flats, specially black ballerinas.

I wouldn't've thought I'd have so much to say about personal appearance and what-all's started to circle around it.

I admit I do wonder whether my hair's going to stay red at all. It use to be kind of light strawberry but now it's auburn. Either way, if I lie in the sun I don't just get hot and sweaty; I get hot and sweaty and *pink*. So I don't lie in the sun. I rather walk and be going somewhere, moving along in the air and talking with whoever's with me. Or walk alone and think. Or imagine somebody nice is walking with me.

Not Wayne, I guess. His legs are too long; I couldn't keep up.

THE McFALL

In every community and town, there're bound to be a few who're just more interesting than most — like Illy. I want you to meet our family friend Miss Illy.

Picture a lady (who seems like a girl) of no paticlar age who for some reason keeps her brown hair in a kind of short curl that always looks the same: like a beauty shop once gave her a permanent and she went home and combed through it. Then notice her kind brown eyes and total lack of makeup, not even lipstick, and that she's a bit stoop-shouldered so that her clothes always look just a little too big for her slim body. I've never known her to go shopping for anything for herself, let alone clothes. She lives with her mother.

Illy found us soon after we got to town. Daddy's known her for years from working on Miss Lillian her mama's heater and refrigerator and air conditioning units, but Illy found Mother because Mother's a cat lover.

Illy must have a hundred cat-lover friends in just Darlington alone, but somehow Mother became her favorite. It's like that: Mother wins people. I think it's her laugh. Not that Mother takes to everybody that takes to her. She's reserved and skeptical, but most people don't know it because she has such good manners.

Illy, though, never knows a stranger. She has a special heart for children and furry animals. She'd've made a great farm girl, if she'd had a chance. She might've taken farm dogs as her favorites instead of cats, or chickens maybe. She might even've been able to love turkeys, and believe me it's hard to love a turkey. Specially gobblers; gobblers can be mean as cottonmouth moccasins.

Illy's kind of famous. Even out on Mineral Springs Road we heard the name "Miss Illy." She teaches pre-school children who'll probly call her Miss Illy for the rest of their lives, and their parents will too. Right now she and Miz Cook run Mother

COUNTY

Goose Play School, cattycorner across from us on Warley, in Parry, Charles, and Peggy Cook's house I mentioned earlier.

Illy started out as Lillian McFall, the cherished only child of Lillian Stem and Harold McFall, owner of the highest-rated hotel in South Carolina -- the Hotel McFall of Darlington. Mr McFall ran hotels in Abbeville and in Hartsville before he bought and took over the hotel here in 1920 and named it the McFall.

Think back to that first meeting that formed Darlington International Raceway: the McFall was where it happened. Mr Mac had already passed away, but he had gotten to be a part of Old Darlington by marrying Fred Stem's sister.

Mr Mac made the Hotel McFall the message and transportation center of Darlington. Its phone number was 52, same as the highway it's on.

You could book straight to the McFall from any location served by either one of the bus lines that passed through Darlington -- Atlantic Greyhound and Queen City. Round trip to Columbia cost $2.70; Charleston, $3. Lots of people traveled by bus and still do, including widowed ladies with no intention of ever driving a car. Daddy's Aunt Minnie rode the bus so much, visiting family and friends, she became a kind of transportation legend. When she died, the bus company in her town sent

150

such a nice floral tribute the family took pictures of it from all sides.

The most lavish social events in the Pee Dee were held at the McFall. Mrs Claussen of Claussen told me (their town house is on Palmetto Street in Florence, across from the Irbys) that she chose the McFall for their wedding reception because it was "the natural choice, simply the handsomest place anywhere near, with the best service."

Before the Crash, Mr Welling the banker put up his guests at the McFall. The Wellings were rich like the Claussens, with a house in town and one in the country. Their town house was the big yellow brick on St John's Street, cattycornered from St John's Grammar School, beside where Mrs P B Childs lives now and up from the Teacherage. Mr Welling specified it would have 2 bedrooms and no more -- huge ones with mammoth 4-posters, they say, with the bathroom in between. (There's another toilet you can get to from the hall, but that's all it is: a toilet and a lavatory.) To look at the Welling house from the outside, the wide porches and a porte-cochere and that rambling Spanish tile roof, you'd never guess there's just 2 bedrooms. Story is, as the richest man in town before the Crash, Mr Welling had plenty of visitors but hated overnight comp'ny. Fortunately, the best hotel in the state was just a couple blocks away. Mr Mac was happy to accommodate.

The Fred Stems live in the Welling house on St John's now and it's true, 2 bedrooms is all they have. When I was selling Buddy Poppies on Veterans' Day, a big girl let me into the vestibule and the front room, both of them wainscoted with that famous dark-varnished white pine, and I saw down the hall toward the rest of the house. I do believe those are as nice entrance rooms as I've ever been in, even counting ones in Orangeburg County. There's a library just off the living room, with dark cabinets built in all around to hold leather-bound books behind glass doors, like at Mrs Douglas's. One day I hope to have a whole room just for books, and if ever I were blessed to get old, I'd keep on 'til I'd read every one worth reading.

When the State got tough on standards, several hotels failed inspection and got closed. Mr Mac, though, he knew what he was doing. The Hotel McFall rated 985 out of a possible 1000. Nobody scored higher.

The hotel's still right where it was in its glory days when Illy's kittens use to tumble around in the lobby in front of the tall pier glass and cascading fountain. She had her first Kindergarten in the hotel. Mrs Claussen says it was a lovely time.

After Mr McFall passed away during the War, Illy's mother Miss Lillian sold the McFall to a Dubose fellow who sold it on to Vance Butler from New York. It's been going down ever since. Now it's named the "Park Terrace."

Some meetings are still held in the lobby and front rooms, and Olan Mills comes sometimes and takes people's pictures. Suers -- people who sue other people or railroads -- go there too, to Senator Mozingo's offices that he set up in the summer of '52. But that's part of another story that's waiting for somebody to write it. Not me, not now.

Nobody I know thinks of staying in the Park Terrace. A few drummers, but they're nothing like the custom the Hotel McFall had. Vance Butler lives in the hotel on the Orange Street side, but I don't know that he'd be paying attention if you needed anything. You'd do better to stay in the Darlington Motel, the new one out Pearl Street close to the Mill.

Mr McFall's pharmacy is in other hands too. He came to town in 1919, won friends, and married into the interesting Stem family. He got lavish praise (including the N&P's) for building up Darlington and made a great success in everything he tried. Then, in 1944, he died.

Illy's 1st Cousin -- their mothers are sisters -- was Bill Farrow. He died young too – died a soldier and a hero. Illy's proud of her cousin Billy—proud in the best way. All of us are who know the story.

Before he was a hero, Billy grew up here taller than 'most anybody his age. He and his mother had a place to live, food to eat and clothes to wear, but nothing much else. The Farrow fellow had deserted them, and they were just scraping by. They say Billy was mischievous, the way a lot of boys without fathers at home are, but he was honorable too, all along.

He graduated from St John's in Depression time, so he went into one of Roosevelt's make-work programs. He joined the one with the roughest reputation -- the CCC. From the other CCCers I know, he must've been one of the few who'd finished high school. The CCC boys built dams, cleared stumps, did dangerous hard work and were tough as whit leather.

After the Japs bombed Pearl Harbor without declaring war, Americans enlisted in droves. Just before Billy went to sign up, his aunt Margaret Stem somehow got some money together and sent him to college. He stayed just until he knew for sure he didn't belong in a classroom during time of war.

Billy enlisted in the Army Air Corps. Almost right off, he volunteered to pilot a plane in Jimmy Doolittle's raid on Japan.

Every man in the Raid knew they could be captured and killed, and they went anyway -- all volunteers, trained for it right here in South Carolina. It was a suicide raid, in a way, to show the Japanese they couldn't bomb and kill Americans and still be safe on their far-away island. The Raiders all went in knowing weather and machinery could doom the mission, but they were willing to die if it had to be that way.

Some reached friendly territory in China; some didn't. Billy's plane ran out of fuel. He managed to land it, but he and his crew were captured.

From prison in Japan, Bill sent brave letters to his mother and messages to his Stem kin, the only family he knew. He didn't expect mercy -- the Raid embarrassed Japan bad, and Japs don't take embarrassment -- so in his letters he tried to make sure his family knew he didn't regret choosing to defend the U S A.

The Japs toyed with him for months before they killed him, like cats with a lizard or dogs with a tethered bear. You don't want to hear the rumor about how they killed him. It was in a way *they* wouldn't call barbaric but we sure would. What the Japs told after he was dead was that they took him to an open space, tied him to a stake, and shot him. We can hope that's really how he died.

Anybody ought to be able to understand why Americans spoke harshly of the enemy. Like the rhyme Miss Isobel Smith of Lynchburg SC (Senator Cotton Ed's daughter) and Walter Chrysler of New York City and their friends danced to, whirling around in a mad circle high up in the new Chrysler building at the end of the War:

COUNTY

> *A tisket, a tasket, Hitler's in his casket!*
> *Eeny meeny, Mussolini*
> *Oughta be there too.*

Some people are beginning to say we should never've had insulting songs and harsh slogans. Okay, but insults aren't terminal like being bombed on a sunny Sunday morning without a declaration of war, and they're not like being held prisoner a long time and then – well, let's just say executed -- for bravery.

Miss Margaret wrote a book after they knew Billy was dead, showing how bad it all made her feel but how proud of him she was. Illy lent me her own copy of <u>Tall and Free, As Meant by God</u>. It's filled with Miss Margaret's religious conviction and gratitude for "our boy." I don't know that her book was actually published, but there's a spiral-bound copy in our Trinity Methodist library you could borrow. Anybody who reads it without tears is either a cold fish or misses the whole picture.

You see why I call the Stem family "interesting." In the case of Bill Farrow, "heroic" fits even better.

Writing's a talent that keeps cropping up in the Stem family. Bill Farrow's letters show it and so does Miss Margaret's own writing in her book about Billy.

Margaret Stem never married, so she was what people used to call a spinster -- a strange term. I have a spinster aunt and 2 spinster great aunts, and Miss Margaret and Illy are spinsters, but if any of 'em ever spun, I never knew it. Did spinsters *use* to spin? If they did, what did they spin? The only spinning wheels I know of are really old or else in fairy tales, to prick a princess's finger and make her sleep 100 years.

The spinsters I know get along just fine. Take Great-Aunt Minnie Dukes. My grandfather bought Lime Cola stock from his brother-in-law, and his money and Lime Cola both disappeared. *She* bought Coca-Cola stock and sent Mother's orphaned 1st cousins through college on her dividends. If Aunt Minnie ever spins, I guarantee it's because she *wants* to spin.

Illy's a writer too – a publicist for cats and children. She sends out articles and takes photographs as illustrations. Lately she's been sending her and Mrs Cook's Mother Goose Nursery news to the <u>News & Press</u>, like about the class's field trip to visit

154

COUNTY

Mr Gene Vaughans' horse and Miss Carrie Reaves' talking parrot. Miss Carrie runs the post office.

Sometimes Miss Illy has articles in <u>Cats</u>, a *national magazine,* and newspapers have done articles about how she would teach kindergarten with her Siamese named Esme sitting by, helping to entertain the little kids. She said Esme provided a good example of patient attention 'cept when he'd fall asleep.

Miss Illy makes sure her cats get recognition for what-all they do. She's like a Little Rascals stage mother. Tinker's been in plays -- one in Columbia and one in Florence. The Florence Little Theatre's out at the Air Field in a Quonset Hut the Army Air Corps put up during the War.

I know all about the FLT production of <u>Bell, Book, and Candle.</u> Illy took me along as her assistant each night the play ran. In October 1953 I was in the 9th grade, but I guess Mother decided it would be a valuable enough experience to justify my staying out late. And it was. Oh it really was.

Tinker got advance articles in the newspapers -- I think Illy wrote the articles -- one with a big up-close photograph of Tinker's face looking slightly cross-eyed. (He's another Siamese.) The <u>Florence Morning News</u> said the play "ran to capacity audiences every night."

Tinker McFall played Pyewacket. There's only one cat role, and it's for a black cat, but Illy prevailed. Pyewacket is the witch's familiar spirit, her buddy. The Friday performance, though, didn't work out that way.

I don't know how much the witch actress knew about cats, but it couldn't've been much. And I sure don't know what she was thinking when she decided to hoist Tinker high up in the air facing downward, but she did.

Tinker re-acted the way any cat *would* that finds itself with nothing to plant its feet on and no arm around it: he spread his claws and reached frantically for the nearest surface, which was the bosom of the actress. In costume that bosom was bare down to here.

Claws contacted flesh -- not deep, but deep enough to draw blood -- and the cat sailed across into the wings just as Illy started out onstage. She was reaching to pluck him out of the air but she missed. He lit running. Illy reversed and snatched

155

him up just in time to keep him from racing out into an airfield full of unfamiliar darkness, and me from having to hunt down a tan-and-brown cat in untold acres of brown-scraggly weeds and briars.

We'd been standing side by side in the wings, Illy and me, intently watching the action onstage, and yet -- it all happened so fast -- I still can't say whether that cat leapt away from the actress or was *flung*.

I missed the final night's performance and so did Miss Illy and Tinker. The actress had requested a stand-in cat and a turpentine-concealing neckline. My guess is, she's sworn off cat hoisting.

Bell, Book and Candle taught me once and for all the superiority of stage plays over picture shows. A picture show is the same every time you see it. Give me live drama any day.

Possibly the cat that should have played Pyewacket. Note its
casual attitude toward the bug in the top of the photo. Or whatever that is.

BEACHES

Illy's got to be the richest former child I know – or anyhow the one with the most generous father. For her 21st birthday, Mr Mac gave her a second-row lot in the most beautiful part of Myrtle Beach and built her a 2-story house on it.

I kid you not.

Being raised kind of poor and normal, I took awhile to imagine how her early years must have affected her.

Thanks to Illy seeing no social distance between her and the family of the man who repairs her appliances, I'm totally familiar with that birthday beach house. She invites Mother and Daddy and me to stay for whole weeks whenever she's there, right upstairs where she stays, not down in the apartment. One week is the longest Daddy thinks he can take off work, but sometimes Mother and I stay a little longer. While he's there, Daddy fixes whatever's broken or breaking. I'm even free to take friends, one at a time.

Illy's birthday house has a clear view of the ocean because it sits on a corner beside a wide right-of-way to the water. She walks Tinker on a leash when we stroll along the strand. Dusty, her blue-gray Persian mix, won't go near the water and clearly regards Tinker as insane.

It's an easy walk from Illy's to the most famous hotel in South Carolina -- the Ocean Forest. It's like a palace gleaming high and white in the sun. But its story is not a happy one.

The hotel was built in 1929 and opened just before the Wall Street Crash. Hindsight's 20-20, and you're right: the original owners went bust.

They say the Ocean Forest has lost money for every owner since. Some of them could stand the loss. Some couldn't.

The Ocean Forest is way bigger than the 40-guest-room McFall / Park Terrace. It has 3 times as many bathrooms as the Park Terrace has bedrooms, and every one of those 121 bathrooms is ventilated.

The Ocean Forest sits forward on acres of Atlantic oceanfront white-sand beach, with its own swimming pool and deck chairs and little glass tables with waiters at beck and call. There are shops in the hotel's tiled lower lobby, and a photography studio.

But the guest rooms are too small to suit the rich people of today, and nobody else can afford to stay there. Some upper-level staff and some who run businesses in the lower lobby live in the hotel – the photographer, the liquor-store owner, the cosmetics-shop lady -- but I doubt their rooms look toward the ocean. Still, there's just too many rooms to ever fill up. The hotel's too big -- too big to last.

The Ocean Forest started out red brick with white trim. Somewhere along, an owner painted it white. It boggles the mind to think how many gallons of white it took to do that, but now it gleams like a fairy palace. Come upon it unawares and it takes your breath away.

Driving north from the Pavilion on 17 (not from the ocean-front street; the hotel's too private to connect with that), turn off toward the ocean when you're in a residential area. You'll find yourself curving past the hotel's acres of tall trees. You might not even notice a round wooden dormitory off to your left among the trees. It's called the Bull Ring, and it's where the workers stay – 'scuse me: the non-management staff.

Then all of a sudden there's the Hotel ahead of you, shining in the sunlight.

The Ocean Forest faces the ocean and turns its back to the highway you've left behind. Out there, motels – low, crouching motels – and restaurants push into what use to be quiet neighborhoods. Along the ocean street in busier, louder Myrtle Beach, taller motels intrude on the old familiar boarding houses like The Darlington and Carter's. The price of oceanfront land is rising. Those higher prices could end the boarding house culture and even take apart the wide acreage of the Ocean Forest.

But not yet.

Like nothing else on the coast of the Carolinas, the Ocean Forest is a legend, a kind of dream. Celebrities book in; you can imagine seeing them in the bar or the sumptuous dining room. Real actors of the "legitimate stage" stay there while they're doing summer stock at the Myrtle Beach Little Theatre. Tourists venture into its forest drive to point out the hotel's glories to passengers.

There's a local ritual, a kind of lame joke: "I stayed at the Ocean Forest," somebody says. The response comes in a singsongy chant: "Yeah, we know: you went to the ocean and slept in the forest."

Even though the Park Terrace is right here in Darlington, just off the Square, I never remember wanting to enter it. But just wait: one day I'll be inside the Ocean Forest, and not just for a touristy glimpse like with Illy one day.

I doubt I'll ever be a paying guest, but I could apply for summer work there; I'll be old enough next year. Waitresses make a dollar an hour *and* get to keep tips. Best of all, I could live free of charge in that round dormitory half hidden in the trees, and get to know professional resort-hotel workers, the ones who move on whenever they get tired of where they are.

Do they worry about tomorrow at all? I want to know some of them before something happens to their world.

It's not that other hotels are a total mystery to me. The red brick Gasque and the white Colonial both belong to Uncle Clarence Gasque's family. He's Night Manager of the Colonial and he's Aunt Tee's husband. They live in the upper floor of a back-yard wooden building, so maybe his job's not so great, but I've gotten to meet some of the staff. Randolph -- last name Howard, I think, from Darlington – he's been Bell Captain there all my life. The Colonial wouldn't be the Colonial without Randolph.

But the hotels most on my mind are the hotel here in Darlington – always there in the corner of my eye without my ever wanting to go inside -- and the big one on the edge of the ocean.

When the Ocean Forest was built in '29, its era was already over. Prosperity was gone from the farms and from almost everywhere else in the US but oblivious Wall Street.

As for the Hotel McFall, it was doomed from 1944 on.

They're out of joint in time, both hotels. Neither one looks to be heading for a happy ending.

160

COUNTY

Don't get the idea that Illy's nice beach is the beach we at St John's know best. We mainly go to the little beaches, the kind of junky ones we can afford -- Cherry Grove, Windy Hill, and Ocean Drive, specially the Pad at OD. They're all north of Myrtle Beach toward North Carolina. The Pad's kind of a dump, with sand and cans and paper cups in the corners of the worn-down wooden floor, but you can dance to the jukebox and sooner or later you see all your friends there. And unless you drink beer, it costs you *nothing*.

Folly Beach is okay, but too far south for Pee Dee people to go in a day and have time to enjoy it. It's a Charleston beach. The only time I ever bowled with duck balls was at Folly.

There's Garden City, too, not far from Myrtle — sort of the poor man's beach. I mentioned Uncle Hart's trailer there that I think he got in a swap one Thursday at the Darlington Auction Market. The trailer's on a sandy lot pretty far from the water, but we get to use it free whenever he needs Daddy to do some work in it. I take a friend. We don't generally hang around much; we light out in the Ford to the Pavilion or OD, depending on whether we're looking for people we already know or people we might like to meet, and how much gas is in the car.

Joyce Anne went with us one of the times Uncle Hart let us use his trailer. The toilet needed a kit to keep it from running over and the cook stove needed a fan, they said.

Joyce Anne and I were getting ourselves ready to head out for the Pavilion when Aunt Opal drove in unexpectedly from Florence. I mean, it's their trailer; she can come when she wants to, but Daddy's right: she hardly ever wants to unless we're there, and it's a real *little* trailer.

So this paticlar day, before we can make a clean getaway Aunt Opal runs out to stop us. She's standing there in the front sort-of-yard waving a half-gone stick of oleo and yelling for us to go get her a pound of butter right away from the Red & White or either the A&P out on 17, she's making a cake. (A *cake*, of all things to *choose* to do at the beach. Even if I get old, I hope I never get *that* old.)

But it's not her we're looking at, it's the huge dog coming up behind her. A Great Dane, or a Mastiff maybe; whatever those dogs of Mr Spillane's are. Most of us know they're there, but they're not supposed to be roaming around. Not that they'd mean to hurt anybody I guess, but they're really big, and he says they're too valuable to risk anything happening to.

You've probly heard of Mickey Spillane, that wrote I, the Jury and the other famous Mike Hammer books they've made into picture shows. Horrible things happen in Spillane's -- gross, actually -- but Hammer's a fascinating detective. He's kind of a Nazi, but there's a real rage against injustice in him, and Nazi's can't have scruples like Hammer because they're followers, not thinkers. Hammer's not named Hammer by accident; he's super tough. To him, crooks are scum, and Spillane's crooks are scum sure enough.

I've read a bunch of his books. What our local librarian doesn't know won't worry her. Spillane's stuff is probly not even in libraries; I've never seen it but in paperback.

Mr Spillane doesn't just have a place at Garden City; he lives there. You don't ordinarily see him, but his hair's light colored and he keeps it so short it lookes shaved. He's all muscled up and looks like he could be Mike Hammer only he's not as tall I picture Hammer to be.

This paticlar day, Mr Spillane's dog is interested in Aunt Opal's hand with the oleo in it -- the hand she started out waving but left stuck way out there while she was standing yelling out to us some other supplies she's suddenly thought of to want.

That's when she must've felt something breathing on that hand.

I wish I'd had a camera. Not because I 'spect ever to forget the look on Aunt Opal's face; I just want you to see it too.

Later on she told us her first thought was, *What's a horse doing loose in Garden City*, and then *It's baring its teeth*. That had to be out the corner of her eye; she still hadn't turned her head to look all the way at it.

Aunt Opal had the presence of mind to let loose the oleo as soon as she felt it being pulled out of her hand.

The dog ate the oleo, paper and all -- kind of inhaled it. Then he looked at her kind of hopefully. But he must've figured she didn't have any more, because he loped on off.

So we went and got the butter and other stuff for Aunt Opal at the A&P, put it into the tiny refrigerator in the trailer (she was still lying down collecting herself when we got back; Mother'd put a wet wash rag on Opal's forehead and was in the easy chair, looking through an old <u>Life</u>), and headed on down to Myrtle Beach.

We'd passed Brookgreen Gardens and were in front of the Air Force Base entrance (it's the Air Force now, not the Army Air Corps) when Joyce said, "I'm looking forward to us speaking only French once we get to the Pavilion."

I mean, I can *read* French and even *write* it okay, but what I honestly think about the French language is, it's embarrassing. I can't get the rhythm, the beat.   They accent the wrong syllable. GuiLLAUME, for Pete's sake, instead of WILLiam, and RoBEAR even though they spell it "Robert." Speaking French makes me feel wrongfooted, so I try not to, 'cept when Miss Douglas calls on me in class.

Which shows you how persuasive Joyce is, to get me to go along with her plan: "It'll be fun. It'll intrigue interesting people."

"How 'bout pig latin?" I whined. "I could do pig latin better."

"Be sane, Memory. Who's pig latin gonna intrigue? Little kids? Even they can speak pig latin. Ixnay on igpay atinlay."

So at least a little while of every single day at the beach around strangers, we spoke French.   She did, anyhow. Trouble was, I'd take so long inside my head translating whatever Joyce said into something I could understand, I hardly ever came up with a French answer before everybody who heard *her* comment had walked too far off to hear it.

Mostly I said, "*Je ne sais pas.*" (You say it Zhuh Nuh Seh PAH. Only quick.)

To me, most people that heard us didn't look intrigued. They looked more like they thought we were nuts.

That was the week I met Joe Thompson, back from Korea and Labrador and planning to enter the University. He'd kind of recognized our French; I don't know anybody our own age who would've -- certainly not anybody else from Red Hill out from Conway. He's mostly lost his Horry County accent and speaks Air Force, which is kind of different and exciting. His dark hair in that military crew-cut looks nice, plus he was Airman of the Month in Labrador and seems like a good guy.

Speaking South Carolina French at the beach was maybe not such a bad idea.

Church Buildings

Churches are maybe the biggest part of the Pee Dee's social life. There's party people -- grownups who throw cocktail parties and what-all at their houses -- but they're mostly not us. With us, it's churches.

Look at the <u>News & Press</u> or the <u>Hartsville Messenger</u> any week, and you'll see church events and guest speakers reported on page 1 and through the whole paper. We all want to know what's going on, who's speaking, who's raising money for what, and what missionary's back in town for awhile. Miss Ethel Williamson that's on the faculty of the University in Havana is Trinity's missionary in Cuba. To look at and be around, she's a mild short lady with kind, patient eyes, and yet she must live an exciting life. When she's home in Darlington County, her talks draw a crowd.

One sleepy morning when I was grumbling about so much church going, Daddy said something I'll probly never forget – not just because he said it and I love him, but because it makes so much sense: "Meb, a town without churches would be a terrible place to live."

It was one of the things he said I know I'll never foget.

Daddy never preaches in words; he's not the type. He doesn't use curse words, either. I do sometimes, but he never does. When I asked him why, he said he doesn't feel the need to. The Bible says let your yes be yes and your no be no, and he does it; he makes it work.

Daddy believes in God and in His Son Jesus Christ, and in the Holy Spirit that Jesus left with us, and he believes in the Church. I do too. The church is people, not buildings. I can't show you all those people, but I can show you buildings. Church buildings can tell about the meaning of churches.

Darlington has some really nice church buildings – old ones with towers and steeples. If you're here for the Southern 500, you'll be here over a Sunday, and you'd be welcome at any of them. I'll put in some pictures of the big ones you'll be passing on the main streets.

Coming in South Main, the first big church you'll see is Macedonia Baptist. You can't miss it; it sits right on your left before you cross the railroad tracks. It's a real neighborhood church. It's good that quite a few of its members live close enough to walk, as houses are built close up around it and there's not much room to park cars. That's the parsonage next to it; the tall white house.

Macedonia must be one of the oldest churches in Darlington. You can't help being impressed when you look up at the towering building.

When you enter the big doors and walk from the generous vestibule into the sanctuary, you realize the inside is even more impressive than what can be seen from the road.

The whole building must've been designed by an inspired architect, somebody who knew how to design the whole so that the parts harmonize completely. Because Macedonia has kept itself original, its sanctuary has all the drama its design was meant to achieve. When you enter and hear their choir already singing its pre-worship service in that high-ceilinged sanctuary, the Spirit comes through.

Macedonia is also one of the churches in Darlington that remind me of pictures of cathedrals in Europe because it has 2 front-facing towers. They're not twin towers: each tower is different from the one on the other side.

In America, the towers are different from each other because one is the bell tower -- built to house a huge bell to ring out evening prayer and the Sunday morning call to worship.

In Europe, towers are different from each other because, centuries ago, it took so long to build a cathedral. By the time another tower was under way, the builders -- architects, artists, whatever they called the designers, as well as many of the early workers who began building the cathedral -- were dead. Dead and gone, but not their work. Those towers stand, and they're massive. They're what you see from first glance. No part of the building overtakes them.

The higher tower at Macedonia is clearly meant to house bells, but they must not be there any longer. The shuttered

Macedonia Baptist Church, S Main, Darlington

tower is a mysterious thing to passersby. In a way it adds to the aura of Macedonia Baptist, making it seem a church that's reinventing itself.

166

Epworth Methodist, across town from Macedonia, is another old church in town that's a true neighborhood church. It's out Pearl Street, almost to the railroad. Cotton Mill workers helped build Epworth soon after the Mill was founded. It has its own cemetery, kept up by the members.

Epworth is in a crisis of survival in 1957, which makes it more precious than ever to the people remaining in the neighborhood, and also to those who had to leave and look forward to coming back for good, or at least to visit and sit in the old pews. They'll be coming back because Darlington is home and because Epworth will always be their home church. Nobody wants to let it die, and God willing, it never will.

Another pressure is coming, too:

With so many more cars around since the War, neighborhood churches like Macedonia and Epworth will get to be rare. They'll have to find other ways to reach out, and they'll need more parking space for cars to bring worshippers from outside. They might buy an old bus from a school and get drivers to make runs out in the area, or buy a house to tear down for parking space.

Still, hearing church bells chime around you on your walk to church must be a lovely feeling. When Macedonia and Epworth were built, town people walked to church. Country people got there mostly by carriage, buggy, wagon, or horseback.

Coming in from the south on 52, first you see Macedonia, then you pass between tobacco warehouses after the railroad track, and then there's First Baptist.

First Baptist is probly the most imposing church building in Darlington, and for sure the most classical. It wouldn't look out of place in old Greece or Rome. Tall white columns span the front, topped by Ionic capitals and a frieze. It has just the one tower – the bell tower, with a huge steeple topped by the Cross. The Cross is so tiny and high up, you could miss it on a misty morning, but keep looking. It's the reason for the church.

Just in case you're here after a hard rain, don't go through the water in front of First Baptist. I've seen cars sitting there in water so high you can barely tell they have wheels. You can make a right turn in either direction, though, and get back to

Main pretty quick. There's lots of parking behind First Baptist, between it and the Baptist cemetery.

Mr Jones is the preacher, and has been for every bit as long as we've been here. (We Methodists don't know how that feels.) The parsonage – or whatever Baptists call the house their ministers live in -- is a nice 2-story brick house nowhere near the church; it's on Ervin Street and backs on Williamson Park. Mrs Jones is a short, comfortable-looking lady. Also there's Billy and then Martha; she's my age. All the Joneses are short and have nice smiles.

Baptists came to America from Wales. In the Pee Dee the first Baptists settled at Long Bluff and Society Hill and built St David's Academy, a famous colonial school that was more like a college for men than like our schools today. St David's attracted teachers all the way from Yale. All the planters' sons who were smart enough to get in wanted to go there, and their fathers were keen to get them in.

Baptists use to not dance. I don't mean just at church; they didn't dance *anywhere*. So because Mrs U S Senator Josiah Evans and some other ladies had married Society Hill leaders (all Baptists) but were determined not to give up their dancing parties, a new church was built in Society Hill: Episcopalian, like the old-Charleston families of Society Hill's new wives.

But old denominations have also had to move over for new.

In the 1870s, a young veteran named James Edward Boone (Mother's "GranPaa") was looking for a fresh start. His wife and children were all dead – killed by scarlet fever during the post-War epidemic in his hometown, Charleston.

At age 15 he had joined Charleston's German Artillery, so he decided to look for a new life among comrades who were now settled in German-Swiss Orangeburg County. He was amazed when he found almost everybody there was now Methodist. Bishop Francis Asbury had been so welcomed into Lutherans' homes and hearts during the 1790s, even the original German-speaking churches converted to Methodism. So Great-Grampaa Boone put the shadow of Boone Hall and the Episcopal Church behind him and embraced his new church and Orangeburg County. Far as I can find out, he was the earliest Methodist on either side of my family.

168

First Baptist Church, S Main, Darlington SC. (Look way up.)

Central Baptist (next page) is in a golden-brick-trimmed-in-white building perched right on the sidewalk on the high ground of a down-sloping lot facing the side of the Public Library. I've always thought of it as "the golden church."

Park leaves Main between the Public Library and Central Baptist. At the back of Central Baptist on Park, you're at J C Daniels Auditorium of St John's High and you're across from Miz Myrtle Jeffords' tall white house.

Central Baptist is another neighborhood church built for walkers. There's no way its members can park on the church's right, because even though Main Street is wide, it's also

169

Highway 52, and the hill there is steep. There's space behind the Public Library; I guess they use that on Sundays and Wednesday nights, and probly they park on the school grounds beyond. The church has a sheltered entrance on Park Street for cars to let passengers out before finding a parking place. You can see it in my photograph, coming into the lower level of the building, at the Sunday School rooms.

Central's earliest members, even those who lived too far to walk, had no parking problem. They'd tie their mules and horses to trees and posts or leave them in downtown carriage barns. Maps from the time of Darlington's oldest churches show plenty of space for churchgoers in the age of horse-drawn transportation. Quite a bit of it was sheltered parking, right off the Public Square.

Central Baptist Church, at the corner of Main Street (Highway 52) and Park Street, Darlington. Hwy 52 is on your right.

Here's a picture I took of the Dargan Street side of Trinity Methodist, the 3rd building Trinity's had. You *could* call it the 4th, because this one burned almost down in the '30s. It faces Pearl Street and the Post Office, but we park mostly at Dargan and Orange. We can park across the street at the Southernaire, too, because it's always closed on Sundays.

One lady left money in her Will to have the tower converted for a clock, but most of us are glad it never got done. We're use to our Norman bell tower. You have to live pretty far out of town not to hear Darlington's church bells on Sundays. Anybody who doesn't come, anyhow they've been called and they know it. Church bells are to remind us Christians not to neglect the assembling of ourselves together.

All Trinity's windows and street doors have Gothic arches with stained glass. The stained glass windows in the sanctuary are extraordinary. Most are what you might call color arrangements, but 3 of ours are actual pictures. The central window in this photograph is of Jesus the Shepherd. The central window on the Pearl Street side is Jesus Knocking at the Door. Behind the pulpit is Jesus in a Garden with His hand raised — some say to bless us and some say to call us to Him and others say to point us Above.

Beside His other hand is a dark shape that's a mystery to me. During some sermons, I'd stare at it and try to figure it out. To this day I haven't succeeded.

Stained glass seems to me the most glorious and colorful kind of art. It can also be the most meaningful. I'm grateful for the wonderful windows of Trinity.

Stored in an underground room, some still in their frames, are the windows salvaged from the '30s fire. The glass is from before 1905, and waves of color wind through each piece. One day the old windows might be sold to raise church funds. By then, maybe I'll be able to buy one. That's a treasure worth saving up for.

Except for her smile that lets you in, our Reverend Llewellyn Pope's wife looks almost imperial. Whatever her birth name was, it couldn't have suited any better than Pope. Mrs Pope wears her thick white hair up and walks tall. Maybe I shouldn't say this about a minister's wife, but Mrs Pope is actually glamorous.

Her poise and confidence remind me of Mama in Orangeburg County, but there's a big difference. Mrs Pope is our choir's lead soprano and sometimes teaches Sunday School. Mama raised 8 church-going children — 9 counting Russell -- and appears to think that's a gracious enough contribution from any preacher's wife.

The philosophy of Methodism charges each congregation with the management and the outreach of the local church, which is why ministers are reassigned every few years by the Conference in consultation with local members. The Popes came here during a turbulent year for the County and the whole Pee Dee. He'll be moving on now, carrying with him a trove of shocking confidences. May he not be borne down by the burden.

The parsonage is a white one-story Victorian over on Orange Street, in easy walking distance. We like that it's close by. Nobody lives in the little Victorian house behind us on Dargan anymore, so we're buying its lot for more space. The house itself'll move to the curve on Spring Street Extension, the street that leads to Mineral Springs.

COUNTY

Like Macedonia's, our sanctuary was designed with a sense of drama. Trinity's center aisle is a diagonal running from the corner entrance, which is the main vestibule, to the Altar. The pulpit looks straight down that center aisle from beside the raised choir loft. During sacred occasions – a wedding, say -- the whole wedding party sweep through the midst of the congregation. They're in clear view from the time they enter and when they gather around the Altar, where the entire congregation can see the ceremony.

During Christenings, some pastors like to walk the long aisle carrying the baby, talking about the meaning of promises the family and the congregation are making for the child's spiritual nourishment. Some people reach out and touch them gently as they pass.

But change is coming. Our Sanctuary is not large like Macedonia's, and now we need more room. The high wooden folding wall that separates the Asbury (Men's) class from the Sanctuary will be taken out, and what Llewellyn Fields Hart nicknamed the "cheap seats" will be part of the Sanctuary. They're a step higher than the Sanctuary floor, but from there you still won't get as good a view of whoever comes down the center aisle 'til they're down front at the Altar rail.

Because Macedonia's dramatic Sanctuary was bigger all along, they've never had to change the original design. Trinity's changes will weaken the visual effect of the central aisle.

Still, it's only a change in the building, not the real Church. When the Church grows, you praise God for the increase. And we do.

No youth program in Darlington draws more young people than Trinity's under Mrs Mincy Copeland and Mr Holley. Some people say we shouldn't be dancing at church (it's really only in the Brunson building), but we aren't really. Folk games only *look* like dancing. Besides, the Bible says King David danced before the Lord.

Right now Trinity has new ministers in Seminary – Dwight Mims and Bundy Bynum. Murray Yarborough and Jimmy Bailey are finishing Wofford, heading for Seminary. Mincy Copeland calls them Trinity's sons, and they probly seem almost like hers. Some of us in MYF feel kind of like we're her children too.

COUNTY

When any local church invites Jimmy or Murray or both to preach, the <u>N&P</u> covers it on the front page. We all try to go hear our own. If you let yourself, you feel the Holy Spirit in the room. You leave with a good feeling. I'd call it gratitude.

Presbyterians were the first to build a church in Darlington. You'd expect that, because it was mostly Scottish people who settled the inland Carolinas including the Pee Dee soon after the English (Episcopalians) settled the coast. Darlington Presbyterians celebrate Scottish heritage with bagpipes and kilts. (I think the kilt belongs to the Ervins. At First Pres in Florence I think it's probly Mr Porter Stewart's kilt.)

Early in the heritage service, the congregation hears bagpipes starting up behind them, along with the sharp beat of drumsticks keeping up a martial rhythm — "Scotland the Brave"-- that stirs up the mind and the heart. Next, member after member walks down the aisle wearing or carrying on a pole a piece of plaid cloth — a tartan plaid — which represents a clan their family claims kin to.

The stirring sight and the sound set me to thinking about not just the Spearses (meaning spies, scouts for the defense of Scotland along the Borders) but also the MacDuffies. *Got to find out about the MacDuffies*, I'm thinking, and *What about McDuff in Shakespeare's <u>MacBeth</u>?* Cap's original name was George MacDuffie Spears. Family and Church go together, especially if you're a Presbyterian. It doesn't hurt to read some historical novels by Sir Walter Scott too. I told you when I was living at the Sand Hill, I found out some farms nearby got their names from Scott's novels. The McIver-Dove-Brunsons' house — you can see the side of it from McIver Road -- is Kenilworth.

Darlington Presbyterian is on Pearl Street, a couple blocks beyond the post office and Trinity. The twin front doors have a Gothic façade, the highest windows have a Gothic arch, and both towers are spiked, something like a fortress. The entire place is a strong reminder of the Scots' reputation as staunch defenders of the Christian Faith, Protestant persuasion.

Like Macedonia, this is another church with two front towers, reminding me of a fortress and of cathedrals in Europe. Even though the bell tower is higher, these tower capitals match. The points above the front entrance doors take your eyes upward to the points on the tower tops.

Anybody who doesn't look up higher every time they see Darlington Presbyterian Church is just not getting the message.

Darlington Presbyterian Church, Pearl Street

Until right recently, when a Roman Catholic Mission opened north of Darlington on 52, the closest Roman Catholic Church was St Anthony's, a gorgeous, high, Cathedral-looking building at Palmetto and Irby, right in the *middle* of Florence. Roman Catholics aren't many in the Pee Dee, so St Anthony's draws from all around. There's a school right in the churchyard.

COUNTY

We see the schoolchildren in their uniforms, going to class. Roman Catholics believe the Church should take charge of the education of children from the very beginning.

The Orthodox Christian Church is the Greek church. It's just as old as the Roman Catholic church, only from a different part of the world — farther east and not under the Pope in Rome. Like the Roman Catholics', the closest Greek house of worship is in Florence, and most of our Greek friends go there. Some Darlington Greeks became Episcopalians, which makes sense, because the Episcopalians have a lot of ritual and so do the Orthodox. But the Demetrious are mainstays of the Orthodox church in Florence. They're close friends there to some of our Spears's favorite people -- the Palles family, the Hobeikas, the Kazantzakises, and the Costases. Pete Costas is Pauline Palles' husband. Uncle Bob goes to Mrs Hobeika's restaurant for breakfast so many mornings, we're thinking they're keeping comp'ny. (He's a bachelor. She's a widow.)

Darlington has a good portion of Jews, a fact I didn't use to know because they're just like us and 've been here all my life. They believe in God differently from the way we do but just as much. They believed in the One God thousands of years ago in the Old Testament, when nobody else had met Him yet. Nobody else. That's why the whole first half of the Christian Bible is the Jewish Old Testament. (To the Jews it's not the *Old* Testament; it's *the* Testament.)

There's no synagogue in Darlington — Florence's Temple Beth Israel (which is flat and modern, not a bit like I'd think a temple would look) is the closest. Jewish children and adults come to our church suppers and events. I've never seen nor heard of any bad feelings between Jews and Christians in Darlington. Until an elderly man committed suicide because some rich people had trusted him with their money and he lost it, I never knew who was Jewish and who wasn't. Daddy says there're plenty of people with no sense of shame about that at all, and that the man never set out to cheat anybody.

We're sad for his widow, who's not well. But it's in terrible times of loss that spiritual awareness is a deep blessing. You'd never give it up once you found its source.

176

Saint Matthew's Episcopal Church, Main Street

St Matthews Episcopal Church is across the street from the Dixie Home Store and right beside First Baptist. They share parking space. The sanctuary is old fashioned – solemn and dark. You just naturally look forward toward the altar area, which is built higher than the pews to concentrate your attention. England is the denomination's birthplace, and St Matthews has a good English look. There it's called the Church of England or the Anglican, but in the US it's the Episcopal Church. When I go there with Marion, she lends me a handkerchief to cover my hair. It's their tradition for women.

From the street, St Matthews has a modest, welcoming look and a nice harmony. The tower and steeple dominate without dwarfing the neat modest building.

If the best architecture in town is not in Churches – if it's in banks, say, or office buildings – something might be wrong with the town's values. Take Milan, Italy. Even though it's the nation's business center, by *law* nothing can be built in Milan higher than the Milan Cathedral.

It's like Papa says: Church steeples and church towers remind us to look higher than this world.

177

THE LAW and LAWBREAKERS

The top laws broken hereabouts are "highway violations." That must mean dirt roads too, because we still don't have many what you would call "highways," even counting all the roads C'n Ben paved in the '30s.

That's Mother's 1st Cousin Ruth Simmons' husband Ben Sawyer I'm talking about. He headed the South Carolina Highway Commission during the Depression. He was the man who persuaded the Legislature that automobile license fees and gasoline taxes ought to go into a state fund for building and paving roads all over South Carolina instead of leaving road upkeep to depend on local taxes. Roads can be hard on whatever you're driving, and states hadn't kept up with the number of cars on the road. Farmers need to get crops to market, businesses need to get and send products, and cars and pickups need to get families where they're going without being broken down by bad roads, deep holes, and flooding on the way.

So C'n Ben got busy and paved roads all over the state with money from the Highway Department fund. But Governor Olin D. Johnston was jealous; he wanted that money to spend on Roosevelt's New Deal, not on roads. So he announced that Ben and the other Highway Commissioners were fired and he was replacing them with his own men.

It didn't take. The Commissioners didn't quit.

Next Johnston accused C'n Ben of skullduggery: the Governor told voters the Highway Commissioner had used state money to pave the street to his mother-in-law's house.

That was a lie.

See, I know that street. Ben's mother-in-law was my Great-Aunt Ada Dukes. Aunt Ada's gone now, but the tall house Mr Simmons built for her when they married is still right where it was then: on that corner *where 2 unpaved streets meet.*

Her son. C'n Bennie that came out of the 1st World War crippled, lives there in mostly 3 rooms on the ground floor with

178

his wife, C'n Bessie Farrell. Pretty soon they'll have to leave because bats have taken over the 3rd floor ballroom and it's starting to sag down into the upstairs, but I use to climb up onto the 2nd-floor gallery to look out over the back lot and the old kitchen. C'n Bennie's trunk with his Citadel uniform stayed out on the top veranda, probly from the very time he left off being a cadet to be a young, strong officer. *I know those streets.* They were dirt streets, and they're dirt streets now.

If you want to know what streets *did* get paved in Rowesville when Ben Sawyer was Commissioner, that's easy, because there's just one: Main Street. Main Street's the only paved street in Rowesville to this day, and the Governor would've stopped *it* getting paved if he could've. He's from the Upstate; what does he care or know about the Lowcountry.

Lies weren't working, so the Governor filed lawsuits. They didn't work either. And then, I guess, his job went to his head and he figured C'n Ben wouldn't have the nerve to stand up to him, so Governor Johnston *called out the National Guard* to occupy South Carolina Highway Department headquarters in Columbia and keep C'n Ben from getting into his own office.

I kid you not, the ol' cuss. (I know; Daddy wouldn't like my calling anybody a name, even a Governor. So forget I said it.)

They say C'n Ben called out the Highway Patrol in the Highway Commission's defense, but I don't know that for sure. Anyhow, the Patrolmen were only too glad to kind of bulge around the place with guns in their holsters.

It was a standoff.

Even the Governor could see he better give up his vendetta before any shooting started. None of his lawsuits, nor Governor Maybank's either, did what they intended. Ben Sawyer was still in office, and the Legislature, not the Governor, was still in control of highway money.

During Ben's time in charge, *our state's road miles doubled, and 2/3 of its miles got paved.* They were needed. Before the '30s, Cap says you couldn't get from the Pee Dee to Columbia in a car if it rained hard. You remember he took the children for their driver's tests during a dry spell.

Three days before Christmas in 1940, C'n Ben Sawyer died. He was in an exercise room -- alone, they said. He was there on schedule, getting in shape to go back on active duty at the beginning of World War II. His throat was crushed.

This book is not the place to go into strange and violent deaths.

C'n Ruth Simmons Sawyer lives in Orangeburg County again, 10 miles from Rowesville where she and Mother were born and mostly grew up.

After Ben was dead, the Legislature changed the law that designated license and gas taxes to go for roads improvement. No telling how long it'll take for any more roads to get paved, let alone here in the farming Pee Dee.

But Ben Sawyer made an almighty start; he did that. For awhile, South Carolina's roads were as good as any state's in the nation. As good or *better*.

The March 20, 1952, issue of the <u>News & Press</u> brought us up to date on what was going on in the County in law breaking and law enforcement.

The most popular lawbreaking activities here in Darlington County were (and still are)

      (1) "highway violations"

      (2) "drunk driving"

      (3) "disorderly conduct"

and (4) "liquor violations."

When you think about it, probly #4 has something to do with the frequency of all the others. Anyhow, Daddy read out the list to Mother and me at the dinner table and said he knows a man that violated all 4 at once:

The man – call 'im Bubba, which actually might be his name -- he started out having a drink or so too many at Griggs's store in the Antioch community. He left in his car (2) and sideswiped another car (1) on the way. Then Bubba got in a fight (3) with the other car's driver, who was a friend of his up 'til then.

Fighting tired Bubba out, so he decided to lie down. That's how come him to fall asleep in the setback.

Some colored men walked up and found him. They shook 'im, but he just grunted and kept laying there, they said. They walked on, came to a store that had a pay telephone, and spent a dime (which the police department refunded) to report it. The man ain't dead, they said, but his car's scraped up and maybe he's hurt.

That meant a deputy got a call to get up out of his bed and go see. By time he'd pulled on his official pants, even the hoot owls had got quiet. It was *late,* and him s'pose to go on duty early next morning.

When the deputy found out he'd been roused out of sleep just to tend to a drunk (4), he whipped his pad from his pocket and started writing.

Fines totaled almost $50, plus Bubba had to straighten out the other car's rear fender and re-attach its running board.

(I should warn you that Daddy enjoys making up parables about things that *could* have happened. This might've happened just this way and it might not. He didn't actually *say* the man was Bubba.)

"Liquor Violations" (#4) includes the illegal distilling of beverage alcohol. I didn't know much about liquor stills, only from hearsay, until Miss Owens' 8th Grade English class. She assigned us to write essays on how to make something, and a boy wrote on how to build a still. I think that's the first time I really noticed that boy. He'd come in from Lake Swamp School.

Miss Owens liked his essay so much, she had him read it to the class. He blushed a lot, but he did it. (Miss Owens blushed too, but blushing's her usual way; half the boys were in love with her.) She said this was the clearest how-to exposition in the entire class and she thought now she might be able to build a still herself.

That boy never built a still in his life; I know that now. Even yet he's not built a still. What's more, I happen to know Mr Francis Blackmon would not be happy in the least to have his son writing about stills, let alone standing up and reading it in front of 30-or-so people, because some of their kin sell liquor and could be suspected of knowing about stills first hand.

It sure was a good paper, though – *1 Plus.* I wrote about how to make an apple pie, and got a 90 (*2 Minus*), which is good considering I've never made one, no more than Wayne Hartwell Blackmon's ever built and run a still.

COUNTY

It's the job of the Sheriff's office not just to keep up with how much moonshining's going on but also to let the public know. The letting-know makes his office look busy and upright.

The 1951 count was 318 stills destroyed, with an average 400 gallons of mash confiscated per still.

1952 was the year I started paying attention to the monthly numbers. I started seeing how moonshining responds to the seasons.

Springtime is when family rations get slim, so more stills are likely to be fired up, found out, and busted up. (That's probly how "busted" came to mean *arrested and charged with a violation*. 'Course it means *dead broke* too.)

That April, the Law busted up 16 stills in the County.

In May, 27.

Then summer came on, with just 14 in June, 6 in July, and 11 in August. Summers, there's plenty work being hired for and done on farms, so there's less need for moonshining income.

The September report was 9 stills confiscated, 2 of them "big-time" and 7 small. White lightning plus 18,800 gallons of mash were destroyed and 14 gallons of whiskey seized, plus some 1,000-gallon vats belonging to the 2 big-timers.

Moonshiners in our county aren't really bad people. Sometimes they'll use contaminated equipment and a customer comes down with a case of lead poisoning, but whether a 'shiner gets caught is not considered major. Moonshining is against the law, but it's not up there in the Ten Commandments like Thou Shalt Not Kill.

In the summer of '52, local minds weren't much on just who was out in the woods cooking mash.

At the top of the front page with one of the still reports is a picture captioned "Darlington County Sheriff Force." I didn't pay a lot of attention to it that day, but since then I've studied that picture I bet 20 times. There's one man in paticlar I've looked at, searching the face.

These were the Deputies in the photograph:

182

COUNTY
Clyde Dudley
Duncan Huntley
Bill Scarborough
Coker O'Neal
Sam Chapman
Ed Bryant
H B Gainey
WW Copeland
Paul Beckham
E W Laney

Johnny Stokes, standing in the middle, was appointed Sheriff by Governor Byrnes on Senator "Spot" Mozingo's recommendation in January of '52. Before the end of the year, he had to run for the office he already had. Somebody was determined he *would not lose*. Somebodies, maybe.

Quite a few others ran for sheriff in '52, including 2 who were sheriff before and been soldiers in the War. The best qualified by a long shot was Wylie Grantham. It was Wylie's older brother "Red" that Daddy joined the Navy with in 1932; that's how good friends the families are. Not that we're prejudiced; just interested. I sure will be glad when I can vote, but that's 4 years away.

Primary's always in the summer, but the only Primary needed is for Democrats. In theory, you could have a Republican Primary, but any theoretical person brave or foolish enough to run in Darlington County as a Republican would have no opponent in the Primary. It'd be unusual even to have a Republican run. A 2nd Republican candidate would be a miracle.

In 1952, so many Democrats had lined up for Sheriff there had to be a run-off. It was between Wylie Grantham and Johnny Stokes.

From then until the run-off and all the way through the election, not a single issue of the N&P nor the Hartsville Messenger missed having a picture ad for Stokes. All those ads in every county newspaper and fliers everywhere must have cost somebody a fortune, not to mention money laid out for "expenses." Walking-around money, it's called.

183

COUNTY

I say "somebody" because Mr Stokes lives on the corner of Cashua and Spain, the next street over from Warley, in a house about the size of ours. He's not rich a bit, unless he's got a trunk like Aunt Ida's. He has a lot of children, which is riches in a way, but in 1952 they were still eating at his table.

It worked, all that outlay of money and whatever else. Johnny Stokes is Sheriff of Darlington County right today.

ASBURY MEN and OTHERS

Mr Thomas Rabb is one of Daddy's closest friends in the Asbury Sunday School Class. The men call him Rabb. Mr Rabb is a kind man of few words who appears to take life seriously.

One hard winter in the '40s, the classroom's old stove had got kind of dangerous, so the men came in to a chilly room most Sundays. One member of the class thought it was about time for that to stop, so he came up with a challenge. He said, "I'll match any amount all the rest of you together contribute today toward a stove."

The man was very well-to-do, as people put it. Prominent. Others in the class were less well-to-do, but most took out their wallets again and starting digging.

Mr Rabb, being the tall silent type, looks you over before he speaks. He looked the challenger over slow with his dark eyes and said, "Well Suh, looks like you and me just bought a stove."

That's one of the stories Daddy tells about their class. It's not the only story where Mr Rabb comes out to be a hero.

Mr Rabb's not a frequent smiler, but when he smiles, it's shy and lovely. He smiles the most when Mrs Rabb is around. And Daddy; Daddy can make him chuckle and almost laugh.

Mr Rabb owns Rabb's Packing Company. Just recently Daddy drew up plans for their new refrigeration wing for hanging sides of meat and oversaw putting it in. Now he says he could build a house so tight that if you took out an ice cube, you'd have to put on a sweater. To raise the temperature you'd just light a match.

"What about fresh air?" I said. If there's anything old houses have going for 'em, it's fresh air.

"Hmmm. Well, I guess we won't build it." And Daddy laughed.

Daddy's laugh starts as an audible grin and turns into pure happiness. Dr John Wilson, who 'course knows all about

185

COUNTY

Daddy's fused back, told me Daddy's the most successful man he knows. He surely can't mean money; he must mean the happiest.

Mrs Rabb was Grace Dawkins. She and her sister Madge grew up in the tall white Victorian house beside the old Trinity Cemetery on Orange Street and became lovely laughing ladies. Madge is Mrs Dana now, with a little boy named Dwight, and Grace Dawkins Rabb and Mother are maybe best friends. They go to the Rabbs' beach house together and cook and walk on the beach and giggle a lot. They're both good gigglers. Sometimes they take me and Barbara, if we don't stay at their house with her sisters Lou and Madge and Tootsie and their brother Calvin that we all call Sonny. Thomas Jr is grown and on his own.

Mrs Rabb says beach water (it's what comes through faucets in beach houses) makes the best-tasting grits in the world. She even brings some back to Darlington in a gallon jug for cooking. The water's kind of gray; you hold your nose when you shower in it. But I have to admit, Mrs Rabb's grits are delicious. Most of us eat grits mornings and lots of suppertimes.

I first met Barbara in Miz Inez Ward's Sunday School Class for Toddlers, with Miz Elizabeth Conder standing at the back of the room with a yardstick to make sure we behaved. Miz Conder is tall and handsome, wears her dark brown hair in a bun, and can give you a *look* every bit as paralyzing as Cap's or Mr Cain's. The yardstick was covered in a pretty-colored soft felt jacket but the look wasn't. We tried to remember to behave.

Barbara was my best schoolfriend through 3rd Grade, before I skipped 4th. When you're not in the same grade, other friends get important. Still, Barbara and I love each other and I'll bet we always, always will. No need for a blood exchange like in <u>Tom Sawyer</u>; we just *will*.

Daddy's other special men friends at Trinity are most of them in the Asbury Class. Mother's in the Ladies' class. There's classes that have men and women both, but those 2 are huge. The ladies' class has 63, and they most of them come. They keep asking Mother to be an officer, saying everybody's

186

s'posed to take a turn. She says she'll do the telephoning the rest of her life rather than be in charge.

Maybe Daddy's *best* Darlington friend, the one he stops by his office during the day and spends the most time with, is John Kilgo. He's lived here all his life, and his people before that. He has Kilgo Oil Company.

Mr Kilgo is married to Caroline Maner Lawton. Isn't that a distinguished sounding name? He brought her here. She was (instantly, I bet) recognized as the most beautiful woman in Darlington. And such a lady. She acts like she doesn't know even how gorgeous her eyes are, like blue pieces of heaven. I don't think she *does* know.

Mrs Kilgo told me that when she married and came here, that very first Sunday, John ushered her all the way down the center aisle of Trinity Church to the front pew on the right, stood while she seated herself, took his place at the end, and turned to the opening hymn. (Each Sunday's selections are up on the walls on handsome handmade wooden hymn boards.) When they stood with the congregation, she felt every eye on her. About 300 eyes that would've been, most Sundays. No – 600, assuming 2 per person, and I'll almost guarantee you she was not just imagining.

On the way home she asked him, "John, does your family always sit where we sat today?"

He looked at her with affection. "Yes," he said. "Why?"

"Well I mean, now that we're a new family, our own family you could say, d'you think could we sit somewhere else next time? Somewhere … not right up front?"

He looked at her mildly – tolerantly, she thought -- and answered her carefully with these exact words: *"I've sat in that pew all my life and I don't see any reason to change."*

That, Mrs Kilgo says, is when she realized how some people feel about their *pew.*

Marion DeWitt runs Dixie Cup – Superintendent, he's called, like Mr Ken Hauck was before he got promoted to Pennsylvania. I don't think Mr DeWitt being in the same Sunday School class with Daddy has a thing to do with me being hired there for this coming summer; I really do *not*. Joyce Anne got her job there first, and they're Central Baptists.

Mr DeWitt is like a lot of leaders of Darlington today: a military veteran. He was a Captain under General Patton -- "Patton's Army." This town is full of heroes.

Mrs DeWitt is a Florence County lady, a Pamplico Coleman. (She says she's really from Hyman, a suburb of Pamplico. Pamplico is *full* of Colemans.) Margaret Coleman DeWitt is beautiful -- tall and more stately than pretty, if you know what I mean. The more I'm around her, the more I notice how fine she looks.

I once hoped to become stately. I might've made it if I'd kept growing tall the way I started out and if my hair was straight enough to put up in a bun. I tried a pony tail for awhile, which straightened it out *some*, but I got tired of fooling with rubber bands. I'll just have to make up my mind not to be stately.

D. L. Holley is our County Superintendent of Schools.

I'm fixing to say the nicest thing I could say about *any*body, and it's true:

If I couldn't have Daddy as my father, I'd want a chance at Mr Holley.

Mr Holley moved here as Principal of St John's Grammar School when I was starting 4th Grade. One of the first things he did was give permission for me, Nancy, and Hubie to skip 4th grade, provided our parents didn't object. Mother and Daddy didn't, and neither did the Rogersons. Hubie Thompson's did, so he didn't get to skip, which guaranteed he'd stay the tallest in his class for *years* and get picked on.

I didn't know about the grade-skipping 'til the 2nd week of school, the very morning Mr Holley came into Miz Baxley's classroom, handed her some papers, and took me out of 4th Grade into 5th. With no warning to me *whatsoever*.

Mother and Daddy are like other parents: they most of them trust school absolutely. If we get in trouble there, we're in trouble at home. I guess mine figured the school would tell me whatever it wanted me to know about me skipping a grade or whatever else it had in mind whenever it wanted me to know it.

188

That's how I came to be plunked down in 5th Grade in total ignorance. Turned out the only big thing Mrs Shepherd, Mrs Davis, and Miss West hadn't taught me in 1st, 2nd, and 3rd grades was Long Division. That must be what 4th Grade is for.

It was *kind* of scary. But it turned out Long Division is Short Division, just longer. I wish I could've learned typing that quick.

Ginny Holley's a college Senior now and a born leader. She was President of our MYF and then MYF State President. Lester won the Soap Box Derby and got to race in Indianapolis. He plays quarterback for the Blue Devils, went to Boys' State (there's no such of a thing as Girls' State), and now he's our Class President. I doubt anybody is more popular than Ginny and Lester. They've both got Mr Holley's kind eyes and nice ways.

Mrs Holley is in the Ladies' Class. She's even smaller than Mother, speaks quietly, and has a nice smile. Smiles matter a lot, I think, but I doubt the class could talk her into being president either.

T C Kistler the Undertaker is the tallest and biggest man in the Asbury Class, with the best singing voice and a kind, kind look. He came home from World War II and is taking over management of his family's funeral home. Mr Kistler his father is Darlington County Coroner and owns the funeral home. It's a handsome white house – almost a mansion -- beside the Presbyterian Church, corner of Pearl and Edwards Avenue.

T C didn't come home alone, not by a long shot. He brought him a wife from Czechoslovakia, a blonde. She's an accomplished musician -- pianist, organist, *and* (would you believe it) *a composer*. She also plans to write books -- novels set in South Carolina -- to be published in her home country in the Czech language. Considering that she knows nothing much about South Carolina and less about South Carolinians, it's a good thing they'll be novels. Novels don't have to have a word of truth in 'em. Besides, nobody in Darlington will get to read them, so nobody'll be mad.

Such an accomplished, well educated lady, and now a Darlingtonian – sort of. But there's a problem with her fitting in, even if she decided she wanted to: to her we're a horde of uncultured barbarians.

189

COUNTY

How do I know the younger Mrs Kistler finds us culturally lacking? Just have a conversation with her and you'll know too.

It does bother me some that C'n Lillian Fair is the only other Darlingtonian as educated in music or any other art as Vera, and neither one is *from* here. . Where are our highly educated local *artistes*?   Maybe we in the Pee Dee do need to learn more art, music, and literature to be able to converse with the younger Mrs Kistler of Eastern Europe.

To C'n Lillian Fair we're not barbarians, though. Even if she thought so, she'd never let on. She's a South Carolinian. Manners, you know. Even if she did think so and said it, she'd be talking about herself. She's *from* here – this state anyhow.

T C would never distress anybody intentionally. Sure he killed Germans in the War, but that's different, and over with, and a case of have-to. It was do it or die.

T C is a fine baritone and can sing bass when needed. Could be that's what brought him and Vera together overseas – music. And the fact that the US Army rescued her entire region from Hitler.

Our choir would be in a pickle without T C, even with Miss Rosa McCall as organist and Mrs Huckabee (Raymond's mother) and Vera that substitute when needed and Patsy Sturgeon that's learning, plus Mrs Pope as star soprano. It takes a strong baritone to stand up to Mrs Pope's volume.

Because Daddy works right in people's houses and businesses, he knows practicly everybody, not just the ones at Trinity Methodist Church. He likes people, and they like to be around him, specially if they've got a sense of humor. It's not so much that Daddy *tells* jokes. He hardly ever does. But he *laughs* at jokes. He has this wonderful laugh that gets into his eyes and his whole self.

Sometimes when he's had a beer or a mixed drink, he thinks everything is funny. That's when Mother gets impatient.

One day she sent me into the Carolina Furniture Company by myself while she waited in the car. Daddy hooks up appliances for Mr Boykin's customers. When the manager Clyde Spivey's off, he works for Daddy installing appliances, like on Wednesday afternoons. That's when all the stores close and give clerks the afternoon off. I was just little then, but she told me to go into Carolina Furniture and tell Daddy to come on.

"Those men are not doing a thing in there but telling jokes and drinking," Mother said to me. We were parked at the curb. "I can hear George laughing all the way out here." She'd finished shopping and was ready to get back to the Sand Hill, plus she really detests drinking. We'd all come in the car; it was a good while before Daddy had got the army-green use-to-be-telephone truck.

He didn't come on, though, so she said to go tell him again.

I wish I hadn't gone and called him, though, even once. Clyde Spivey and Mr Linton Boykin and Daddy were having a good time together. It wouldn't've hurt Mother and me to wait.

Daddy didn't talk a bit on the way home.

Daddy's best Negro friend is Roosevelt Goodson.. He's with Darlington Construction Company, so he works for the Psilloses. Roosevelt's an expert concrete finisher.

In spite of his name, Roosevelt must not be a Democrat. He and Daddy can talk politics and religion or whatever, and always end up agreeing. Why, is they're both conservatives, which means they take each person as a separate person who has to be respected or disrespected according to how he acts, not what group he claims to belong to.

Freedom has to go along with that. Neither one of them thinks we have enough freedom in Darlington County. They hate that some people get favors and others get k.... others get bad treatment.

Democrats run everything here and always have, ever since soon after the War Between the States. The Union Army's marauding and burning made everybody so mad down here, Negroes and Whites both have voted Democrat ever since. It's only now they're beginning to see how much power having only one Party gives the top officeholders in each County. Daddy and Roosevelt think the State has to get back to a 2-party system somehow, and they think General Eisenhower opened the way when he decided to be a Republican after winning WWII. That's the kind of talking Roosevelt and Daddy do – that and helping each other out with work and stuff. They don't mind me listening.

Roosevelt Goodson is a very handsome person, with high cheekbones like some Indians in pictures I've seen – dignified like that. Mr Rabb claims Indian heritage too, so so does Barbara. She says Rabb probly use to be Rabbit, to fit with the outdoorsy names of their People.

I don't know of any pure-bred Indians right near here, but there're lots in the Upstate and just over the line in North Carolina. Aunt Myrtis Dukes Johnson in Red Springs has an Indian who lives in her back yard and takes care of the grounds, but he's prejudiced and scares her cook away. He's got rid of 3 so far, she says, and he won't leave, and Dr Johnson won't make him leave because where would he go. (She calls him Dr Johnson, so so do we all. It's a holdover from when she secretaried for him after they got married.) Aunt Myrtis has to fold her lips and look for a new cook each time the yardman goes on the warpath and clears out the kitchen. This latest cook might stay, though. She looks to me like she might push back as hard as she gets pushed.

Mrs Roosevelt Goodson -- Virginia -- is handsome like her husband, and gracious and friendly like him. Their children seem nice, but they're younger than I am and of course go to Mayo. The oldest boy, Roosevelt Jr, goes by the name of Bunny, which I expect'll change as he gets older. I doubt they know Mr Cain, or I spect they'd pick another nickname.

Another of Daddy's best friends is Gus Demetriou, who talks with a Greek accent because he's from Greece.

Gus is what everybody around town calls him and what he says for people to call him, but Daddy says for me to call him Mr Demetriou.

Mr Demetriou owns the hot dog stand that's built onto the side of the tobacco warehouse on Main at the train track. If you want a really good hotdog, that's where to go. People call it Gus's or "the Greek's." Say "Let's go get a Greek hotdog" or "a Gus dog," and everybody knows what you mean. Mouths start to water just thinking about it.

What makes them wonderful, if you ask *me*, is the bun warmer.

When you order, Sanders (Gus brought him over from Greece) slices open the buns and presses them just so

192

between the warm metal plates of a bun-pressing machine. He stands there and probly counts, because they come out the same every time: perfect. Soft and just the slightest bit moist.

Then he slaps just the right amount of mustard (and ketchup if you ask for it) inside as a bed, puts in a baked weenie, and hands the hotdog to the helper lady.

She puts in slaw and chili (they make their own; everybody does, but theirs is just the right spicy) and whatever else you say you want, most likely diced onions and pickle relish.

Through the walk-up window, you hand the lady 15 cents, plus a nickel for your drink. They hand your order out to you, with your hotdog in a made-for-it, pleated, white-paper trough.

Ordinarily people order outside and eat in their pickup truck, but you can come in and sit in a booth or at the counter on a leather seat on a shiny chrome stool. When I was little I'd go round and round on mine, trusting somebody to say "Quit" and stop the stool before I got dizzy and fell off. Somebody always did, thank goodness, usually Daddy.

If you come inside, you get a dill pickle slice and some potato chips on the plate, no extra charge.

Daddy does all Gus's electric work.

Gus told Daddy he might have to raise his hot dog price to a quarter, and some drinks have gone to a dime, which would make 35 cents in all and might lose him some business.

"Go ahead," Daddy said. "They'll still come. They know nobody's hotdogs are as good as yours, and you can't cheat yourself and stay in business. There's your overhead every day. Power's not free, and neither am I and neither is the rest of your help -- 'specially if you have to send to Greece for it."

And he and Gus just *laugh*.

Not that it's so funny, far as anybody else can see, but they just like being together that much.

When Daddy went to the hospital with a kidney attack, Mr Demetriou sent flowers *every day*. Kidney stone operations take a long time to get over, and pretty soon we had to set flowers on the floor. When Daddy got out, we took the latest ones around to rooms that didn't have any. I've never seen a more generous man than Mr Demetriou. When he likes you, he *likes* you.

The actual name of Mr Demetriou's place is the Carolina Lunch. They even serve meals. There's 3 nice booths tucked in at the far end of the counter next to the restrooms. Gus comes and sits with us when everything's running smooth.

Eating at the Carolina Lunch is a treat. We don't eat anywhere much but home, 'cept when we go to Sister and Ellison's in Cottageville for Thanksgiving, and in Rowesville whenever the Dukeses or the Boones get together or we're at Mama and Papa's.

Uncle Bob's friend Edwin Turner has Turner's Chicken Basket, a really nice restaurant out the other side of Florence -- on Irby Street almost to Cole's Crossroads. We go there sometimes. One time Mother ordered the Danish Lobster Tail dinner. It's their most expensive 'cept for "Fillet Mignon 3.00." Someday I hope to go and order a fillet. Anything costing that much has got to taste amazing.

There's another man I didn't mention when I was talking about the church, but he was in the Asbury Bible Class with Daddy and them. He was called "Red" -- Red Watts. He was Daddy's same age.

I didn't know him all that well, but I doubt I'll ever be able to forget him.

He's not there any more.

Teachers Good and Scary

St John's has got some scary teachers, but I want to start off by telling about a good one: Jane McIver. (Say McEEver. The Scots say i's like we say long e's.)

McIver's a local name. There're plenty of Scottish names around here, like ours: Spears that's spelled Spiers in Scotland but pronounced *spears* just like we say it.

Mrs McIver married in; she's from Pennsylvania. Instead of "hey" when she meets you in the hall, she says "hi," only she says it fast and pronounces it "hah-ee." She told us that when she came to South Carolina, she'd be startled whenever somebody on the street said "hey." She thought it meant she was doing something wrong; like it was the beginning of "Hey, quit that."

Yankees speak English but not really *our* English. They don't even say "I reckon." We do and so do the English, the Irish, and the Scots, but not Yankees. Mrs McIver's not really a Yankee any more, though; she's great -- dark-haired and nice and *interesting*.

Mrs McIver's course in American government is an eye-opener.

The first day in Democracy class, she told us the course is named wrong. She told us it ought to be titled "US Government" because the USA is *not* a democracy; it's a republic, and the class is on how the whole American government works, plus the states and even Darlington County.

She's *good*. She woke me up and made me care about our system of government. Then she said this: most states have more than one political party.

Now I realize why whoever named the course got it wrong: growing up in the Solid South he'd only ever heard of Democrats.

What I remember her saying on Day One is this:

COUNTY
"'Democracy' is a class about the political system of the United States. Our nation, however, is not a democracy. It's a republic.

"We vote for our representatives and send them to Washington, or to Columbia if they're state officials, and they vote instead of us. We ourselves seldom vote on issues directly. We elect others to vote for us.

"We hope our elected officials will vote responsibly; we can tell them what we want them to do, and they're supposed to listen because we sent them there and theoretically we can refuse to send them back. We're the voters, and elected officials can be replaced.

"You are soon going to be voters. Living in a free nation means you have a duty to learn how to function in a republic.

"The reason we cannot function as a democracy is that there are so many of us who know how to read and write and let our wants and opinions be known. Also, we're a huge nation, spread from sea to sea. We couldn't possibly all gather at the same place; nor could we all be heard if we did. Our elected representatives go instead of all of us. As I said, they are supposed to discuss, debate, and then vote their understanding of how the majority of the people who elected them would vote if they were there to hear the discussion. Failing that, they are supposed to vote their conscience.

"The United States was founded on the concept that every voter is equal in value to every other voter, which is the democratic ideal. Therefore you can call us a democratic republic, if you like; that's accurate. As you know from history classes, that's what Thomas Jefferson called the party he founded and believed in: the Democratic Republican Party.

"Remember, the United States is a republic."

And here I am, living in a state filled with life-long Democrats as far as the human eye can see. A few farmers think outside the crowd, like Daddy and Roosevelt Goodson and the Williamsons, but they're too few to be heard.

I went home that day enlightened but puzzled. Why is every elected official in Darlington County and I guess in the whole State a Democrat?

Even if she hadn't taught me another thing that whole year, I learned more in one day in Mrs McIver's class than I remember learning in that short a time in anybody else's.

196

That's when I got ready not to have my thinking done for me by politicians any more.

Mrs Jay Ervin, known to her friends and her husband's multitudinous relatives as "Mary Jay Ervin," is my favorite history teacher of all time because not only does she know history, she also brings her subject alive by quoting from great writers of what we call literature.

Let's face it: history books are usually dull. The great writers aren't the ones who write history for classroom use. About the only way you can keep your mind from wandering off is to take ceaseless notes or to underline, and then if you don't get it erased, you can't sell your history book back at the end of the year.

Mrs Ervin taught me American History, which is what we most of us take when we're Juniors. Colin Jordan was a Senior but he was in that class too, and kept turning around to talk. Mrs Ervin was on top of that the minute she saw his head turn. So he got in the habit of slouching back and leaving one hand on top of my desk (they're all connected, front to back) and when I took a notion to, I'd write on his hand. But I'm falling off the subject.

Mrs Ervin wouldn't bring in literature just by quoting lines; she'd *declaim* them, the way contestants did in the high school Declamation Contests they'd bring us in from grammar school to hear. There was a tall red-headed girl – an Howle, I think -- who chose an Edgar Allan Poe story. I still remember how wild and low-pitched and crazy she declaimed that final line: "It's the beating of his hideous heart!"

Back when Mrs Ervin was in high school, I bet *she* won their Declamation Contest every single year.

Say we'd get to Indians: she'd have lines ready from Hiawatha -- "By the shores of Gitchee-Gumee [or however you spell it] / By the shining Big-Sea Water / Stood the wigwam of Nokomis -- Daughter of the Moon, Nokomis -- "

Say we'd get to a famous battle; she'd have a poem ready: "Into the jaws of hell / Into the valley of death / Rode the 600!" It didn't have to be American literature, you see; she knows it *all*.

Say you had a ship at sea; she'd bring in "The Ancient Mariner" for sure, and some Moby Dick. I can't wait to read

197

Moby Dick this summer. Even though Mrs Ervin says it tells more about cutting up whales' bodies than she ever wanted to know, still it must be interesting, with Queequeg and his coffin that he sleeps in every night after he happens not to die, and obsessed Ahab, and "Call me Ishmael" like Hagar and Abraham's wandering son.

I love a teacher who makes me hungry to learn more and to read more, and shows me where I can find the good stuff.

And then there's the other type of teacher entirely. Or rather, the other types. Just like there's more than one way to be a good teacher, there's more than one way to be a bad teacher.

You don't talk back to teachers, and you expect them to respect you too. You know they *know* more about their subjects than you do, but you also know they're not necessarily *smarter* than you are. Before long you can tell which are and which aren't, but you can learn from every one of 'em. They've completed a college major or they wouldn't be teaching in high school.

Helping us use our minds better, that's the most important job of any teacher, far as I'm concerned -- that and giving us accurate facts to think *with*. But I don't want them trying to tell me *what* to think. If I'm ever a teacher, I'll always respect a student's need to think.

Here I am, sounding like I'll be a teacher. I'm *not*.

The worst teacher I had at St John's was never even my teacher. She had me in Homeroom one year, which is not a subject. But I still call her the worst because she plays favorites. A teacher that picks pets and enemies, watch out.

What this paticlar teacher did to me didn't turn out to be all that important really: she made sure the teachers' committee didn't choose me into National Honor Society as soon as others in our class did.

Until right after the NHS election when Mrs Ervin warned me to steer clear of her, I didn't know that paticlar teacher ever thought about me one way or the other. I certainly wasn't wasting much thought on her when Mrs Ervin caught me in the hall and told me I hadn't been chosen for National Honor. Mrs

E said she'd expected me to make it as soon as Nancy and Edwin and Mac and anybody else did, but that I hadn't been elected. And that if that paticlar teacher hadn't argued against me getting in, I would've made it easy.

"Character" is listed equal to grades, so maybe she said I have a bad character; maybe that's how she shot me down. I really don't know, and I didn't want to ask Mrs Ervin, who probly was sticking her neck out even to say anything to me, specially before other students knew the results of the choosing.

I went on down the hall feeling a kind of cold chill. I don't think I even thanked Mrs Ervin, I was so confused. Did teachers do mean things like that in public? Yes, they must. This one sure did. And I'm not her first victim.

What made her go against me, assuming it's not just because she's a snob (she *is* a snob; anybody can tell that just from the way she walks down the hall), might be this:

She knows I don't like her. And she knows it's because in Homeroom I saw and heard her do something really mean to Bobby Smith. She saw me looking surprised while she was doing it. I'm not good at hiding my reactions; I don't try, really. I think it's better for people to know who you really are, so why pretend. (Which'll probly dog me my whole life.)

That day she threatened to have her sister who works in Washington DC fix it so Bobby won't be able to get a good job after graduation. I missed the start of whatever went on between her and Bobby, but I remember her threatening him with her powerful sister in the Government.

At home I asked Daddy if Mrs [blank] really has a sister in Washington, and can somebody who works in the Government really hurt a student's future? Daddy knows her whole family; her brother and sister-in-law are his customers. That might be part of her snobbishness: my father repairs appliances. I needn't say that to him. He didn't grow up poor; he grew up as a farmer's son. He says to never dignify snobbery by recognizing it.

So I asked him, and he frowned and kept frowning. He finally said, "Yes, her sister does work in Washington, and no teacher ought to threaten a boy that way. The fact that there's probly no truth in what she said is not the point. Point is how it affects Bobby, like leaving him with a bad feeling about school."

199

I don't know what effect she had on Bobby. I didn't want to let him know I'd heard.

I made NHS the next semester. Not because I had any better record; I didn't. And I probly had a worse attitude by then, once I found out that some bad teachers are not just bad, they're bullies. I bet when she was a girl in school, she longed to be a bully but nobody was interested. Now she's got the power. It's good that snobs don't go into nursing; a snobbish teacher is bad enough.

No need to give you her name. I never even told Daddy about her keeping me out of National Honor. He'd've maybe gotten mad, which he almost never does.

Miz Lucile Edwards is a completely different case. Her problem is, she doesn't like us – any of us. Far as I can tell, there's not a one of us she likes as much as she likes algebra, and I'm not sure she even likes *it* on her bad days.

Nancy Rogerson is a math whiz. I'm not bad at it, but I don't like it. You can *learn* a subject, but it's hard to *like* a subject when you're put off by whoever teaches it.

Miss Carolyn Rogerson in Senior math, I've got no problem with. What she does is teach; she's not emotionally involved with math nor us either. If you get it, you get it; if you don't, you flunk. I can handle that and respect it as fair. No favorites played, and no craziness.

But Miz Edwards, she's kind of a crazy woman. I had her for Arithmetic my 1st year in high school and again for Algebra.

I wasn't good at Algebra nor bad either; I was there in the middle. It was the ones who were either good or bad, specially the ones who were super good and actually liked math, like Nancy Rogerson (no relation to Miss Rogerson in Senior Math), that Miz Edwards seemed to kind of hate. Nancy specially.

Miss Rogerson, she puts problems on the board herself in Plane Geometry and Solid Geometry and Trigonometry, and we can ask questions about how she worked them if we want to, but going to the board's not the big thing.

In Miz Edwards' class, though, seems like we were sent to the board all the time. She'd stand at the back of the room, pleating and unpleating the pull cord and staring out the window while the ones at the board were sweatin' bullets. That's how

200

she teaches. She must've explained things sometimes, but I honestly don't remember it. I read in the book and did the homework, and in class I did my best to lie low.

Not Nancy. Nancy waved her hand to get to answer up or put a problem on the blackboard. No bull; that's what she did.

One day she got a problem wrong. Anyhow Miz Edwards said it was wrong. And it might've been, for all I know.

Nancy argued. She turned around toward the board, still arguing, to show Miz Edwards how she was doing it right. (Nancy wears loose unbuttoned cardigans; they're her thing.) Miz Edwards reared back and threw an eraser at her so hard it left an upright chalk mark the exact image of the eraser on the back of Nancy's sweater. Right in the *middle*.

You don't want to mess with a teacher with a throwing arm like that, not when she's liable to use it at you.

I've finally found a math I like, right here at the last, when I'll never have it again. It's Geometry. It's got shapes and logic and makes total sense to me. The only thing I really liked in Miz Edwards' class was word problems. Trains approaching each other, sacks of different weights, towns x far apart, rivers to cross.

I hear there's a math in college called Calculus. I hope if I meet it in a classroom, there'll be nobody throwing erasers if I get it wrong.

OUR MUSIC

Remembering:
Mid-afternoon in the Dixie Home Store parking lot, across from St Matthews Episcopal Church. I'm 14. I'm sitting in the driver's seat of our mint-green '53 Ford, listening to music on the radio and waiting for Mother to come out with groceries.

Out of the clear blue sky descends one of the most meaningful moments in my musical life.

I had my license (finally!) and was in the driver's seat because Mother doesn't much like driving anyhow. I was playing the car radio, the way anybody would, and there it came:

Heartbreak Hotel.

I felt my heart rise into my throat.

It was perfect; it *is* perfect.   Love that's left only pain; bleakness that won't allow release; an invisible wound; the urge to hide among the other silent wounded; universal sorrow – all in a melody and words that try to speak for a heart too stunned for anything but tears.

Ah love and loss! Ah universal sorrow!

Nobody had to say, "Girl, that is a song never heard by you before and a voice never heard by you before, but you'll never forget either one." I *knew.*

I started digging through the car pocket and under the seats and everywhere and wouldn't you know, I couldn't find a scrap of paper to write anything on, even if the only pencil I found hadn't been broken off halfway down. My brain was doing its best to memorize the words. I was in a sweat for the record not to end before I could get them all in my head.

Because it was so *good.*

I didn't know a thing about Elvis, not even what color he is. I was kind of guessing he was a Negro because I never heard a

White man sing like that before. Not that I'd ever heard *anybody* sing like that before, but everybody I've heard singing on the radio has been one race or the other and I thought I had to make *some* kind of guess so I could find the singer and the song again.

The name Elvis gave me no clue; I'd never heard it before. Was he from some other country? Couldn't be; not a sign of a Yankee twang, and no foreign sound. Elvis sang Southern.

The record ended.

I didn't know whether to change the station in hopes of coming up on it, or to leave the dial there and hope the disc jockey would tell me something – anything (I hadn't even caught the last name) or what. I just kept singing what I could remember so I wouldn't forget what words I knew.

You'd think, crazy as I am about music and as many songs as I already know by heart, words so wonderful and imaginative and haunting as "Heartbreak Hotel" would just've engraved themselves on my spirit. But it hadn't happened, not all of them. I couldn't wait to hear "Heartbreak Hotel" again.

Then Mother came out of the Dixie Home and first thing she did was change the station to Bing Crosby or Frank Sinatra or some other crooner. Not that it mattered; Elvis was gone from the airwaves. Elvis was all I could think about; his sound, his song.

I had to have that record.

I'm not saying everybody was as impressed right away when they heard Elvis, but I was.

Next morning at school all I could talk about was "Heartbreak Hotel." One of the people I generally talk to is Wayne Blackmon because he somehow finds things out before I do. Turned out I guessed wrong: Elvis is White.

Whatever color -- purple, plaid, or transparent -- Elvis sounds perfect. Southern for sure. And a man's voice, I'm telling you; the voice of a *man,* Man.

Since then, Wayne's picked another singer to like: J R Richardson, the Big Bopper. 'Course the Bopper's not better than Elvis, nobody is, but the Bopper's good and he's from Texas. Wayne's a nut about Texas. He saw a lot of Westerns on Saturdays like Eltas Jean and me.

COUNTY

The Bopper and a lot of other new singers are just riding on Elvis's coattails, is what I think. I won't say that to Wayne, though; I don't want to make him mad. He hardly knows I'm in the world anyhow.

This is some of what I found out about Elvis:

He grew mostly up in a tiny shotgun house in Tupelo, Mississippi, that his daddy built by hand. He had one brother but he died, so Elvis is almost an only child. He got use to singing in church, which is what you'd expect of good Christian people. Right before he got famous, he was singing in a roadhouse for teenagers called the Louisiana Hayride. (Say LOOzy-anna.)

Once he started making records that got played on the radio, Elvis was instantly recognized as a musical genius who had blended the South into song. (Anyhow, that's what I say he did -- and keeps doing.) He's got our maverick country sounds and the sounds of both races (we all sing in our churches) and down-home sassiness and deep-down feeling for another human being and sorrow and loss and church-going and the way you feel when you pray in need. Where else in the world could he've come from but here? Rye-cheer, as we say at St John's, mainly to get English teachers' goat.

Somebody told the most famous showman on tv about Elvis, and Ed met Elvis and liked him a lot in spite of what he'd heard about Elvis' dancing, so (poof! it felt like) Elvis was on the Ed Sullivan Show.

I was watching, naturally. The whole world should 've been. It was like watching the world shift.

I remember that first night, Mr Sullivan called Elvis "a nice young man." And he is. You can see it 100 ways. Elvis Presley signed up to serve his country in the Army when he could 've been making thousands -- or millions, if you can make millions singing -- by not interrupting his stardom. But he up and left his brand-new mansion in Memphis, Tenn., and went into service. Elvis has that clear a sense of God and Country. I hope show business doesn't hurt him, he's so real, so actual. He even gives away new cars to reglar people and says nothing about it. I hope to be able to give a car to somebody who needs one someday. Not a new one, a dependable one like I'd want to drive myself.

204

COUNTY

Even though Mr Sullivan saw right away that Elvis is a good boy, he fretted over the way Elvis moves his body while he's singing. He solved that problem by not showing him on tv from the waist down. The human body is synchronized, so you knew anyhow what was going on. You can't just loosen yourself from your own hips.

Elvis is like us and 'most everybody else our age; he moves with the music. There's nothing dirty about the dancing Elvis does, far as I can tell. Northerners just aren't use to the rhythms of the South. Or they weren't until Elvis.

Thanks to Ed Sullivan and Elvis, our Southern country sounds are getting out to the rest of the world. You hear people say, "Soon, every band'll have to have a guitar. Don't, and they'll be nowhere." Good thing guitars are light and don't cost like pianos.

Strummers and singers are all over the place. Most don't ask for pay; they come ready to play their hearts out, aiming (I guess) for the big time, whatever the big time turns out to be. Meanwhile, other boys slap 'em on the back and buy 'em beer, and girls sit with their chins on their hands and gaze, each one imagining the song's meant for her. Every singer and player and songwriter wants to be on the radio or tv now, I guess, 'stead of doing what they do mainly for the music's sake.

I'm not the only one in the Spears family that takes music seriously; we've got Saidee's husband Win, who's been in the family almost as long as I have. He plays piano by ear, and he's always composing songs for Saidee and my cousins Dick and Rizzie.

Uncle Win's in the Air Force; stayed in after the War ended. He's working on a novel now. He's never written one, but he's sure he can. That's pretty unusual for a military officer. Add writing music, and he might even be unique.

Last year Eagle Books published <u>Winston in Wonderland</u>, which is not a novel; it's a true book, kind of a comedy. I've read it. There's funny parts, but we aren't so sure the higher-ups'll think so. It's not a novel and might be a little too real and uncomplimentary about how things work (or don't) at The Pentagon, a place he got really tired of before he was reassigned. He may've written it as a boredom antidote. For men in uniform during WWII, the Cold War's pretty tame so far.

Uncle Win''s been sending his songs to Jo Stafford. He thinks she's the best. She didn't take any yet, but she might. She can sing any style of song, country or city, and make it sound good.

So if one day you hear the name Winston Estes as a songwriter, that'll be Uncle Win. Or a novelist either.

We sing together, some of us at St John's, after school at each other's houses. Not usually Elvis songs; he's too good to imitate.

So is Johnny Mathis, really. His voice is like cream -- smooth, tenor cream. Nobody sings a creamy song any better. Like this:

(Read from left to right, the way you normally do, but don't expect to stay on one level. Lower notes are lower than higher notes, so go down for the down words and up for the up. I went to a lot of trouble to plan this out, in case you don't know the melody already. The *ly* *-he* on the next page is NOT a typo.)

```
                              wear
Chan      are ,   though              a
     ces                  I              sil-
                                             ly
                                                grin


                         come            view,
                    you        in
the          ment                  to
     mo


              you
         are      think
     ces              that
Chan                   I'm
                          in
                             love
                                 with
                                     you
```

Then listen to the Platters. "Only You" is just as loving in its message as "Chances Are," but the Platters don't sing it that way. They're not conveying feeling; they're mostly giving out sound because what they *do* is dance music. A song's a gig to them, so their style's easier to imitate.

Here's a few lines. Shiver your voice and draw some words out, and then spring away from some other words like you're kicking away from a diving board:

```
        youuuuu              the
                       make[!]
      ly          can-nuh        daaark[!]
On                                      ness
                                           light.



       Hone!     you
Oh        ly-    hoo
          he          hoo
                     can-nuh   [etc etc etc]...
```

The dancing you do to the Platters is different, too. When some of us were at the Booth farm and Vivian's mama was watching us dance, she said, "Some of y'all, far as I can see, it's no dancing to it. You *don't* dance, you just lay up there and twitch."

I figure she was comparing slow dancing to the Charleston or the Black Bottom or some dance from her generation. I can't imagine it, but she must've been a Flapper, like Mother. Which is hard to imagine too — those long beads flapping around and little patent-leather heels kicking up.

Actually that must've been fun.

But my cousin Lillian Fair's music might be the best even though it's way different from ours. It's been around for centuries, before anybody here was born. Famous composers from all over the world wrote it.

COUNTY

Hers is music grownups dress up and go out to sit in auditoriums in reglar towns and concert halls in big cities to hear, and come out talking about the performance and the *repertoire*. (That's one of those words I took French so I could pronounce.)

Lilllian's kind of music is called classical.

Classical music will go on forever. One sign of that is, its melodies keep coming back in popular music. The composers didn't put in words, and if they had, the words wouldn't usually've been English and weren't necessary anyhow because it's the music that speaks. Today's songwriters take those tunes and put in words. Most people my age didn't grow up around classical music, including me, so to us it's all new.

Even without words, a given piece of classical music can speak clearly. When we hear the William Tell Overture, 90% of the US population (everybody with a radio) will think right away of the Lone Ranger galloping up on the Great Horse Silver with a silver bullet, and yet most of those don't know they've ever heard any part of the William Tell Overture.

Darlington has ladies who teach piano and voice. C'n Lillian taught, but then she retired and spent her time inspiring others to appreciate great music.

Mrs P B Childs started teaching piano when her husband got sick, and then he died. She teaches piano in her living room on St John's Street, in a tall white Victorian beside the Stems' house that use to be the Wellings'. I starting taking from her while we were still living on Mineral Springs Road, and I'd get recital solos like "Deep Purple," and duets. Whoever you had a duet with, you were supposed to get together at your house and practice, like when Anna Jeffords came out to Mineral Springs Road to practice with me. The audience seemed to like the music we played okay we thought, but they were easier pieces. You work *up* to classical.

Hymns can be grand (some religious music is the grandest of all compositions, I've found out), and you know I like Popular and some Rhythm & Blues and I've grown up around Country, but since I've been taking from Mrs P B Childs, I've started to appreciate classical music and even love some of it. Last year my Spring Recital piece was the Third Movement of Rachmaninoff's Second Piano Concerto. I wish C'n Lillian had

208

been there to hear me play it. I'd practiced and practiced, and I know I did it right at recital: I felt it.

Even though the J C Daniels Auditorium nowhere near fills up for our recitals, it's still scary to play there. When you're on the lit-up stage and all out there is dark, for all you know the place might be packed. What if you forgot the piece halfway through? I've seen a girl have to stop and then limp on to the end of a piece and leave the stage in tears. It can happen.

But the music I'm playing now is too important to forget. If I messed up a great piece, I'd deserve banishment.

Last year my recital solo was by Beethoven. I read his letters (there're not many; he was too busy writing music) and found out he started to go deaf at age 29 -- Deaf! -- and kept on writing great symphonies all his life 'til he died at 57. He suffered for his art. You can feel the suffering in his music, and the overcoming.

The only living composer I can think of in America who can write anything near as brilliant as Beethoven is George Gershwin. (He's not just *in* America; he's American now.) Think about Rhapsody in Blue and some of Porgy and Bess. They can stand up against Beethoven's -- well, maybe not his 5th piano concerto, but say his 4th -- not his best, but anyhow his mediums. To me, Porgy and Bess is an opera. It's called a "folk opera," like it's less than an opera, but how many *European* operas aren't folk operas? The Gershwins are Jews who fled Russia when George and his brother Ira were just little.

Rachmaninoff lived in Czarist Russia, before Russian or any other kind of Communism got called Communism, so he didn't have to emigrate. His music is Rich. Gorgeous. Powerful. There was one good thing about Czarist Russia: they didn't try to get into everybody's head. Leo Tolstoy's War and Peace came from Czarist Russia. It's so long it 'bout kills you to read it, but it's as good as even the best novels of William Faulkner of Mississippi. And Faulkner won the Nobel Prize for Literature for the whole world.

If there'd been a Nobel Prize back then, I'm pretty sure Tolstoy would've won it too, if it was done fair.

I've tried but can't think of any Communist who writes great music. Russians might still, but are the composers Communists, or are they their own selves? Great music or great anything comes from individualism, not out of socialism or any other politics. In the Union of Soviet Socialist Republics, "good citizens" are at the service of the State. Don't, and they're ostracized. Or banished. Sent to Siberia. Liquidated. The Communists are famous for getting rid of inconvenient people, so they might've liquidated the very ones who'd've been their great composers today.

Great music comes from individualists wherever they are in the world.

1st-Cousin-Twice-Removed Lillian grew up in Newberry and studied at the Chicago Conservatory of Music to be a classical pianist. She loved music, not just for herself, there playing the baby-grand piano in their house behind those tall magnolias on Cashua, but for everybody. She wanted us all to know and enjoy great music.

She and the Music Club brought famous musicians to perform in town. When we were in grammar school, performers of great music came here -- violinists, pianists, even groups that did chamber music meant for small gatherings, but in Darlington all the ones I heard were in the same public place: the J C Daniel Auditorium. We flocked to listen. We may have had no choice about going when we were little; I don't recall whether we did or not. What I remember is sitting enchanted as they played.

After her only child left home for good, C'n Lillian Fair lived on alone in that house the size of an orphanage. Mother says she's hardly ever seen a house that big, even in Orangeburg County. The house C'n Monroe Spears built for his family has 14 rooms and almost as many fireplaces. It's easily the biggest house on Cashua and probly in Darlington.

When we moved to town in 1950, Lillian Fair had stepped down from most of her work for the Music Club. I think it was Mr Jack Frierson the insurance man who took over as President.

Near the end of September 1952, C'n Lillian passed away in McLeod's Infirmary. Mother's sister Marie Dukes Bowie, A B and R N, is Floor Supervisor there. C'n Lillian's passing was peaceful.

COUNTY

Lately Darlington's had a falling off in classical music presentations. Don't take my word for it; ask anybody, and compare the front page of the N&P ten years ago with 1957's.

Where is Rubinoff, the great violinist? And the musicians who took time to come play for us in grammar school and junior high, and made us aware of great music? I don't know who paid for them to come here; I just know they're not here now that C'n Lillian's body is beneath the tall graceful stone in Grove Hill -- the monument her son C'n Monroe K chose for her.

The write-up says she was in The King's Daughters (she and Mother were, together), the DAR, the Garden Club (it didn't need any other name), and Trinity Methodist Church. Mostly, though, you noticed the music.

I see some gravesites as stories in stone. They almost speak.

Cn Lillian's monument is stately and formal but beautiful, like music she loved.

C'n Mamie Agness's monument is the lovely mourning woman.

Lillian Fair's gravestone is classical, you see, and Mamie Agness's is romantic. Exact opposites, there on opposite sides of C'n Monroe.

FAST

The Race has become our yearly end-of-summer reality that borders on fantasy. Every Labor Day from 1950 on, the Darlington 500 swirls the central Pee Dee into an alternate orbit.

Almost from the start, the Race spawned a procession of showy events. Brash newcomers vied with staid citizens for leadership, and groups came up with idea after idea for big, shiny events. The thousands who reglarly popped up here early each late August looking for excitement ate it up, and so did most of us.

The Chamber of Commerce has been shot out of the saddle by the once-shy Jaycees. Dick McKelvey, a quiet recent graduate of St John's, is now a mover and a shaker. So is Catherine Sansbury Cross, civic leader and dignified Director of Nutrition for the public schools. Time Trials keep the racetrack humming in the background, but Time Trials are for honest-to-goodness Racing Fans. Most of us locals never get to a Time Trial because there's too much else going on.

Each Saturday morning before Labor Day, the Southern 500 Parade forms on our side of town's farthest-out long street, which is Warley. The Celebrity slot is just this side of the cemetery gate, after Broad Street ends after its dip-and-climb past Diamond Hill Plywood. The nearest units to the Celebrity convertible park and wait in numbered slots right in front of 120 Warley. Yep: our house.

Each Southern 500 had its own Grand Marshall, usually an actor from a popular television show. It's like a Christmas parade, only a tv star takes the place of Santa Claus. Matt Dillon – you could say James Arness but who'd ever've heard of James Arness if he didn't play Marshal Matt Dillon of Gunsmoke's Dodge City – was Grand Marshall one year. Another year Festus and Doc were a kind of twin Marshall. So far we've not seen Miss Kitty. She might not like racing.

213

COUNTY

I get to see the parade celebrity up close just by walking a short block. I can tell you Matt Dillon is even taller and wider-shouldered in real life than he looks on tv, and handsomer, but he rode on a convertible in our parade, not on a horse. They said he said you can't trust horses in a crowd.

We were pretty disappointed. You heard some grumbling and a few snickers. I mean, Matt Dillon in a *car*? It just didn't seem right. We thought he should've tried.

He wouldn't've had to bring his famous buckskin from the show. The horse wouldn't've even had to be a stallion, for Pete's sake. Big as the Marshal is, he could've ridden one of the super-tame Clydesdales or some other dray horse use to taking orders. And use to being in parades.

Come to think of it, maybe that horse wouldn't've been so easy to find.

The celebrities aren't all the onlookers hauled their lawn chairs out to see. Being up on a float every year (not because I'm anybody, but there I was), I never saw a whole parade, but I got filled in by the members of St John's Band, which usually marches near the front. They get to see everything that comes after they pass the break-up point and hurry back to the Square.

School bands march in a gorgeous variety of uniforms, none of 'em smarter than St John's royal blue with gold braid. Whenever a band would come to an intersection, they'd break out into blaring music and dip their trombones and toss their drumsticks in rhythm. Some from Negro schools, including Mayo and Wilson, their whole band would go into synchronized dancing -- trombone, Drum Major, Majorettes and all. Folks along the curb would applaud like crazy.

The Shriners brought honking squeeze horns and bright-painted cars that reared up and spilled clowns onto the street. Riders on ponies and horses pranced by in fancy western fringe. (Apparently they didn't share Mr Arness's concern.) Floats came from all over, alternating with cars with handwritten signs taped to their doors to identify the important person waving from up on each folded-down convertible top.

Those parades transformed normal female kids into float-riding, candy-tossing Miss Prisses -- me included -- zipped tight into our wide-skirted taffeta-and-net dresses meant to be worn

214

to fancy dances. It was a good thing I got to see the end units before the Parade got going, because once I hoisted my voluminously decked-out self carefully up onto whatever float we (whatever squad of girls I was with) were assigned to, that was the most I saw of the other floats and units 'cept for when we would finally be circling the Public Square.

With my skirts draped just so over the uncomfortable box underneath me, I was shown just how to smile, act, and how much to chunk of whatever the float builders had accumulated for me and the other girls to chunk. They didn't want us to run out of stuff before we arrived at the Square in front of the biggest collection of people who weren't actually *in* the parade.

Up there on our float we'd wait and wait for the front of the parade to get going and get out of our way. I don't ever remember it raining on those Saturday mornings – after years of that, Cat Cross got to remarking on it -- but it was always hot. I'd slather on anti-sunburn cream. I knew not to put much makeup on my face and eyes or I'd sweat and cake up and smear. (Some float riders didn't think of that, I noticed.)

Finally the pickup hitched to our float would crank up, the float would lurch, and we'd begin to glide along. No matter how many times it happened, that was the high point of the day for me. Being in front of the crowd never matched the moment when the float began to roll.

Mother and Daddy would've left the house in plenty of time to station themselves in folding chairs and chat with friends someplace along Cashua, but some of the neighbors would be there to wave as we passed along Warley, which was nice. That's when we'd start tossing out our Tootsie Rolls, Squirrel-Nut Zippers, little cellophane bags of popcorn, tiny plastic cars – whatever was supplied -- to the people on the curb. Little kids would jump up and down and call out our names (if they knew us, and lots did) to get us to pitch something their way. I was always out of stuff to throw before we reached the Square.

By time we got to the Square and around it, the first units were already dispersed and standing around watching the rest of the parade. Wayne, Jimmy, Kent Ham, Kathy, Betty Byrd, Richard Hyman, and lots of the rest of St John's band would wave to us and make faces to make us laugh. Then we'd all go home, change out of costume, and collapse.

COUNTY
I honest-to-goodness don't remember what any float I rode on was sponsored by. Ungrateful brat, you could call me. Now all that part of life is over for me – for the Class of '57. We most of us'll be out and gone before Labor Day gets here.

The Miss Southern 500 contest follows that same night, to choose the swimsuited contestant who'll congratulate the winning driver on Monday evening. This contest doesn't bother with fancy attire; it gets right to the skin. Beauty-title holders come from all over the Southeast, some with near-unbelievable bosoms that bring forth *risque'* (a French word, you notice) remarks from male observers. (I told you one of 'em.) Needless to say, they're kept a safe distance away. Each beauty queen hopes to be the lucky winner who gets to shove the victorious driver's wife or girlfriend aside and give the sweaty victor a well-photographed kiss.
You might not like hearing the word *sweat* so much, but hey, in Darlington on Labor Day it's <u>hot.</u>

Sunday is quieter, being the Lord's Day, but all over town people are picnicking and having a good time. The traffic sounds outside our church services never stop, but race fans are courteous. There's not much horn blowing, whoopin' an' holl'rin' during preaching.
Then it's Labor Day Monday and the reason for this whole shebang: the Southern 500 itself.

By 1955, when Mother saw her first (and probly only) race at the big track, its founder was no longer one of the owners.
If I tried to tell you how that happened, how painful it must've been, I'd just be guessing. What we know is, Harold Witherspoon Brasington dreamed up, negotiated, and built the Darlington Raceway when no other raceway like it existed, and 7 years after he created it he's not even on the Board of Directors.
All Daddy's ever said about it is, "Not everybody's as good at business as they sometimes need to be."
They say Harold won't come into the track any more. If he's got business there, he'll drive up and sit outside in his pickup.

216

To me that shows a lot of hurt.

Harold's got other interests, like looking into building a track up in North Carolina. It won't be like this one, though. There's no other track like Darlington, and won't be.

As far as I'm concerned, the whole sport of big-time stock-car racing and NASCAR and all the other tracks built to copy Darlington will owe more to Harold Brasington than they'll ever owe to any other man.

Bob Colvin's not a peanut broker now; he's President of Darlington International Raceway. I don't think anybody holds it against him, because he's a really nice man, a likable person, and a good friend of Daddy's. So is Loomis -- Mrs Colvin. They live just as modest now as they always have, in a neat brick semi-modern house on a corner of North Main. Mr Colvin was in the right place when the change came. Nobody blames him.

Here's part of the story behind that story:

You remember Harold's nephew from Conway who left college to enlist as a combat pilot, the one I said was close to Harold's own age and they were friends and almost alter egos? That one.

Well, he moved here and worked at normal jobs awhile after the War, but couldn't stay away from airplanes. He took to flying again for a living: he re-enlisted. Harold and Boyce both lived with the throttle full out.

During the most disastrous month in local memory, the Brasingtons had their own separate disaster.

On the 17th of April 1952, WWII veteran 1st Lt Boyce Allen Brasington was a crew member on a flight out West. The airplane went down outside Golden, Colorado, on Golden Mountain. All 11 crewmen and passengers died.

The pallbearers Anne Wilson Brasington asked to serve were Curtis Allen, Glenn Howle, Joe Moody, and Bob Colvin.

"Uncle Harold" takes a fatherly interest in the fatherless boys left behind. The baby boy was barely a year old. His big brother -- Boyce Allen Brasington Jr – was 3.

We call him Allen.

When Mother and I went to the race together that one time, we sat up in the stands. That was new for me.

COUNTY

Before, I was always in the infield with Daddy. He always gets tickets, maybe some of 'em free for being the track electrician, but he gives those to Russell, who brings buddies from Orangeburg County. The infield's cheaper and for Daddy it's better than a concrete bleacher, no matter what kind of folding seat or pillows you put between you and it.

We sit in fold-up chairs on top of Daddy's converted Southern Bell truck, and we watch for a while and walk around for awhile; that eases Daddy's back. We bring sandwiches and picnic food from home and a drink box full of ice and bottled drinks. If he's needed outside during a race, he can get there through the underground tunnel.

So last year Mother decided finally she wanted to see a race, see what all the hoopla is about and why 10,000s of race fans come every year. Daddy got us good seats, as good as anybody's 'cept for the ones up high behind glass. We were able to see everything without being close to the dust kicked up from the track.

The main thing Mother enjoyed that day didn't have anything to do with racing. I told you about her weird sense of humor -- the one where somebody gets embarrassed but not actually hurt. She'll laugh 'til you think she's not going to stop, and she laughs about it again every time she remembers it or somebody brings it up. It's a blessing, a mirthful memory that comes back and brings the laughter with it.

This time the memory happened the 2nd row below us and down a few seats.

Right there sat a stylish lady with an elaborate hairdo, the kind just coming in style. It's got a French name: *bouffant*. You could tell it had been put up on those new big rollers the size of Weinberg sausages. The result was high, w-i-d-e, and fixed just so, curved and set and then sprayed stiff. It was, let me tell you, *glossy*. And blonde. You could even say it glowed.

Behind this lady was a beer-can beer drinker.

I have a feeling I don't even have to fill in the rest of this little scene for you, but I'm going to anyhow. Just in case, you know -- in case you never saw a NASCAR race or never saw "mad as a wet hen" acted out.

His first couple of beers went down fairly fast; it was (as Labor Day in Darlington always is) a hot day. I wasn't keeping count, but Mother was. Mother's not really a race fan; she's more of a crowd observer.

She saw the beer drinker getting a little careless while opening what must have been his 3rd. She punched me hard in the side, and I looked where she pointed, just in time to see a stream of beer shoot into the back of the glossy lady's hair.

Soaked it.

Hit a few others around, but as practicly the contents of the can looked to be in the lady's hair and dripping down her bare back into her flowerdy sundress, there wasn't all that much left over for her seatmates. They didn't seem to care, or even to notice it much. Things were heating up down on the track.

That lady, though, she cared; she noticed. BOY did she care.

She stood up, whipped around, and with beer still foaming in her wilting hair and meandering down her back, she gave that man whatfor. Her voice rose above the roar of the cars as they hurtled by.

The beer drinker naturally wanted to see what was transpiring down on the racetrack, but he couldn't get away from the lady with the beer hair because she was between him and the track action. After while he gave up trying to peer around her and just sat and hung his head until she got through.

She blew his doors off.

Her final statement was something like, "And I dare you to open another (blurred) beer the whole rest of this (blurred blurred) race, or my husband [she pointed to him; I don't think he'd opened his mouth the whole time] 'll drag you out of these stands and beat your ......"

Mother had both hands over her mouth the whole time to keep her giggling down so she wouldn't miss anything. I doubt she caught every word, but she picked up enough to give an entertaining account to Daddy that night at supper in spite of giggling and having to stop and drink ice tea.

I remember looking at the lady's husband. A big 'un he was, with a large rose tattooed on his near arm. Strange I hadn't even noticed him 'til then, sitting there so quiet on her other side.

I'd almost bet her name is Rose.

COUNTY

That was, as I said, a hot day, and lots of beer was being consumed. When we were first walking into the stadium, I saw one man who'd already passed out. He was sot on the ground, propped up against a little asbestos-sided building marked MENS TOILETS. Apparently he'd started his race a little early and forgot to pace himself.

It was a HOT day.

Meanwhile, things had been heating up elsewhere in our town.

The Textile Workers Union of America was going after Darlington Manufacturing Company.

It would be their first mill in South Carolina -- a top prize if they could pull it off here in a new Right-to-Work state. Deering-Milliken mills being well respected in the textile industry, they're a hard nut to crack. Roger Milliken loves South Carolina and moved here in 1954, to Spartanburg. He's the Big Cheese. There's no Deering; it's just the Millikens. Others can buy in, but the Millikens hold the majority of stock in each factory. You can't mess with canny Irishmen.

What I didn't know then is that the person who was doing as much as anybody in Darlington County to further the Union's efforts was Mrs Weatherford of Mineral Springs Road, our next-door neighbor for the first decade of my life.

Agitation

When the textile industry began bailing out of the Northern states in the late 1800s, South Carolina put out the welcome mat. Some of New England's factory abuses and strife made it into our history books at St John's; some of the strikes did too. But by 1956 the Cotton Mill had been Darlington's main industrial source of income for 3/4 of a century. We figured we'd have it forever and ever Amen.

World War II was a boom time for textiles and other materials, but 'cept for a short, sharp uptrend brought by the Korean Conflict (the Government's not calling it a War even though it killed quite a few boys of our generation), the textile boom soon went away. After Armistice opened up trade worldwide, textiles made in the US would be at a disadvantage against textiles made in poorer nations. Change was reaching into Darlington, along with the news. But how many people were listening and watching?

Roger Milliken, President and majority stock holder in Darlington Manufacturing Company, was doing both. He'd also give speeches and write about the situation of textiles in the nation and the world. You could read his articles and interviews in the Darlington paper and in other local newspapers wherever the company owned mills. He always conveyed respect for the textile industry and all who worked in it, but he made no secret of the negatives.

Meanwhile, times were good in Darlington. Cotton Mill weekly payroll had been $28,000 by the end of 1950, the silver dollar spree; it was over $32,000 by late 1956. 500 workers and almost that many families depended on the Mill. Most of the 8,000 total population did too, but Darlington as a whole hadn't yet thought about what that meant.

The Weatherfords' farm is separated from what use to be our farm by the Unnamed Road, the same road that separated the other side of our farm from Henry and Lila Stokes's. The Stokeses face the Weatherfords – Elmer and Essie -- across Mineral Springs Road. Beyond the Sand Hill -- what use to be the Sand Hill I mean -- are the Moise Jameses and the Swinneys and the Drews. All those families use to be our next-door-farm neighbors. They're all still there and still full-time farmers today, 'cept the Albert Drews, the late comers. After a start at farming a poor piece of land he bought after the end of the War, Albert Drew is breaking up the place into house lots. But what can you say; it was Cap that sold out first.

Our Mineral Springs Road neighbors still call Daddy when something breaks they can't fix. He hears what's going on out there the same way he gets to know what's going on all over Darlington, whether he wants to or not. If it's going to hurt anybody to tell or it's bad news, he generally keeps it to himself.

When somebody calls, Daddy'll try to name a day but you won't know just when in that day he'll get there. That's how it happened he was still there working at the Weatherfords' when some men in white shirts showed up. They made like it was a social call, but Daddy knew who they had to be and what they were there about and left 'em to it.

When he came back the next afternoon to finish up, Essie seemed to want to talk about what he'd seen the day before.

Daddy let some days pass before he told Mother and me what Mrs Weatherford said that evening and what he thought about it. He wasn't happy.

Daddy said this:

Essie is being used by people she doesn't understand, against other people she doesn't understand. The Union's using her to get at the biggest, most progressive textile firm in the South, and the richest. She not only believes in the Union, she believes everything the Union reps tell her: that once the Union's voted in, everything will be better; everything. Conditions, machinery, and pay. For her, for everybody.

All she had to do was believe in the Union, they said.

And oh, she did, she did. She does to this day.

If she and some others who met with them out on Mineral Springs Road would work hard and make it happen, the men said, the Union would right away push for improved working conditions and the pay the workers deserved.

"I imagine the Union would be mighty grateful to you, Essie, if you could get them their way." That's what Daddy said to her then.

Well, George, she told him, the Union hadn't exactly promised her anything; they really couldn't yet. But, well, they'd said they'd have some local positions to be filled, and they'd be just like Daddy said -- grateful.

She felt like one of them, already. They were going to be the best thing for the Darlington Manufacturing Company.

The Union spent long months working to get in here. It converted Essie Weatherford and a few others into petition-carriers and cheerleaders. That in itself was an amazing feat, considering how "union" has been a nasty word here ever since the Union Army invaded in the 1860s and left a forest of burnt-out chimneys that kept reminding the South never to forget who did it.

It was one of those chimneys that sparked fire in Atlanta reporter Margaret Mitchell. When she was a little girl driving with her grandmother in their horse-and-buggy, her Gran pointed to a blackened chimney (I see it almost covered with yellow-flowering honeysuckle), and told her, "Never accept defeat." During the '30s Depression time, Margaret put that memory together with other facts about the South's time of rebellion, loss and humiliation, and wrote her only novel -- Gone with the Wind.

COUNTY

Will the Unions get in here, when the South hates the very word "union" and has for almost a century?

But Unions or not, what can keep textile manufacturing in the US? WWII taught us there're nations sprinkled all over the world where people work for little or nothing. Probly they can learn to grow cotton or import it or whatever they need to make cloth from, and set up factories. Heck, we'll help 'em, us generous Americans.

Japan -- think about Japan. They've stopped studying war and now they're studying us, figuring out what made us the winners. Americans are teaching them how to set up factories. There's one they've hired to be there with 'em while they do it (I'll probly remember his name later). To the Japanese ready to start businesses, he's like a pagan god of manufacturing.

That's not all: they're learning English so they can read our books, even our literature. Us now -- what other languages are *we* learning well enough to read or speak?

I probly picked the wrong language to take. I don't think the US is interested in competing in the perfume market, and Voltaire's and Baudelaire's writings don't mean much to Americans. (Ever read his masterpiece, "Flowers of Evil" – Fleurs de Mal? Me neither.) The French are more likely to follow *our* writers than the other way 'round. Take Poe; he was BIG in France. Today French writers consider Edgar Allan Poe the father of what they call the Art for Art's Sake movement. (What they don't understand was that he was writing whatever he could sell, to keep from starving in a cold house.)

Latin? Even dead, Latin's the basis of medical and legal terms and all the Romance languages. They're called that because they're based on Latin (*Roman* speech), instead of on early German the way English is. Spanish is a Romance language, and it's almost everywhere in Central and South America because the Spanish and the Portuguese (their languages are much alike) conquered all that part of the world while they were looking for gold and riches. Knowing some Latin helps us learn Roman-based languages easier.

Not that many Americans will bother. We'll sit around and wait for other nations to learn English, which means they'll be able to figure us out before we figure them out.

COUNTY

After William Faulkner won the 1950 Nobel Prize for Literature, Japan invited him over. Our State Department sent him, all expenses paid. (The speakings Faulkner did in Japan are collected in a book; you can read them yourself.)

The Japanese came to hear Faulkner in numbers that amazed the Mississippi writer. He started out not knowing a word of Japanese, but some of his audience had learned English just so they could read his *novels*! He met Japanese who'd read them all, and his stories too. <u>Intruder in</u> <u>the Dust</u>, <u>The Hamlet</u> trilogy, and other books of his had taught them our War Between the States from the South's point of view. They knew about deep-woods hunting from "The Bear," and "Old Man" showed them the great Mississippi River flood. They'd puzzled through <u>The Sound and the Fury</u> and were ready with questions, always expressed courteously.

(I understand <u>The Sound and the Fury</u> perfectly, by the way, because I met those people in Orangeburg County. Here's the key to the tragedy: it's Quentin's disappointment in their father. Nothing Caddie does changes anything important, nor Benjy nor Dilsey and certainly not Jason. No matter who his father is, Jason's pure Snopes.)

Even so, I'm in total awe of somebody who can penetrate Faulkner's Southernness through another language. An American lady told Faulkner she'd read one of his novels 3 times and still didn't understand it. He told her, "Read it 4 times." All true authors have arrogance. Have to, or they'd quit.

Here's the point about language, though:

While Mr Faulkner was in Japan, he found out why he'd been invited: the Japanese *identify with the South -- with us -- because they fought the US Army and lost, and so did we.* In Faulkner's books, the ones he set in Reconstruction time, they see a defeated people who're determined not to make defeat a way of life. They admire us, the South. Yes, *us* the national red-headed stepchild.

Never thought I'd use that phrase. My own hair's reddish, and I like it. It's just a saying; you know that.

I love Faulkner and hope someday to show you why. I admire the Japanese who admire Faulkner, but 'course I can't like them all yet. It's hard to forget that even the children and the old ladies were ready to spike us through with sharpened sticks.

The Japanese -- we aren't calling them Japs any more -- they're not just making pretty porcelain figures for us to buy and set on a shelf; they're setting up real factories and reading English and understanding democracy all of a sudden. What's going to stop them from taking the textile industry as part of their rising and having it spread all over that part of the world?

But here in Darlington, we thought because we "always" had textiles, we always would.

I don't know whether the Union organizers discussed with Mrs Weatherford the textile big picture. It's not likely they brought up how the textile industry deserted the New England states after Unions took over and brought in the Closed Shop. Not likely they talked about other countries where factories pay much, much, much less than we do in the United States, and whose products compete directly with American goods since the War made us a smaller world.

Mainly they convinced her to be against the bosses, especially Mr Milliken and the local manager Mr Oeland. Could be they even brought in optimistic predictions from 4 years earlier, when there were high (and mistaken) hopes for the US textile industry.

Daddy believes that even if Roger Milliken were the best, most benevolent, worker-oriented textile mill owner in the entire world -- and maybe he is – our textile industry won't be able to stand for long against Asia's low standard of living and wages. If Daddy knows that, Roger Milliken knows it in spades. Ireland never had a great economy, but the Irish in America – including the Millikens – hadn't just now got off the big boat.

Roger Milliken is rich -- born that way, like the young Rockerfellers -- but Darlington's cotton mill didn't make him rich. *He could do without it.* That's the rumor we kept hearing out in town: *Roger Milliken can do without Darlington Manufacturing Company if it turns out to be more trouble than it's worth.*

If I know my father (and I do), he told her all that. Daddy would've said every bit as much of it as he thought she could put up with hearing. He'd've said it gently and nice, but he'd've got it in.

226

COUNTY

When Daddy finished with the repair and was ready to go, she was kind of smiling. (I've seen her "kind of smiling" a hundred times. It always means "you don't know what I know.")

Well, she said, Millliken can't do anything if the Union gets voted in. Not a thing.

And, she said, it will.

About *one* of those, she was right.

SHUT DOWN

The <u>News & Press</u> almost never pulls its front page. This time it had no choice. What happened, happened on a Wednesday, and the N&P's a Thursday weekly. They hit us with it all at once: the shutdown, the finishing-up plans, and the auction.

When the news came in, did the Coffees actually shout HOLD THE PRESSES? Even if they didn't (and I can't imagine them shouting), they set a headline that's as close to a scream as the N&P ever comes:

Darlington Cotton Mill To Close; Directors Order Immediate Halt Of Production; Purchaser Sought

The 2 subheads that followed were smaller but almost as awful. They told us it was all a done deal; no turning back.

December 12 and 13 Set As Dates for Public Auction of Mill Property

Oeland Anticipates Final Production
1st Week of November; To Clean
Plant for Inspection of Buyers

Darlington's main source of income is gone. A few more weeks to finish orders in process, then a few days for a clean-up crew to do their last job here, then no more Darlington Manufacturing Company.

Hard for us to believe. *Hard* to believe.

The date of the meeting that closed the Mill was Wednesday, October 17, 1956. Charleston's <u>News and Courier</u>

covered the vote and workers' reactions, and published some of the many comments the Union immediately gave out. The Union was loaded, cocked, and firing at will.

The Union began by calling the shutdown "an outrageous example of industrial feudalism at its worst." Also, "Never has there been a more brutally clear example of an employer's determination to prevent collective bargaining."

Union President Pollock had clearly expected the outcome he got. He admitted he'd contacted Labor Secretary Mitchell "some time ago" to ask for "an intervention." The election was on top of us – Eisenhower's second campaign for President -- so Pollock hadn't got his meeting yet.

Maybe we could call it a tragedy, the struggle over the Mill and who would control it. Maybe "black comedy" -- painful farce interrupted by moments of comic relief -- a tragi-comedy, except that Darlington doesn't much feel like laughing.

Darlington's not the nation. It's just a smallish town trampled by corporate elephants.

To the Textile Workers Union of America, Essie Weatherford was a means to an end.

The Union appeared to be surprised at the closing of the Mill, but ... *was* it surprised?

Could this shutdown be the very outcome the Union wanted? So it could file the Big Lawsuit that will surely reach far beyond little Darlington – the lawsuit aimed at the new Right To Work laws recently passed by most Southern states?

The very day of the shutdown, Union spokesmen were talking lawsuit: "A denial of the legal right to organize and bargain collectively is an infringement on workers' individual freedom and perpetuates the low wages and inadequate living standards that for years have been a blight on textile communities." Its President said specifically that the decision "flouts the spirit and the letter of the law,"

I mean, who could think up those words on the spur of the minute? They got *denial, legal right, infringement, perpetuates,* all in one sentence. Even *individual freedom,* for Pete's sake, a concept foreign to stated Union goals. Look at the word: Unions are intrinsically collective, not individual. Individuals inside Unions go along to get along or they get out.

COUNTY

As for inadequate living standards on the Mill Hill, maybe even most of our living standards in Darlington are inadequate. I'm pretty sure the Union bosses would find plenty on this end of Warley Street to sneer at. Does our 1-bathroom, 2-entry frame house meet the Union standard of adequacy? Do all of us need a Union but are too dumb to know it?

On the day the shutdown came, the Charleston <u>News and Courier's</u> "roving reporter" Eldridge Thomson talked with some men who were gathered "at a small store uptown." They were trying to get it through their heads they didn't have jobs any more. Every one of 'em felt he'd been shafted.

One that wouldn't give his name told Thompson, "If the manager had resigned before the election the union would not have gotten a half-dozen voters."

That's the kind of comment the N&P, an old fashioned newspaper, would've shied away from. It tries not to embarrass local people, let alone a whole family. Maybe that comment reflected only one man's disgruntled opinion, although the reporter didn't present it as though nobody there agreed. Was resentment against the manager a factor in the vote? If so, did it start from agitation by the Union, or was it already there?

Mr Oeland's daughters Jimsie and Helen are nice people, both graduated now from St John's. He's out in the community speaking to church groups (they're Presbyterians) and presenting awards to Mill workers; we see his name in the paper. Could be he was a victim of the rumors set up by the Union.

One thing you can count on: the local boss gets plenty of blame when things go wrong. And wrong they've sure gone. Mr Oeland will probly be out on the street with the rest of them. The owners can't be that happy with him: he lost.

That same day, the Charleston paper built an article around Mr Frank Kinsey. It said once the owners realized the Union was determined to force a vote, they got in there and talked with loyal workers they knew would never go for the Union.

One was Mr Kinsey.

Frank Kinsey "wasn't bitter but he didn't try to hide his disappointment," was the lead.

230

Frank Kinsey sat in his comfortable living room and discussed the situation. He had faced problems before, but none so grave. For 40 years he has worked for the same mill. He is now 63. His job is gone. He has a little general merchandise store in his front yard but with the Mill closing he stands to lose that business too. Most of his trade comes from Mill employees.

"Company officials told me and 40 other employees if we opposed the union in its effort to organize the workers that we would be taken care of," Kinsey related. "We fought the union. We lost the election. Now we are losing our jobs."

Kinsey said he believes today's decision of Darlington Manufacturing Co. stockholders to liquidate the 75-year-old plant is the "town's biggest blow. Right now is Darlington's darkest moment."

When I think of Mrs Weatherford, I see nice brown eyes twinkling behind rimless glasses. I see big, doughy breakfast biscuits kept on a plate in an overhead cabinet for whatever time of day we got the urge to clamber up onto the counter to get at 'em. I see a tallish, strong, dark-haired farm wife who runs the house, anchors the children, and helps out cheerfully with the crops and the chores.

She's even a romantic figure, in that she's clearly the love of handsome, volatile Elmer Weatherford's life. He's the family romantic -- the one who pledges his life of hard work to those he loves. In all my years inside their house including spend-the-nights, I never saw him go against any plan of Essie's. If he wanted to, he never said so, out loud for us to hear.

(Mr Weatherford cherishes no human being more than he cherishes our Eltas Jean. I love him for that and for his hopeful, old-school, trusting heart that his hot temper almost never overcomes.)

Now that the Mill's closed, Mr Frank Kinsey seems to blame the owners -- the ones whose side he was on. He feels lied to and used.

But Mrs Weatherford does not feel lied to and used. She still believes in the Union, in spite of having no Mill job any more

231

and no future as a Union Rep. She's more than willing to keep blaming the owners and only the owners because they did what they said they'd do and what the Union said they would not: close the Mill. It's like she didn't hear Daddy at all, that afternoon at her house, and has a cloudy memory of what she was told by her Union colleagues.

But then she hadn't put in 40 years of her life at the Mill like Mr Kinsey, and she's not the support of her family. Mr Weatherford and the farm are still there.

All through the '50s, the N&P's been running articles on the textile industry. Taken together, they showed shutdown coming -- not this soon, but coming. One way you could look at it, the Union only sped up the inevitable. It's just that it's hard to believe in the inevitable until it falls on top of you.

We forget that cotton can go bust, even though it went bust before, in Mrs Weatherford's lifetime. Investors and speculators who missed the meaning of 1926 fell hard in 1929, which was followed by a starving, desperate decade in most of the nation. Much earlier even that that, textile mills shut down in the Unionized North, and now we're learning that cotton mills can shut down in the South.

We don't intend to let anybody starve, but some lessons cost a lot. Under the wrong leadership, they can gut a town.

Roger Milliken watches international trends in textiles for a living, but sometimes a clue appears to the rest of us.

Like my new blouse.

My new blouse is not made of cotton. I don't know what it's made of, really; chemicals mostly? Because it needs no ironing at *all*.

Iron it, ruin it. Wash it, hang it to dry, shake it out, wear it.

Mother says it's just the thing for me to take when I leave. She figures once I'm away, I'll wear my clothes rough-dry rather than pick up an iron, and she might be right. Forget to unplug an iron and a scorched ironing-board cover's the least disaster that could happen. Dangerous things, irons. Heavy. Nothing like the weight of old *iron* irons, but heavy aplenty.

COUNTY

It's just one blouse, but the more I think about the Mill, I think this blouse is bad news for the textile industry and worse news for cotton farmers.

Where do they make this new cloth? At munitions-and-chemical factories, like DuPont de Nemours up North in Delaware? Even across the Pacific Ocean? Can't tell from the label, but I know it's not any kind of cotton material. It's not nylon either, nor rayon; they stick to your skin in warm weather, which is 3/4 of our South Carolina year. This cloth's crisper than nylon.

What *is* this new stuff?

I think soon everybody might want to buy clothes made out of this new kind of cloth. How many people like to iron? Don't bother raising your hand; I wouldn't believe you.

Not just cotton mills but cotton itself might be in trouble.

But I'm a farm girl, and here's what I think:

Cotton might take a hit in the near future, but cotton as a crop won't go away. Some other kind of material could be mixed in, but cotton makes the cloth that breathes. Cloth has to breathe or it stifles your pores. Comfort counts.

Clothes aren't the only use of cloth; they're just what we think of right off. War uses lots of cloth. Uniforms, parachutes, tarpaulins, tents all need to be strong, and the industry gears up in time of need. Cotton's the mainstay. Whatever they add, cotton's in there.

Dungarees, work shirts and pants, coveralls all need to be strong too, and I don't know any *comfortable* cloth stronger than cotton. Daddy buys his work clothes from a traveling salesman; lots of working people do. Are traveling salesman jobs about to disappear too?

And underwear! Crinolines without any cotton wouldn't stand; they'd just wilt and hang there. Underpants and slips and camisoles and undershirts -- nobody'd want strange cloth next to their *skin*. Not for long, they wouldn't.

I'm not about to go into a speech on female hygiene, but my plain-talking grandmother in Rowesville made sure I know the facts. She's got the confidence to say things most ladies won't say, and she says without enough air flow you could break out or even get a private disease that has to be examined by a doctor.

233

And looks -- I can't picture how anything unnatural could compete with the look of a crisp-ironed cotton shirt or white cotton blouse with ruffles. Cotton's the best thing for dresses and skirts, too.

It's a pretty blouse, though, this new no-iron one. A really nice blue with big mother-of-pearl buttons.

Or maybe they're plastic.

I bought it uptown in Darlington at Coggeshall's, on sale because nobody much wants to buy these things yet. They will, though -- and where will cotton mills be then.

Perish the thought.

The Mill Directors weren't near as prepared as the Union was with a flood of statements, let alone accusations, after announcing the shutdown. Just their time-schedule statement was startling enough to us locals: that the Mill operation would end in a couple of *weeks*, and the property would be offered at auction in less than 2 *months* later – before the end of 1956.

Why so soon? Were there buyers waiting to come in? And if that was so, why didn't anybody seem to know it? And what would make another company risk coming in if the Union (or some other Union) had to be part of the bargain?

One of the Directors (they're all South Carolinians, we think) is Mayor Tom Buchanan. His wife Joanne is in The King's Daughters with Mother, and Joanne says the Mayor's as shocked as anybody.

"He's hopeful to be seeing a white knight galloping this way any day now, coming to the auction to buy the Mill and rescue the town -- not to mention him and the other owners, who the last thing they want is a ghost on their hands."

Plus, there're always the optimists that say there'll be a buyer for the Mill even if nobody buys on auction day. They believe there won't be much of a time lag at all before a new owner comes in and starts hiring.

Most of those believers also believed that voting the Union in would make everything better.

The auction's come and gone. The galloping knight never showed up. Nobody bought the Mill -- the updated textile equipment in 200,000 square feet of manufacturing space in a

234

tall brick building plus 50,000 square feet warehouse capacity on 31 acres of land. Nobody bought any of the carefully presented and divided bid lots that could've been useful to a rich bidder.

One of the bid lots was the big brick building on your right as Pearl Street starts to slope down to the railroad tracks: the Company Store, as handsome as any store on the Public Square, and bigger than any except Belk-Simpson. Mr Coker put it there so there'd be a general store in easy walking distance of the Mill. There's even a full auditorium upstairs for the workers and some office space. Surely somebody could buy it soon and open a store for that end of town.

While Mayor Buchanan and other local stockholders were hoping another textile operator would buy the mill for its up-to-date equipment, the Union was undercutting the chances for a happy outcome. It was putting out a different story, painting the worst possible picture of conditions at Darlington Manufacturing Company.

After the vote, the Union could point to another evidence of problems at Darlington: a *dissatisfied work force* that had appealed for help from the Union.

But what the Union says about the Mill might not matter. The US textile industry's not expanding. As for converting such a huge Mill for any other work, that effort could cost any new business a fortune. To do any good, it would need to handle the factory and the warehouse too, and to absorb the workers who're still here needing jobs, and maybe the ones hoping to come back if the opportunity offers. *If.*

Local hope for another company bringing good wages -- or anyhow subsistence -- is dying. Six months after the shutdown, generations that lived close together for decades are splitting up to find work. Some women and men both who never needed to learn to drive are having to pay somebody to get 'em to where work might be.

It's dawning on all of us that what might come next is liable not to be as good as what we've lost.

Or might be nothing at all.

So the Union was voted in, and the owners – or majority stockholder Roger Milliken -- closed down the Mill.

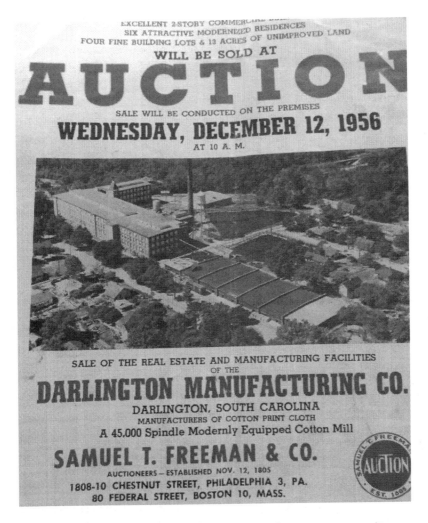

The Darlington Manufacturing Company, as it was named and as it's continued since Major Coker started it in the 1880s, fell.

The owners responsibly filled the last orders -- that took precious little time -- and had the final clean up done.

Then the doors shut.

Then came the auction.

Then the doors shut again. And locked.

236

Not everybody went for the Union, but everybody's paying the price of the shutdown, including us right here at 120 Warley Street.

People who lost their jobs still need their appliances to run, so Daddy spends more time working for no money. You can't let a family's food spoil because the refrigerator broke down, and you can't let them burn the house down with a bad space heater because the furnace quit working on a cold, cold day. Those are facts.

Mother says we could end up broke ourselves if Daddy won't pay more attention to paying customers.

Daddy knows he has to take what Mother says lightly, to get her back in a good mood. So he just says since we've always been more or less broke, it wouldn't be much of a change.

What next?

Frank Kinsey is concerned about workers who're heading out, leaving families behind. Some've been looking for other jobs since the very day of the vote, maybe some even from the first hint that the Mill would close. They didn't believe the Union, and they were right not to. The Mill closed, didn't it?

Some have found work in the Carolinas; they're the "lucky ones," with "only" a couple hours drive to and from work each day. Some are working at Springs Mills (that's at Lancaster) and a cotton mill at Bamberg in Orangeburg County. Neither one's close by, so they won't be seeing their children and grandchildren and parents, aunts and uncles as much, nor nieces and nephews and the neighborhood. No telling what harm family separations do in the long run to people who're use to living close and taking a hand in raising each other's kids. But they've got work. Those who don't have drivers' licenses nor cars either will get in on a carpool. People'll help each other out.

"But they aren't all going to find jobs," said Kinsey. It's a chilling thought. Every grown person around here remembers the Depression.

Some are heading way away. Some went east in search of a living. A few started northward toward Detroit and

237

COUNTY
Cleveland. They might find jobs. They might not. Don't, they'll move on.

They're not bums; they're workers. They're looking for work. Until they find it, the nation calls them hoboes.

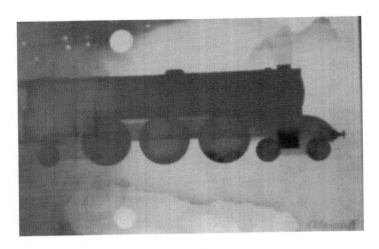

A Russian emigrant in England (you can see his name: Alexieff) submitted this painting in a poster contest to announce the run of the Night Scotsman. It left at midnight (maybe it still does) from the station called King's Cross, to run between Scotland and England. He imagined a locomotive airborne between mountains moon and waters, freed of the earth like a train bound for the Promised Land. This might be the most famous train poster ever. It could be titled Moving On. It's not, but it could be.

The Wabash Cannonball

What happens to out-of-work people leaving an out-of-work town? Is that one of the ways a worker gets to be a hobo -- when a factory closes down because of a fight between powerful people? Or because an industry can't thrive much longer and its factories start falling?

Could be there's just as many hard luck stories confided around a hobo camp as the number of hoboes there. Or maybe they get tired of saying; maybe nobody listens. One hobo is like the next: just trying to find the next meal (or money to send home) by finding work.

But they've got a song -- a song that hangs in my mind. It's full of loss like the hobo's life and hard like his lot. Still, in its own way, it's a happy song because it's moving toward the hoboes' heavenly destination. All mortals are moving toward a destination, happy or not and heavenly or not. And we're all mortal.

"The Wabash Cannonball" is a song so famous it's got places and trains named after *it*, not the other way round. There's a Wabash River in the Midwest, but until the song came along, nobody ever heard of a train of that name because there wasn't one. It's called a folk song, which means nobody knows who wrote it. It can't be *older* than the 1850s, because trains weren't up to much 'til then, not having many tracks to run on, let alone to cross the entire nation, which is probly just a dream anyhow for any one train.

It had to be hoboes that made the song. *Had* to be.

Some nameless-to-us 'bo riding the rails in hopes of the next job must've started it, others added to along the way, and way later the money-singers got ahold of it and took out what they didn't like or didn't understand, but it made its way across the nation on the rails.

239

The nameless-to-us 'bo would've been listening -- and not listening -- to the rhythm of the wheels along the pieced-together metal track up on cross-ties cut by farmers and hauled by mule and wagon to lumber mills all over the nation until finally there was the sound everywhere, day and night, of train cars passing over the crossties (they call them sleepers) and moving on down the line.

COUNTY

Ever slept sitting up on a train? Ever got to feeling the clack-clack in your head and inside your bones? I rode to Washington one time wearing a little red hat, and still I felt it. There's something mournful in it, and at the same time it's picking up speed and taking you with it, faster maybe than you meant to go, so you get the excitement of it too.

When it slows, the click of the rails, you know somebody's getting on and somebody's getting off, maybe mail is being hefted on board to be sorted by the train's mailman.

Mother's grandfathers both ran general stores and bought crossties from farmers and sold them to the railroad. In that day, more and more lines -- 'roads, they were called then -- were being laid everywhere.

So here's the nameless-to-us hobo who's jumped on without the detective seeing him and he's in a 'car maybe alone, maybe not, catching 40 winks before he gets to some place there might be some work for him.

After while (he won't know just how long; he's got no watch anymore and nobody expecting him when he gets to wherever) he's feeling rested and reasonably awake.

But he gets to feeling mortal the way the clack-clack of wheels on rails can make you feel -- time moving along, moving on. That's what a train sound says to a person who listens, who feels it. There's these deep sad feelings but all along the tempo's picking up and taking you with it, God alone really knows where.

The clack-clack rhythm gets into his head and his mind comes along, and his bones too. He likes to sing -- use to be quite a singer before maybe he got tired of his woman and lit out, or before maybe she threw him out with nothing but places to go, or earlier when he finally realized his mama (the only human he knew to depend on) had lit out for good this time, or before maybe the Mill closed down and the Ol' Man couldn't feed that many mouths any more, or before whatever it was that divided his life.

So he starts to put words to the railroad rhythm.

From the great Atlantic ocean
to the wide Pacific shore
She climbs the flowery mountain

241

COUNTY
> o'er hills and by the shore
> She's mighty high and handsome
> and she's known quite well by all
> She's the 'boes accommodation of
> the Wabash Cannonball.

He saw the Wabash River once, and he likes the wailing start of its name. "Shore" gets in twice because nothing else makes sense and rhymes, both. An accommodation train's made up special, and this Cannonball's a dream train just for hoboes. They don't get off to look for work this trip; they stay on to the end of the line.

> Oh listen to the jingle,
> the rumble and the roar
> As she glides along the woodlands,
> o'r hills and by the shore
> As she climbs the flowery mountain,
> hear the merry hoboes squall
> She'll reach her Destination,
> the Wabash Cannonball.

He likes that part so much, he decides to make it the chorus, the part you sing over after every verse. Oh, he knows his way 'round music, our nameless 'bo.

Sure, it's kind of a sad song. Everybody knows the Destination's death. But this train is worthy to be the hoboes' last train, their last journey. *Ain't it mighty high and handsome, and ain't we all headin' to the end of the line?*

So maybe he decides not to make up any more verses right now; a stop's coming up, looks like. He'll try out his song tonight, or whenever he gets some rest after he does what work he finds during the day, at whatever place he swings down from the railcar when the railroad dick's back is turned.

He figures it's a good song. He figures he'll sing it when he finds some other boys, maybe in a camp not far from a 'yard. Maybe he'll find one that can make up some more words, some more verses, and hand it on to the next.

That day, or however many days it was until he was satisfied with his new song, was the day a nameless-to-us hobo became as nearly immortal in this world as a man without a name can be.

Dizzy Dean does love that song. He sings on the radio whenever some game he's announcing goes into the 7th-innng stretch or some other lull, and "Wabash Cannonball" – that's his favorite. That's how I first heard it, listening to games with Daddy, growing up.

Dizzy Dean is my idea of a real country maverick: he means no harm but means to be himself. He might comment from his own baseball experience or say something so funny you'll get to laughing and miss the next play. Point is, he'll say whatever's on his mind about the game (even if it makes a sponsor mad) or – no need to have a great voice if you're strong to carry a tune -- he'll break out and sing whatever he feels like singing.

Dizzy Dean was a great baseball pitcher, maybe the greatest of all time. Then he got hurt and lost his fast ball after he tried to keep on playing with a bad foot. Now he calls baseball games and we sit and listen. He and my Daddy, whose back won't let him play any more either, taught me to love baseball as a thinker's game.

A lady told Dizzy he was a bad influence on children by using *ain't* on the radio. He said, "There's lots of folks that ain't saying *ain't* that ain't eatin."

COUNTY

He's right. Grammar's good, but don't lose your background, your *people*. And you got to keep eatin'.

Out where Mr Dean came from and where he lives now, the Depression's not that far back. It's not so far back around here, either, that we can't remember grits-and-whatever every night for supper.

What makes a man a hobo, separated from family most of the time, roaming the country's railroads, picking up work where he can?

Maybe a shut-down factory.

SENIOR PLAY

Christmas came, and my 17th birthday. The biggest changes in my life will come before I'm 18 -- bigger even than being pulled up by my country roots when I was 10. I can't go right on writing it the same time I'm living all those changes; I've got to wind this book up before long. A writer needs time to think, or her writing's worth nothing.

Since the Shutdown, St John's goes along as if Darlington's the same as ever. We can't solve it, and what you can't solve, you can't let stop you.

This year's been a procession of surprises for me because of the new National Merit Scholarship competition. We took a test during fall semester, and then 5 of us got letters saying we were Semi-finalists. The letter said the next stage was the College Entrance Examinations in January. Our scores on the CEE would decide between the Semi-finalists and the Finalists, plus it would decide if any of us got full scholarships to the college of our choice.

Mr Cain was already struttin' like a peacock about having 5 Semi-finalists. He said he always knew St John's was the best school around, and this proves it. Another thing that proves it – and he made sure the newspapers got this in the story too – is that Nancy Rogerson is another semi-finalist. She's lived in Columbia since summer, but Columbia had nothing to do with her test performance because Mr L A didn't get transferred until this year. So that's SIX of us out of our class of 72. Mr Cain says no graduating class in the nation matched that.

On January 12 in Florence I took the CEE. Even without the Merit competition, what I made would matter. The national entrance exam can decide who gets into college at all, and I always knew I had to go to college. I want a good job -- an interesting job. But once a test is over, you can't change what you made, so why let it linger on your mind?

Then results came in: Mac Willcox and I were Finalists. Nancy was too – the only Finalist at her high school.

COUNTY

Not only that, Mac won the full scholarship – 'cept that as the son of Dr Mac, he was too rich to get it. I think he received the minimum: $100. We all got congratulatory certificates. But his and our names went out to colleges and universities all over the nation, I guess, because even though I didn't win the Merit Scholarship, offers of scholarships from private colleges all around started coming in the mail. Good enough offers that Daddy said to take my choice; he'd make up the rest somehow.

I picked the one that sounded best to me -- Virginia Intermont in Bristol, Virginia. We can get there in a car. And it's in the Virginia mountains. And it's 2 years, and I already know I want to transfer and finish at the University of South Carolina.

Uncle Bob saved up enough from working at Dr Perritt's Drug Store in Lamar to go to Carolina for one semester, made all A's, and came back to Lamar and went to work again. Daddy went to Carolina a whole year (1932-33) and lived with the Sig Eps (he couldn't afford to join but they liked him). He couldn't find work to support himself, so he enlisted; signed up for the Navy because he heard it has the best food. Russell moved in with Uncle Bubba and Aunt Mary Haiglar Dukes in Columbia and went to Carolina a couple years at the end of the '40s, then dropped out and headed to New Orleans to his Uncle G W's and the Mardi Gras. But so help me God and Daddy, I'll be the one to go the distance and get a degree from Carolina.

Virginia Intermont's up in the high mountains. I love the mountains. That's where Daddy and Mother and I take off to when we get a chance -- not the beach, but the cool green-and-rock mountains that turn bright red and gold come late September through October. We stay at Maggie Valley or Cherokee, North Carolina, and drive up higher, carrying gallon jugs of water for when the car runs hot.

The main street of Bristol's right on the line between Tennessee and Virginia, where we've never been. We can't afford a trip up just to look, so I won't see VI 'til I'm actually a Freshman. Daddy says our '53's not strong enough to haul us and my typewriter and clothes up in September, but by then the '58s'll be out (they're coming out earlier and earlier), so we'll borrow Uncle Hart's mint-green-and-mink-white Ford station wagon he's got ordered.

COUNTY

VI is a girls' school; that's the only way to satisfy mother. Her sisters went to Columbia College, and she's disappointed I'm not going there. But ... well, Aunt Rosa and Aunt Myrtis and Aunt Marie all went there, and Cousins Mary and Cornelia and Margie, all on Mother's side of the family, and ... well, *they* went there. I want something different.

I think I do, anyhow.

Watch me go 'way up to Virginia and then hate it. Oh, Lord, please don't let my hard-headedness make me miserable.

But I've made my decision. Intermont's expecting me and offering to pay my tuition and some of my board and books, so that's that. Bristol and around there can't be anything but beautiful, judging by the pictures in the brochures they sent. Intermont's even got an equestrian center. You can keep your own horse there if you decide to.

Like *I've* got a *horse*.

But I did get to the Camden Races last month! Kathy's mother, Martha Graham, use to work as secretary to one of the directors, Mr Skiddy von Stade -- the kind of name that stays in your head. Skiddy can't be his Christened name, but Von Stade is German; sounds like Stoddy. He invited her, and she took us, me and Kathy and Laura the little sister.

I've never seen such dressed up people not on a Sunday. And the *hats*! The men in white slacks and British shoes (I know because Uncle Ellison orders his from there) and the ladies in flowing dresses and lovely wide hats. Chapeaus, I guess you'd call them – or rather *chapeaux*. You could never wear those hats in church; nobody behind you could see. At a horse-race track, though, they're the *thing*.

None of us were dressed up, not even Mrs Graham. She's tall and graceful and just strode along leading us just like she belonged there. And she *did,* of course. The Grahams moved to Darlington from Sumter, remember; they've been around. They even use to live in another state -- Georgia. We still tease Kathy about the Georgia way she says the word *rinse*.

The Camden horse race was an experience I might never have again. I kept my program. Springdale Course, it says. 25 cents just for the *program*. No telling how much Mrs Graham would've had to pay for our tickets if they hadn't been free.

247

COUNTY

Only a week later, the 5th of this very month, we put on our Senior Play, *Galahad Jones*. I wanted to go to the house party afterward but knew I better not get involved in any real work with the <u>Bulletin</u> on top of me. So I read for the shortest part. Since I was the only one who did, I got it.

Tickets were 75 cents for adults and 50 for students and children, and every ticketholder got handed a program free at the door. 60 businesses bought ad space in the program, including a dozen from Society Hill, and we got lots of offers of furniture and props and free publicity. It was all amazing.

The *most* amazing thing is, practicly the whole Senior Class put on that play. If you live far out of town on a farm without a car or you can't stay after school because of a job or you're due at home to take care of somebody, you miss out on some fun happenings. It's nobody's fault, but I hope not getting to do these kinds of things won't hurt anybody along the way. Some people just don't sign up; that's okay too. Bobby Jolly and Belva Jean Story were busy with other stuff.

Carolyn Honney was Line Coach, Mac Willcox was Stage Manager, and Betty Byrd did the lights.

Richard Bailey, Clyde Lane, Lester Holley, Wayne Norwood, Betty Lou Abbott, Edna Earl Godbold and Vorn Bairefoot built the set. Betty Byrd was involved with that too.

Richard was another one doing more than one job. He and Mary Ghent, Hanna Adams, and Grace Gardner did the programs.

Betsy Banks, Sally Hyer and Anna Jeffords did Properties. Sally and Anna are more or less best friends; they signed up together. Just those 3 somehow got everything we needed donated or lent.

Betty Lou Abbott and Betty Byrd both helped with the set building, like I said, plus they worked on Publicity with Linda Moody, Anne Weaver, Betty (Bobby's twin) Jolly, Conrad Hoffmeyer, Lavon Kelly, Jimmy Perkins, Martha Boyette, Shelvie Jean Anderson, and Anna Lee James. That group did Tickets too. They were the ones that got the businesses, including so many in Society Hill, to buy ads, plus getting every drugstore on the Public Square to sell tickets.

COUNTY

Eltas Jean Weatherford, Marilyn Lewis, and Edna Earle Godbold ushered. Mr Finn directed. Mrs Finn did our make up (stage make up feels really odd and heavy).

Lots of people came. It's like that in Darlington; grownups like to encourage you.

It's kind of overwhelming to know that after we graduate, we won't be the town's senior young people any more. We'll just be people.

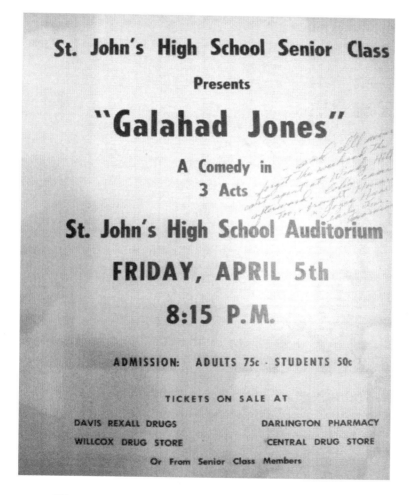

St. John's High School Senior Class

Presents

"Galahad Jones"

A Comedy in
3 Acts

St. John's High School Auditorium

FRIDAY, APRIL 5th

8:15 P.M.

ADMISSION: ADULTS 75c - STUDENTS 50c

TICKETS ON SALE AT

DAVIS REXALL DRUGS   DARLINGTON PHARMACY

WILLCOX DRUG STORE   CENTRAL DRUG STORE

Or From Senior Class Members

The night of the play, Kathy Graham stole the show. The audience loved her. She was the Swedish maid, and couldn't have been better suited for the part. I already told you Kathy's

COUNTY

tall, blond, and 'way more than pretty, and yet she's not stuck-up a bit. She got into that role: every time she lounged in from the wings and opened her mouth, waves and trills of laughter came from the audience. *Trills.* The way she looked and moved and spoke -- all just perfect. If the playwright had been there, he'd've immediately rewritten the whole play around her character. Not that every cast would have a "Swedish" maid as talented as Kathy, to make a limp play so much better.

As it was, the rest of us didn't mind a bit being put in the shade. Not even Bobby James, I bet, and he was the title character, the lead, the actual Galahad Jones.

Vivian Booth and Pim Booth played Mr and Mrs Jones, but they aren't actually even kin, far as anybody knows. Pim's real name is Paul. He's the only one in our class who has a nickname that *everybody,* even his family, calls him. It's for his initials: P M (Booth).

Roger Hathcock played Olaf, the boyfriend of Lena the maid. Roger's not *from* here, and his New Jersey accent kept overcoming his s'pose-to-be Swedish brogue, but probly the audience didn't care. I kind of wondered if Mr Finn (he not only directed, he picked the cast) chose Roger because he figured at least he talks different and the audience wouldn't worry whether his accent is Swedish or what. Or maybe because he just thought Roger ought to be on stage because he's so good-looking. Assuming teachers can tell.

The others in the play were Joyce Medlin and Faye Byrd (they're 1st cousins; their mothers are Privettes), Betty Charles Baxley, JoAnne DeWitt (the only member of the class who has 4 capital letters in just 2 names; she's also President of the National Honor Society), Philip Campbell, Charles Bradshaw, Bobby Smith, and Edwin Williamson.

Oh, and me.

The Senior Play house party afterward at Windy Hill was okay – I mean *good*; it was good. But I already don't remember for sure who all was there, so many showed up. Some slept in cars and some on the downstairs screen porch. Boys, that was; most boys are too tough to care about comfort;.

The house was the usual weekend rental -- a white-board 2-story, blocks away from the ocean. We don't go for luxuries, just a bottom floor for the boys and an upstairs where the girls can slop around and whisper and giggle. Besides, you're not in the house 'cept after you're so tired your eyes keep crossing, and soon as you fall into bed you're asleep. We had chaperones -- we always do or none of the girls could go -- but I don't remember seeing them the whole weekend.

I'm glad I went. It's not the beach house party I'll remember so much as one thing that happened: Philip Campbell and I took a walk on the beach that Saturday night.

We'd never even had a conversation in all our years at St John's, Philip and me, but for some reason – fate, I s'pose -- we paired off together for that walk and found out we're friends. We talked the whole time, never shut up, about stuff that matters to people about to leave classmates they've been with for 100s or 1000s of days but might not ever be with again. We knew we couldn't slow down time but somehow managed to grab a piece of it before it left us.

We said – me and Philip both -- we can't believe we took this long to realize we're friends. We never even went out on a date together, and now it's too late; we're going in different directions and time's too short and dating would be too complicated because we're both seeing other people anyway. Funny how you miss meeting people you've known forever.

Then again, dating each other could've ruined it. Kissing (you got to kiss; it's part of dating, seems like) interferes with communication. Some people even kiss not to have to talk.

I get letters from 7 people that aren't even here -- 1 in the Coast Guard, 2 in military schools, 2 at Clemson, 1 at the Citadel, and specially Colin Jordan in the Air Force since July – but have I even bothered to get to know the rest of the class?

That next morning, here came Colin, home on leave from a Texas AFB, driving up to the beach house with Joyce Medlin and Howard Goodson in Colin's old black Oldsmobile 98 that's big as a boat, honking the horn. My time was taken up from there on, and 'course I rode back home in Colin's car that night.

I bet I could run into Phil 50 years from now, if we live that long which I'm not sure I will because I can't imagine being over 25, and we'd both remember that nice walk on the beach at Windy Hill.

April's Ending

After these last weeks – final grades, big decisions, practice in the amphitheatre, Class Day, the Baccalaureate Sermon, all the fanfare and rigmarole – we'll graduate. All of us will march up the aisle to *Pomp and Circumstance* and take our seats on the stage. Some of us have to make speeches (Lord, don't let me faint on stage), and we'll listen (or not listen, but the train will be moving along whether we listen or not) to the other speeches, including Mac's Valedictory and Grace Gardner's Salutatory and Mr Cain's remarks. Finally our names will be called out one after another, for us to come get our diplomas.

By nightfall on May 31st, those heavy royal-blue velvet curtains on stage in the J C Daniels Auditorium will have opened and closed for us one last time, and we'll be outside, in a different place.

What I hope is, the good things here won't go away while I'm gone. I've seen other towns lose the best part of themselves. Lamar grew up on railroads and then the railroads – both of 'em -- pulled out. Darlington depended on the Cotton Mill, and the Mill's empty. Spring weeds grow fast around deserted buildings and a cemetery.

But we've still got Dixie Cup, maybe even expanding, and the cotton-seed-oil mill. Perfection Gear's coming, planning to build on 52 at the Dovesville end of Mineral Springs Road. It'll bring bosses from up North but it'll be hiring local workers. NuCor Steel's out past there. It could turn out to save Darlington, but it's a long way out. Strange name for a steel mill, too: Nuclear Corporation. It's different from steel mills up north; it's a re-cycling mill. The head office is in Charlotte, and the bosses are Southerners that like to fish. Good signs.

Darlington's still a pretty place at its center, the Court House Square, with the Town Hall and the stores, all with Victorian fronts, some with dates engraved high up. Just not as busy is all. None've closed down or even changed hands, but then it's only been a few months since the shut down.

'Til lately I didn't pay much attention to how the stores look, and the whole Public Square. It was just there, the place to go for whatever items you needed or wanted to look at or think about buying. Now I see that it's old, dependable, clean, beautiful, and home.

But there's the Hotel, fading away in the corner of your eye every time you go to town, and yet when Mr McFall died during the War, it looked as stately as the Court House. All it's got now is Senator Mozingo's law offices and every once in a while the odd business gathering and a few days of Olan Mills. As a place to stay, you could call it a flophouse working its way over to being an eyesore.

I look at it and feel ... not depressed exactly ... more like a foreboding. To me the hotel shows how fast things can change. Edgar Allan Poe could've looked at the Park Terrace the way it is now and made a horror story out of it, like that actual building at his school in London. He moved it mentally out to a weird tarn and *presto change-o!* it's the doomed House of Usher.

Whole towns can get like that. Timmonsville's no older than Florence, but the heart of downtown is shaky. When a filling station turns into a used-furniture store and the main business street gets to be mostly empty plate-glass windows, downtown's pretty well lost. For small towns, that's the ultimate tragedy because for them, downtown's all there's ever likely to be. Their only (sad) chance is to be close enough to a big town to survive as a suburb. Ever been to Dentsville? That's where the first higher-education school for girls was established before there were any women's colleges; Daddy's great-great uncle Elias Marks founded it. His niece, my great-aunt Katie Reckling finally moved away, into Columbia. And they say Eau Claire use to be the prettiest town in midstate. You wouldn't know that now.

When he retires from minks or chinchillas or whatever furry animals he raises in El Paso, C'n Byron Copeland plans to move back to where he grew up -- Timmonsville. I don't think he will, though. When he comes to visit family like he's planning to this summer after so many years, I don't think he'll want to stay. The railroad that built the town is gone and nothing's taking its place.

COUNTY

Florence's downtown is still the place to shop, and their big sales are getting better and better – but come to think of it, the stores on Evans can't be making good profits if they have to drop prices so much after Christmas. If shopping centers keep cropping up around and about, the downtown of even Florence could be in trouble. Five Points might get to be the center of town, the way it started to be when the 1st railroad put its depot there – the railroad from Wilmington NC that made Charleston notice the Pee Dee. Those 2 'roads created Florence.

Darlington could fall too, easier than Florence, now that the Mill's jobs are gone and if the Chamber of Commerce and the Jaycees don't stop turning over the decision-making to Mozingo. He doesn't even like Right To Work. Politicians don't know business, most of 'em, unless they're business people.

Doggonit, I might have learned too much about business, running the newspaper. I can't vote for another 4 years and might as well hush.

If everything works out, I'll leave here after graduation at least for a few years. Next year in the mountains is the start, later in other states, maybe even other countries once I start working (God knows at what; I don't) and save my pay. If I keep in good health (no more malaria, bronchitis and hepatitis slowing me down), I'll live awhile in another country and see what that's like.

But I know I'll still care what's happening here, back home.

And be keeping up with it all.

And coming back.

Some day I might come back for good. Nobody's certain of a day, no more than hoboes out there on the road. It's all in God's hands.

But if I live, I'll be back. I believe that.

Maybe even if I don't live. Maybe after I'm through with this life I'm living now, that's when I'll come back.

With all the serious things I've been telling you, all that philosophical part, I almost don't want to let you know what just happened today at school. It might seem trivial, but to me it's not. No more trivial than the economy of the United States.

COUNTY

If Mrs McIver and Mrs Ervin hadn't taught us about Communism, Socialism, Capitalism and what makes nations go to war, I wouldn't know how to think about money past the price of a 45 rpm record. Yesterday, real life poked me in the eye. Now I'm not just educated, I'm mad.

So here it is:

Mr Cain informed me during 3rd period that the <u>Bulletin</u> Staff won't get to use any of our earned profit for a party! Says he won't even consider it.

He says we're the only <u>Bulletin</u> since he's been Principal of St John's High School that's operated at a profit, and the school's been subsidizing the newspaper all these years at a loss. Therefore, he's confiscating our profit. (He avoided that word; he said he's "returning it to school funds." *Returning*, would you believe. Like we *filched* it.)

He also said that our ability to turn a profit for '56-'57 does not mean next year's staff will.

Which of course it doesn't mean any such of a thing; who ever said it did? Let's talk *sense* here.

All I could think of to say was, "What? WHAT?"

I said it loud too, but it did me no good. He just turned around, walked into his cubicle at the back of the office, and got busy with matters that were clearly more important than the morale of the newspaper staff and our thinking in future.

What *I* think he should've been doing is feeling ashamed of himself instead of (silently) calling me a bunny one more time. *The bunnies are running the school newspaper*, that's what he was thinking. I could read it just as clear as it'd been written on the back of his gray suit or up on his bald spot.

So now I've got to tell the Staff that *made* the profit, that worked their behinds almost off and walked their feet almost numb to ask the generous businesses of Darlington County to buy ads, that we can't have a party. *Me*. I've got to tell them they might just as well've lazed around or been as untalented as all the <u>Bulletin</u> business staffs apparently were that went before them, because the school would've gone on making taxpayers eat the yearly loss and would've published our '56-'57 <u>Bulletin</u> all year *anyhow*.

Funny how a little thing can make a big difference in your thinking; mine, anyhow. Not having a party from the profit the
255

COUNTY
<u>Bulletin</u> made this year -- we'll forget it between now and graduation. Maybe.

But it's tied to a bigger thing: whether people in charge discourage good work or encourage it with rewards linked to their success, the way our staff party would 've been.

Our only real chance to get together as a staff for something other than work. Drat!

After we leave St John's, whatever we do, I hope our rewards are for something worthwhile done, not for knowing how to float along on the system.

Does that seem harsh? Do I sound hard? Well, sticks and stones can break my bones, but words . . . . .

Go ahead, *call* me a Bunny. See if *I* care.

I've slept on it, if you could call it sleep. Maybe I'll just tell Vivian, and she can help me decide how to handle it. I don't want a staff meeting that turns into a cuss-Mr-Cain frenzy.

He's not such a bad guy. This is the first time he's actually disappointed me, really.

I can see his point about me giving out the <u>Bulletin</u> at the end of Chapel. And him signing me up for Physics against my will turned out okay; what would I've learned in BFL anyhow? Nothing about the internal combustion engine, for sure, and probly nothing else that'll be helpful any time soon. Maybe never, if I don't get married.

But you kind of do get married, don't you. Survival of the human race and all, and besides, you probly fall in love.

It's just that I never suspected before that Mr Cain was a Socialist. Maybe he has to be. Maybe everybody that lives on the taxpayer's dollar has to think incentive is nothing and neither is motivation. Some public employees must work hard, but they must do it out of good character or habit from childhood like on a farm, or maybe just to be promoted, not because working for the taxpayer calls for it. Tax money keeps flowing into their pockets regardless.

I'll be a taxpayer myself this summer, God help me, when I'm a computer-billing girl at Dixie Cup, and not a St John's Senior.

St John's never rewarded us just for showing up. The school was like our parents: it knew we were capable of more

256

Last year's Senior girls practicing for Class Day '56. Our turn's here.

than that. Most of us grew up working for what we got or we didn't get it. At St John's it was the same way – real life.

Not that we picked on each other – at least, not past grammar school. Awkward, intelligent, athletic, pretty, brave, shy, or quirky – so what? Differences tell us who we are. Our beauty queen was just as friendly to the NHS president as to the drop-out as to the tennis whiz. Our builders of midget racers and carvers of rabbits got along fine with the men who blocked for the backs. It's all good.

Okay, I admit there's a few snobs, or seem like snobs, but I never thought they meant to be. I figure they're just awkward and unsure of themselves, like me when I'm in a new situation. Vivian told me a couple years ago she use to think I was stuck up.

"Good grief," I said, gobsmacked. "Me, stuck up? What did I ever have to be stuck up about?"

We laugh about that now, Vivian and me. I'm glad she felt okay about telling me, meaning she's over it. And whatever I was doing that made her think that, I hope to goodness I've quit.

257

COUNTY

I'm not saying we're perfect. And nobody's *every*body's favorite except Anne Weaver. We all know she deserves it because she's the perfect generous soul. That's the pure truth.

Perfection's not required, though. Some of us had to work a few things out, but we did it, or grew past it. We accepted each other, pimples and all.

It's been years since anybody in our class even got into a fistfight at school, and you know boys: that's remarkable. Nobody in the Class of '57 even got a bad-sounding nickname. We all go by reg'lar names. There's been some in other classes -- Rat Bait, Fudgie, Cootie – but they seemed okay with that. Name-calling, though -- that's different from nicknames. We don't do it. Name-calling's a jealous thing, and jealousy's not *our* thing.

My class ring says St John's has been here since 1818 – might's well say 140 years. May it last another 140. If classes that follow ours match our determination, and if politicians and bureaucrats don't take it down, St John's won't fail and it won't fall.

If I'm being mushy and sentimental, well hey, that's how I'm feeling. I'm feeling emotional, and proud too – proud of *us*. Maybe every graduating class feels this way; I hope so, anyhow. We like ourselves. We're okay people.

I think we're ready.

A toast to ourselves and those like us: too few.

25701825R00147

Made in the USA
Charleston, SC
12 January 2014